Discursive Perspectives on Education Policy and Implementation

Softcover reprint of the hardcover 1st edition 2017

W0192975

Discursive Perspectives on Education Policy
and Implementation

Jessica Nina Lester • Chad R. Lochmiller •
Rachael E. Gabriel
Editors

Discursive Perspectives on Education Policy and Implementation

palgrave
macmillan

Editors
Jessica Nina Lester
Indiana University
Bloomington, IN
USA

Chad R. Lochmiller
Indiana University
Bloomington, IN
USA

Rachael E. Gabriel
University of Connecticut
Storrs, CT
USA

ISBN 978-3-319-86524-9   ISBN 978-3-319-58984-8   (eBook)
DOI 10.1007/978-3-319-58984-8

© The Editor(s) (if applicable) and The Author(s) 2017
Softcover reprint of the hardcover 1st edition 2017
This work is subject to copyright. All rights are solely and exclusively licensed by the Publisher, whether the whole or part of the material is concerned, specifically the rights of translation, reprinting, reuse of illustrations, recitation, broadcasting, reproduction on microfilms or in any other physical way, and transmission or information storage and retrieval, electronic adaptation, computer software, or by similar or dissimilar methodology now known or hereafter developed. The use of general descriptive names, registered names, trademarks, service marks, etc. in this publication does not imply, even in the absence of a specific statement, that such names are exempt from the relevant protective laws and regulations and therefore free for general use. The publisher, the authors and the editors are safe to assume that the advice and information in this book are believed to be true and accurate at the date of publication. Neither the publisher nor the authors or the editors give a warranty, express or implied, with respect to the material contained herein or for any errors or omissions that may have been made. The publisher remains neutral with regard to jurisdictional claims in published maps and institutional affiliations.

Cover Design by Thomas Howey

Printed on acid-free paper

This Palgrave Macmillan imprint is published by Springer Nature
The registered company is Springer International Publishing AG
The registered company address is: Gewerbestrasse 11, 6330 Cham, Switzerland

PREFACE

In May 2014, we gathered at the *International Congress of Qualitative Inquiry* held at the University of Illinois in Urbana-Champaign, Illinois, to discuss the possibility of a special issue of *Educational Policy Analysis Archives* (EPAA) focused on the use of language-based methods for the study of education policy. At the time, our vision was to create a forum where scholars using language-based methodologies and methods could share their policy-related work. We recognized that new approaches to the study of policy were necessary and that qualitative scholars could contribute to the generation of these approaches. At the time, we had no idea how many scholars saw this forum as valuable. Indeed, as we have learned throughout this process, scholars using language-based methodologies and methods have much to say about this topic! We were astounded to receive more than 50 individual submissions for what became a two-part special issue of EPAA, covering a variety of language-based approaches and policy issues. The special issues, along with our own reading and research, highlighted the need to say more about these approaches as they relate to education policy. Could, for example, a focus on discourse become popularized in policy research? Might these approaches serve to support education scholars in unpacking issues of power, privilege, and (in)justice related to the design and implementation of policy issues? Could language-based methodologies and methods open new and potentially fruitful sources of data? In reflecting on these questions, we collectively agreed that more scholarship was needed on this topic and thus we began shifting our attention from our EPAA special issues to the development of this co-edited volume.

Our vision for this volume thus developed in parallel with our efforts to complete the special issues of EPAA (Lester et al. 2016, 2017). Many of the authors included in this volume also appeared in one of the special issues we generated. The first focused on critical discourse analysis and the second focused more broadly on varying approaches to discourse analysis. Thus, we readily acknowledge that this volume is part of a dialogue that we began before, and we further acknowledge the assistance of the editorial team at EPAA for supporting us at the earliest stages of conceptualizing these ideas.

The primary purpose of this book project is not simply to repeat what has already been said by the authors included in the EPAA special issues; rather this volume serves to extend and solidify our argument that language-based methodologies and methods are valuable to the study of education and are especially so in relation to education policy issues. In particular, we see these methods being particularly valuable for implementation in different policy contexts. Equally important, we view this volume as an opportunity to introduce novice and experienced scholars to the use of language-based methodologies and methods. No such volume currently exists. Scholars generally focus on language-based methodologies and methods without resources exploring the link between these approaches and the study of education policy in particular. We see this gap as particularly concerning, given the popularity, utility, and relevance of these approaches. Finally, we also view this volume as a resource for experienced scholars to identify potential policy topics, methodological approaches, and questions that may be explored using these approaches. Indeed, the topics covered within the volume are vast and thus encourage scholarship within and across a variety of policy domains.

As we prepared this volume, we each adopted unique roles. Jessica Nina Lester, Assistant Professor of Inquiry Methodology at Indiana University, served as the methodological expert. Her own work using language-based methodologies and expertise about them served as the technical base for this volume. Further, her keen editing skills proved essential to the overall management of the project. Chad R. Lochmiller, Assistant Professor of Educational Leadership and Policy Studies at Indiana University, served as the primary policy expert on this volume. His expertise in issues related to policy and leadership provided guidance that helped steer the chapter authors toward meaningful policy issues that spanned both policy and institutional contexts. As the second editor, he provided support and assistance to the first editor, as well as recommendations for external reviewers with policy expertise. Finally, Rachael Gabriel, Assistant Professor of Literacy Education at the University of Connecticut, served as a policy expert on issues related to teaching, learning, and literacy and contributed her own scholarship to this volume as a model for others to follow. Collectively, the editors created a balanced editorial team that reflected methodological and policy expertise. Indeed, it was this balanced team structure that supported the initial development of the EPAA special issues upon which this volume is based. Further, it was the co-mingling of knowledge bases that supported the needs of chapter authors.

While each reader will undoubtedly bring a different lens to the reading of this volume, we think it is appropriate for most scholars to use this book as a resource and reference. The chapters presented herein focus both on policy issues and on background information designed to support deeper understanding of language-based methods. This is not a traditional research textbook, however. Scholars will not find step-wise instructions that describe how to conduct policy research using these approaches. Rather, this volume should be seen as a compendium of model studies that aim to inspire scholars to pursue research using one of these approaches, in addition to several chapters that offer methodological perspectives related to language-based methodologies and methods. Indeed, we hope this book serves as an invitation to readers to not only consider the utility of language-based approaches in their own policy work but also see the empirical chapters as exemplars for how such work might be conceptualized and carried out.

Last, we are indebted to the authors who contributed chapters to this volume. Were it not for their willingness to share their ideas, we would not be able to offer this resource. Our hope is that using this volume and studying the various examples presented within it will yield opportunities for scholars with various interests to examine policy issues using language-based methodologies and methods and to use these methods as an opportunity to open up new analytic approaches, data sources, and questions pertaining to the design and implementation of policy. In the current political and policy environment, we see any perspective that brings a critical lens to the work of education as important. As many of the scholars within this volume highlight, the types of issues that language-based methodologies and methods enable scholars to examine provide fuel for those who seek to ask whose interests our education policy serves.

Indiana University   Jessica Nina Lester
Bloomington, IN
USA

Indiana University   Chad R. Lochmiller
Bloomington, IN
USA

University of Connecticut   Rachael E. Gabriel
Storrs, CT
USA

References

Lester, J. N., Lochmiller, C. R., & Gabriel, R. (2016). Locating and applying critical discourse analysis within education policy: An introduction. *Education Policy Analysis Archives, 24*(102). doi:10.14507/epaa.24.2768

Lester, J. N., Lochmiller, C. R., & Gabriel, R. (2017). Exploring the intersection of education policy and discourse analysis: An introduction. *Education Policy Analysis Archives, 25*, 25.

ACKNOWLEDGMENTS

We wish to thank those who have contributed to the development of this book. First, the idea for the book grew out of our work as guest co-editors for *Education Policy Analysis Archives*, a journal which supported and became invested in a two-part special issue focused on discourse analysis and education policy. We thus thank Gustavo Fischman and Audrey Amrein-Beardsley for their encouragement and support in bringing these ideas to fruition. Second, we thank the anonymous peer reviewers who provided rich and thoughtful feedback that carried each one of the chapters forward toward its full potential. We also thank the Palgrave Macmillan team, specifically Milana Vernikova and Mara Berkoff. Finally, indeed this book would not be possible apart from the thoughtful work of the contributors. We thank each of them for sharing their work and engaging with us in thinking about possibilities for language-based methodologies and methods and education policy scholars.

CONTENTS

LIST OF FIGURE

LIST OF TABLES

An Introduction to *Discursive Perspectives on Education Policy and Implementation*

Jessica Nina Lester, Chad R. Lochmiller, and Rachael E. Gabriel

INTRODUCTION

This co-edited volume brings to the fore possibilities for employing language-based methodologies, specifically discourse analytic perspectives, to the study of education policy and its implementation within particular policy contexts. Education researchers have long been interested in the study of the design and implementation of policy and more broadly the impact of education policy on students, teachers, and/or educational organizations. In this volume, the contributing authors illustrate the varying methodological, analytical, and substantive possibilities found when foregrounding the study of discourse (defined in varying ways). Building upon a long-standing tradition of employing critical discourse analysis for the study of education policy (see Lester et al. 2016, for a brief overview of critical discourse analysis and education policy), this volume aims to spark further conversation about the

J.N. Lester (✉) • C.R. Lochmiller
Indiana University, Bloomington, IN, USA

R.E. Gabriel
University of Connecticut, Storrs, CT, USA

© The Author(s) 2017
J.N. Lester et al. (eds.), *Discursive Perspectives on Education Policy and Implementation*, DOI 10.1007/978-3-319-58984-8_1

1

usefulness of and myriad possibilities for working at the intersection of education policy and language-based methodologies (e.g., critical discourse analysis). We thus intentionally invited scholars who engage with diverse methodological perspectives, data sources, and policy issues to contribute to this volume, and believe readers will find their contributions to offer rich examples of discourse analysis studies within education policy alongside several methodologically oriented discussions. Thus, the contributing authors provide a range of perspectives, examining education policy using both micro-analytic traditions (e.g., discursive psychology) and more macro-analytic traditions (e.g., critical discourse analysis). Further, some of the authors work to move beyond traditional conceptions of discourse, data, and even policy, and, thereby, "push" the conversation to the methodological "edge" and invite readers to envision new possibilities.

We begin this chapter by providing an abbreviated discussion of the place of language in education policy. Then, we offer a description of the structure of this volume and provide the reader with key "signposts" that might serve to support their engagement with this volume. Finally, we offer a detailed listing of the chapter abstracts.

DISCOURSE AND EDUCATION POLICY: WHY LANGUAGE MATTERS

Talk and text (both defined broadly) have always been central to the development of educational policy and its implementation in various organizational settings. From the initial framing of particular policy problems (Coburn 2006) to debate, discussion, negotiation, and decision-making inherent in the policy-making process (Boden 1994), talk and text often serve as the primary vehicle through which the policy-making process is made visible and its related outcomes understood by external actors. Likewise, talk and text also shape the dissemination and appropriation of policy ideas within organizations and the context of educational practice. Thus, within this volume, we take the view that language is both constitutive and constructive. Language creates, codifies, and conveys policy while at the same time macro and micro features of language—from broad rhetorical techniques to specific word choices—shape meanings and understandings of policy. Consequently, we argue that the application of language-based methods to the study of education policy signals an interest both in the material construction of policy itself and in the medium of policy processes. In other words, language-based methods, including discourse analytic perspectives, allow for investigations of both the substance and the systems of policy in action.

This perspective reflects current trends in education policy research, which increasingly attend to policy as a social process, often foregrounding issues of sensemaking (Spillane 2004) and resistance to policy mandates (Terhart 2013). This has often involved macro-level investigations of policy issues (e.g., studying professional behaviors of teachers and administrators, descriptively examining program structures, evaluating interventions on student learning outcomes, etc.). Indeed, early education policy researchers attributed variation in policy implementation and outcomes to confusion, miscommunication, or a lack of skill or will on the part of those responsible for policy implementation (McLaughlin 1987; Odden 1991). This generation of policy research is distinguished from more contemporary approaches by the assumption that relationships between policies, implementation efforts, and outcomes were knowable, straightforward, and largely causal. More recently, scholars have expanded on this understanding. Specifically, they have applied cognitive perspectives to policy implementation (Spillane et al. 2002) and have thus positioned teachers, administrators, and other "street-level bureaucrats" as sensemakers in their own rights, who understand and implement policy ideas through unique lenses which have been shaped by their particular knowledge, experiences, and contexts (Coburn 2001; Jennings 1996; Spillane 1999).

Increasingly, researchers have thus turned their attention toward the study of practices influenced by policy as well as the ways in which these practices influence policy development. This research has highlighted the central role that "street-level bureaucrats" play in shaping the implementation (Weatherly and Lipsky 1977) and the importance of "sensemaking" in understanding how educators think about the implementation of policy and more broadly make sense of their work (Spillane 2004). We assert that the use of language-based methods is uniquely suited to understanding the processes by which street-level bureaucrats collaboratively make sense of policy and the resources used to (re)frame and communicate policy messages (Coburn and Woulfin 2012). We argue that a turn toward theories and methodologies that foreground the discursive is a natural extension of something similar to a cultural turn (Jameson 1998) in education policy research. In the social sciences more broadly, a turn toward attention to cultural topics and methods was followed by a discursive turn (Howarth and Stavrakakis 2000)—a steadily increasing and sustained interest in the role of discourse in social processes and in the construction of the social world. Indeed, Howarth and Stavrakakis (2000) noted that recent research "shows a proliferation of studies that deploy the concept of discourse and the methods of discourse analysis" (p. 18).

This proliferation of interest is visible in the production of new journals, handbooks, and textbooks devoted entirely to discourse theory and analysis in the social sciences published in the 1980s and 1990s. This broadly described discursive turn is deemed by some to be a natural extension of an earlier "cultural turn," a movement within the social sciences that began in the 1970s and involved a shift from positivist epistemologies toward critical and post-structuralist understandings of the meanings of cultural processes and systems of signification (Steinmetz 1999). Influenced by cultural studies, literary criticism, and linguistic analyses, the notion of "the discursive as a horizon of meaningful practices and significant differences" (Howarth and Stavrakakis 2000, p. 3) is a logical extension of an interest in the meaning rather than only the measure of objects, actions, and relationships. A discourse analytic perspective takes as its focus the ways that social practices construct and contest social realities using "systems of meaningful practices" (ibid., p. 4), such as talk and text.

As described above, policy processes are often distinctly rhetorical (e.g., proposal, debate, discussion, negotiation, decision-making, writing, and revision) with choices about the linguistic representation of ideas and ideals holding central importance. Within a framework informed by post-structuralism and contemporary social science research, we understand that the social world—the context within which policy is constructed, negotiated, and enacted—is both constructed by and constructive of language use. For example, by taking up discourses of economics and competition, Race to the Top policies were framed as reform efforts, understood as federal intervention, and enacted as part of a new generation of accountability policies (Steinberg and Donaldson 2014). Language is used to construct and convey the policy to practitioners and the public, but also used by these audiences to understand, (re)frame, and enact or resist it.

The same transitions from a focus on measurement to an interest in the cultural and, finally, the discursive aspects of education policy and policy studies more broadly can be found in Honig's (2006) explanation of the two generations of policy research: the first generation was primarily concerned with measuring the impacts and outcomes of policies with a positivist orientation to the identification and measurement of good policies and intended outcomes. According to Honig (2006), the second generation is distinguished by three specific features:

1. An interest in increasingly complex policies and their association with specific organizational practices or contexts;
2. An interest in those aspects of implementation that explain variation in the results of policies across settings; and
3. An epistemology focused on revealing the complexity and contingency of policy implementation such that variation is assumed to be the rule rather than the exception to a truth-finding effort guided by positivist epistemologies.

In other words, "contemporary education policy implementation research can be distinguished epistemologically—by its orientation to the nature of knowledge and knowledge-building about implementation" (Honig 2006 p. 20). Just as the discursive turn may be viewed as a natural extension of the cultural turn in the social sciences more broadly, we argue that increased interest and use of discourse theory and analysis within education policy research is a natural extension of what Honig refers to as second-generation or contemporary education policy research. Perhaps, we could even name it a "third generation" of policy research. Language-based methods offer inherently more complex understandings of policy formation as well as its implementation within organizational contexts.

Using a broad definition of policy, we argue that language-based methodologies, specifically discourse analytic perspectives, are essential in helping the field understand substantive policy matters given the breadth of disciplines upon which policy research may draw (Cibulka 1994). Across many subfields of policy research, there are a growing number of examples of discourse methodologies being employed, including those in political science (e.g., Bhatia 2006; Townshend 2004), sociology (e.g., Perez 2013), and educational psychology (e.g., Lester and Gabriel 2014), among many others. As we demonstrate in this volume, the breadth of possibilities and the power of findings produced through the analysis of discourse signals the primacy of such analytic approaches within the education policy research endeavor.

STRUCTURE OF THIS VOLUME

The structure of this volume supports both novice and experienced scholars in their efforts to understand how language-based methodologies might be used to study education policy, particularly education policy implementation. A central aim for this volume is to provide the reader with an introduction to language-based methodologies as well as to situate these approaches within the broader context of policy literature. Yet, we offer a caution in noting that this is not a textbook, as we do not include discussion of the nuanced details related to designing and carrying out a discourse analysis study. Rather, we hope this volume serves as a useful starting point for those new to discourse analysis and, perhaps, a tool for sparking new possibilities for those already familiar with the work produced at the intersection of education policy and language-based methodlogies, more particularly discourse analytic perspectives. Thus, to lay a foundation for the volume as a whole, Chap. 2 provides the reader with an introduction to recent education policy research and highlights the dominance of the qualitative case study as the primary methodology used in policy analyses. This chapter serves as a call for new approaches to the study of education policy and offers language-based methods in response to this call. Chapter 3 then introduces language-based methods and serves as the technical and methodological core of this volume. Further, Chap. 3 offers important methodological context related to language-based research methods. In particular, the third chapter highlights the applicability of critical discourse analysis, discursive psychology, and conversation analysis as three potential methodologies. Some of the other included chapters point to possibilities for the use of other language-based methods. Notably, several of the chapters offer methodological discussion through empirical examples, pressing the reader to consider new and emergent perspectives that could further advance the use of language-based methods. Other chapters present empirical examples that demonstrate how language-based methods can be used to study particular policy issues.

To assist readers in accessing the content of each chapter, we asked each chapter author to incorporate some common elements. These include an introductory box highlighting Chapter Contents as well as a concluding box that highlights Key Connections to Policy Research. These features are designed to assist the reader in both identifying the topics included within the chapter and positioning the chapter in relation to the broader policy literature. As we hope this volume provides scholars with insights about how these methods might be used, the Key Connections to Policy Research box serves as an important avenue for scholars to consider current and future research that might employ language-based methods. Each chapter also concludes with a Summary, which is designed to bring the main points from the chapter together. Readers may first wish to read across the summaries to determine the overarching message and scope of this volume. Indeed, one of our aims for this volume was that each chapter stands alone with respect to its message and content.

CHAPTER ABSTRACTS

For ease of referencing and to offer more particular details on the individual chapters, we provide a listing of the chapter abstracts.

Chapter 2: Education Policy Implementation Research: A Call for New Approaches

Chad R. Lochmiller and Samantha L. Hedges

In this chapter, we present a literature-based argument for the adoption of language-based methodologies to study education policy implementation. The chapter summarizes recent policy implementation literature. Within this review, we highlight the ways in which this research positions policy actors in relation to policy implementation. We find that scholars have examined resistance to the adoption of policies, the alignment between policy goals and local organizational values, and the role of policy actors who are both internal and external to the organization. Across these studies, we assess the methodological similarities of recent research, finding that scholars have widely used the qualitative case study as the dominant methodology for studying implementation issues within localized contexts. We highlight the strengths and weaknesses of this approach. Finally, we conclude our discussion by advocating for the use of language-based methodologies to examine policy implementation issues which are bound within sociocultural and sensemaking contexts.

Chapter 3: Language-Based Approaches to the Study of Education Policy

Jessica Nina Lester, Francesca A. White, and Chad R. Lochmiller

This chapter provides background to some of the methodological perspectives taken up in this volume, with a general emphasis on discourse analysis and a more particular emphasis on critical discourse analysis, discursive psychology, and conversation analysis. Of these approaches, policy scholars have used critical discourse analysis most extensively in the study of education policy, and thus it represents the dominant approach to language-based policy research. Our discussion describes how the analyst approaches their work within each of the selected methodological perspectives, provides insights into the key features of the approach, and integrates examples from published literature to illustrate how policy scholars can use these approaches to study education policy. The chapter concludes by discussing the implications of using these approaches in policy research.

Chapter 4: From Subjectification to Subjectivity in Education Policy Research Relationships

Erica Burman

This chapter evaluates what a Foucauldian discursive approach brings to analysis of educational policy-related material. It focuses on a specific textual example from a local, UK-based study of educational impacts of welfare reforms on poor families that is spoken by a parent of three children in the context of a research interview. Her statement, "Tell your professor we are good mothers," is discussed in relation to four features: (1) the range of subject positions elaborated; (2) the incitement to "confession" and investments in being seen as "good mothers"; (3) the articulation of a collective subjectivity that repudiates the surveillance and regulation of working-class communities; and (4) an ethical-political demand addressed to the researchers to challenge the dominant discourses to which this mother and others like her are subject. Distinct practical-policy contributions of Foucauldian Discourse Analysis are identified, including indications of discursive shifts and possibilities of resistance.

Chapter 5: Membership Categorization Analysis for Education Policy

Justin Paulsen

Membership Categorization Analysis (MCA) is a language-based approach that provides unique insight into education policy research. At its most basic, MCA is concerned with identifying the patterns with which individuals or organizations develop categorizations (e.g., teachers, students). Everyday categories can be analyzed to understand the way a particular culture bounds categories to particular activities, attributes, and relationships. Such information can allow education policy researchers to hypothesize about the effectiveness of policy, adapt policies to the particular constraints of the culture, or assess how policies change cultural categorization. This chapter illustrates the usefulness of MCA. The chapter analyzes the way different educational organizations in Bangladesh with differing degrees of international connectedness construct the category teacher. As relative connectedness to international organization decreases, the nature of the teacher construct differs more significantly from a preeminent global construction of teacher, suggesting the validity of the global policy flows argument.

Chapter 6: A Mangled Education Policy ~~Discourse~~ Analysis for the Anthropocene

Ryan Evely Gildersleeve and Katie Kleinhesselink

In this chapter, we present policy discourse analysis (PDA) as a method for critical policy studies in education. After reviewing key tenets, core principles, and exemplars of PDA, we suggest a post-humanist (and materialist) addendum to the method, emplacing it within our current geologic period, the Anthropocene, in which humans are the primary agents of affect and effect on the planet. Applied to PDA in education, the Anthropocene begs attention be paid to non-human agencies produced through policy-as-discourse and the consequences thereof. We build upon the discursive commitments of third-generation policy research by insisting—and illustrating—how discourse and materiality are entangled in the production of realities. We first explore post-human ontologies of *becoming* (Bennett 2010; Braidotti 2013). We then demonstrate how a post-human, materialist PDA might operate using analysis from Gildersleeve et al.'s (2015) project on the discourses of opportunity for Latino (im)migrants in higher education policy and Ulmer's (2015) application of Malabou's concept of *plasticity* to policy analysis.

Chapter 7: Plays Well with Others: The Discourse and Enactment of Partnerships in Public Pre-K

Bethany Wilinski

Partnerships between school districts and community early childhood education (ECE) providers have been promoted as part of the recent expansion of publicly funded pre-kindergarten (pre-K) in the USA. Although they are positioned as beneficial to a range of stakeholders, pre-K partnerships can also be sites of conflict because they bring together two distinct systems: ECE and K-12. In this discursive analysis of data from a yearlong study of pre-K policy implementation in Lakeville, Wisconsin, I use Bakhtin's (1981) notion of dialogism to demonstrate how a local pre-K partnership deviated from a state-level vision of partnership. As a result of the power dynamics that animated school district-ECE provider relations, partnership in Lakeville came to look and feel very different from the state-level discourse of partnership. Findings from this study complicate the notion of partnership, challenging its position as a straightforward policy solution.

Chapter 8: Reframing Misbehavior: Positive School Discipline and the New Meaning of "Safety" in Schools

Hilary Lustick

The Supportive School Discipline Initiative, launched in January of 2014 by the Department of Education (ED) and the Department of Justice (DOJ), has released a School Climate Guidance Package. The Initiative frames high suspension rates as a matter of poor school climate. However, federally mandated zero-tolerance discipline policies caused a spike in suspensions and exacerbated racial disparities in disciplinary outcomes. Zero-tolerance policies were themselves a response to perceived violence in schools. While those policies framed misbehaved students as threats to their classmates and teachers, this new package frames misbehaved students as victims of dangerous educators. At stake is the adequate implementation—and funding—of discipline policy reforms that may have the potential to improve school climate and reduce suspension. Examining discursive mechanisms such as intertextualization, grammatical construction, and word choice, this critical discourse analysis unpacks the Guidance Package's underlying ideologies and concludes with implications for research, policy, and practice.

Chapter 9: Critical Discourse and the Twenty-First-Century Education Report Policy

Jasmine Ulmer and Sarah Lenhoff

In this chapter, we examine how the discourses of education reform intersect with the twenty-first-century policies that purport to prepare students to be productive members of a global economy. Through the example of a national reform organization that promises to deliver twenty-first-century skills and competencies, we demonstrate how discourse shaped and revealed the aims of the program as it was implemented in three high schools. By approaching policy language as a form of critical discourse, we were able to compare official program goals with the language of implementation, uncovering a misalignment between stated goals and teachers' perceptions. We show that education discourse shapes policy initiatives at the same time that it influences practices of schooling and society that prioritize commercial interests over social improvement. Critical research on school reform and implementation can play a transformative role in questioning policy discourse and suggesting new possibilities for situated pedagogies.

Chapter 10: Reading and Dyslexia Legislation: Analytic Techniques and Findings on the Framing of Dyslexia

Rachael E. Gabriel and Sarah Woulfin

Reading achievement is often used as a barometer for the success of schools and the efficacy of reform efforts. As such, it is often the target of education policy mandates at the state and federal level. Over the past five years, more than 24 states have considered revisions to laws concerning the education of children with dyslexia (Youman and Mather 2013). In this study, we review recent legislation and analyze transcripts of public hearings and associated legislative documents (e.g., bills, revisions, and press releases) using frame analysis (Benford and Snow 2000; Goffman 1974) to understand how reading has been constructed as a policy problem. We then engage in a discourse analysis of frames by examining constructions of reading as a policy problem and the positioning of stakeholders made relevant within written testimony. We then discuss the various constructs of reading/reading difficulty in legislative documents within a single state and discuss their implications for implementation and future policy-making.

Chapter 11: Constructing Teacher Effectiveness in Policy-Making Conversations

Rachael E. Gabriel

Over the years since the Race to the Top competition (2009), 46 states and the District of Columbia revised state policy regarding the measurement of teacher effectiveness thus ushering in a new generation of tools and approaches for teacher evaluation. State teacher evaluation policies codify definitions of what it means to teach (Raudenbush 2009), what teachers are expected to do (Darling-Hammond 1990, 2013), and which ways of teaching and learning are to be encouraged or resisted by articulating a set of values for classroom teaching and student learning. By identifying tools and approaches for the measurement of teaching quality, such policies inscribe particular definitions of teacher effectiveness—a construct that has often been debated and reconstituted over the history of research and evaluation in US public schools (Grant et al. 2013). In this study, I analyze transcripts from the Teacher Evaluation Advisory Committee (TEAC) meetings in Tennessee, an influential case of teacher evaluation policy-making within which the discourses of evaluation and effectiveness policies can be examined.

Chapter 12: Future Directions for Education Policy Research and Language-Based Methods

Chad R. Lochmiller and Jessica Nina Lester

This chapter seeks to bring together the key contributions that the individual chapters make at both a methodological and substantive level. Specifically, we offer a summary of what we interpret as the key points or primary considerations of the individual chapters. Then, we discuss key methodological contributions that readers might identify when engaging with this volume. Notably, this volume seeks to examine possibilities at the intersection of education policy and discourse analysis. Thus, we also consider the key contributions the individual chapters make to education policy conversations. From here, we offer considerations for next steps—noting possibilities for future directions for policy scholars interested in taking up language-based methods writ large.

SUMMARY

In this chapter, we provided a general overview of the volume. To do so, we began by highlighting the potential for engaging in research at the intersection of education policy and language-based methodologies, specifically discourse analytic perspectives. We highlighted the possibilities of using language-based methods as part of a new generation of policy research. We then offered a general overview of the structure and key features of the volume. Finally, we concluded by providing a listing of the chapter abstracts.

Key Connections to Policy Research
1. Language (broadly defined) both constructs and conveys policy to the practitioners and the public at large.
2. Language (broadly defined) can be employed by varying audiences to understand, (re)frame, enact, and/or resist policy.
3. Language-based methods, including discourse analysis perspectives, allow scholars to investigate both the substance and systems of policy in action.

REFERENCES

Bakhtin, M. M. (1981). Discourse in the novel. In M. Holquist (Ed.), *The dialogic imagination: Four essays by M. M. Bakhtin* (pp. 259–422). Austin: University of Texas Press.

Benford, R. D., & Snow, D. A. (2000). Framing processes and social movements: An overview and assessment. *Annual Review of Sociology, 26,* 611–639.

Bennett, J. (2010). *Vibrant matter: A political ecology of things.* Durham: Duke University Press.

Bhatia, A. (2006). Critical discourse analysis of political press conferences. *Discourse & Society, 17*(2), 173–203.

Boden, D. (1994). *The business of talk: Organizations in action.* Cambridge: Polity Press.

Braidotti, R. (2013). *The posthuman.* Cambridge: Polity Press.

Cibulka, J. G. (1994). Policy analysis and the study of the politics of education. *Journal of Education Policy, 9*(5), 105–125.

Coburn, C. (2001). Collective sensemaking about reading: How teachers make reading policy in their professional communities. *Educational Evaluation and Policy Analysis., 23*(2), 145–170.

Coburn, C. E. (2006). Framing the problem of reading instruction: Using frame analysis to uncover the microprocesses of policy implementation. *American Educational Research Journal, 43*(3), 343–379.

Coburn, C. E., & Woulfin, S. L. (2012). Reading coaches and the relationship between policy and practice. *Reading Research Quarterly, 47*(1), 5–30.

Darling-Hammond, L. (1990). Teacher evaluation in transition: Emerging roles and evolving methods. In J. Millman & L. Darling-Hammond (Eds.), *The new handbook of teacher evaluation: Assessing elementary and secondary school teachers* (pp. 17–34). Newbury Park: Sage.

Darling-Hammond, L. (2013). *Getting teacher evaluation right: What really matters for effectiveness and improvement.* New York: Teachers College Press.

Gildersleeve, R. E., Cruz, C., Madriz, D., & Melendrez-Flores, C. (2015). Neoliberal futures and postsecondary opportunity: Janet Napolitano and the politics of Latina/o college choice. In P. Perez & M. Ceja (Eds.), *Higher education access and choice for Latino students.* New York: Routledge.

Goffman, I. (1974). *Frame analysis: An essay on the organization of experience.* Boston: Northwestern University Press.

Grant, L. W., Stronge, J. H., & Xu, X. (2013). A cross-cultural comparative study of teacher effectiveness: Analyses of award-winning teachers in the United States and China. *Educational Assessment, Evaluation and Accountability, 25*(3), 251–276.

Honig, M. I. (2006). Complexity and policy implementation: Challenges and opportunities for the field. In M. I. Honig (Ed.), *New directions in education policy implementation: Confronting complexity* (pp. 1–24). Albany: The State University of New York Press.

Howarth, D., & Stavrakakis, Y. (2000). Introducing discourse theory and political analysis. In D. R. Howarth, A. J. Norval, & Y. Stavrakakis (Eds.), *Discourse theory and political analysis* (pp. 1–23). Manchester: Manchester University Press.

Jameson, F. (1998). *The cultural turn: Selected writings on the postmodern, 1983–1998.* Brooklyn: Verso.

Jennings, N. E. (1996). *Interpreting policy in real classrooms: Case studies of state reform and teacher practice.* New York: Teachers College Press.

Lester, J. N., & Gabriel, R. (2014). The discursive construction of intelligence in introductory educational psychology textbooks. *Discourse Studies, 16*(6), 776–791.

Lester, J. N., Lochmiller, C. R., & Gabriel, R. (2016). Locating and applying critical discourse analysis within education policy: An introduction. *Education Policy Analysis Archives.* doi:10.14507/epaa.24.2768

McLaughlin, M. W. (1987). Learning from experience: Lessons from policy implementation. *Educational Evaluation & Policy Analysis, 9*(2), 171–178.

Odden, A. R. (Ed.). (1991). *Education policy implementation.* Albany: State University of New York Press.

Perez, R. (2013). Learning to make racism funny in the 'color-blind' era: Stand up comedy students, performance strategies, and the (re)production of racist jokes in public. *Discourse & Society, 24*(4), 478–503.

Raudenbush, S. W. (2009). The Brown legacy and the O'Connor challenge: Transforming schools in the images of children's potential. *Educational Researcher, 38,* 169–180.

Spillane, J. P. (1999). External reform initiatives and teachers' efforts to reconstruct their practice: The mediating role of teachers' zones of enactment. *Journal of Curriculum Studies, 31*(2), 1–33.

Spillane, J. (2004). *Standards deviation: How schools misunderstand education policy.* Cambridge, MA: Harvard University Press.

Spillane, J. P., Reiser, B. J., & Reimer, T. (2002). Policy implementation and cognition: Reframing and refocusing implementation research. *Review of Educational Research, 72*(3), 387–431.

Steinberg, M., & Donaldson, M. (2014). *The new educational accountability: Understanding the landscape of teacher evaluation in the post-NCLB era.* Storrs: Center for Education Policy Analysis [Policy brief]. Retrieved from http://cepa. uconn.edu/wp-content/uploads/sites/399/2014/02/The-New-Educational-Accountability_policy-brief_8-19-14.pdf

Steinmetz, G. (1999). *State/culture: State-formation after the cultural turn.* Ithaca: Cornell University Press.

Terhart, E. (2013). Teacher resistance against school reform: Reflecting an inconvenient truth. *School Leadership and Management, 33*(5), 486–500.

Townshend, J. (2004). Laclau and Mouffe's hegemonic project: The story so far. *Political Studies, 52,* 269–288.

Ulmer, J. B. (2015). Plasticity: A new materialist approach to policy and methodology. *Educational Philosophy and Theory, 47*(10), 1096–1109.

Weatherly, R., & Lipsky, M. (1977, May). Street level bureaucrats and institutional information: Implementing special education reform. *Harvard Educational Review, 47,* 171–197.

Youman, M., & Mather, N. (2013). Dyslexia laws in the USA. *Annals of Dyslexia, 63* (2), 133–153. doi:10.1007/s11881-012-0076-2

Jessica Nina Lester is Assistant Professor of Inquiry Methodology in the Department of Counseling & Educational Psychology in the School of Education at Indiana University. Much of her research is positioned at the intersection of discourse studies and disability studies. Lester recently co-edited a book focused on performance ethnographies and co-authored a book focused on the use of digital tools across the qualitative research process. She also co-authored a research methods textbook and is the co-editor of *The Palgrave Handbook of Child Mental Health: Discourse and Conversation Studies* and *The Palgrave Handbook of Adult Mental Health: Discourse and Conversation Studies.* Her most recent article has appeared in journals such as *Qualitative Inquiry, Qualitative Research,* and *Discourse Studies.*

Chad R. Lochmiller is Assistant Professor of Educational Leadership in the Department of Educational Leadership and Policy Studies in the School of Education at Indiana University. His current research focuses on education policy issues, particularly those related to school finance, human resource management, and leadership development. Lochmiller's research has been published in *Educational Administration Quarterly, Journal of Educational Administration, Journal of*

School Leadership, Education Policy Analysis Archives, Leadership and Policy in Schools, and edited volumes. Lochmiller is also a co-author of a research methods textbook, *An Introduction to Education Research: Connecting Methods to Practice,* designed for practitioner-scholars.

Rachael E. Gabriel is Assistant Professor of Literacy Education at the University of Connecticut. She is an associate of the Center for Education Policy Analysis and the Center on Post-Secondary Education and Disability at the University of Connecticut. Her research interests include teacher preparation, development and evaluation, as well as literacy instruction, interventions, and related policies. She is the author of *Reading's Non-Negotiables: Elements of Effective Reading Instruction* (2013) and co-editor of *Evaluating Literacy Instruction: Principles and Promising Practices* (2015) and *Performances of Research: Critical Issues in K-12 Education* (2013). In addition to serving as an associate editor of *Educational Administration Quarterly,* Gabriel is also on the editorial boards of the *American Educational Research Journal, Educational Policy Analysis Archives, Journal of Literacy Research,* and *Reading & Writing Quarterly.*

CHAPTER 2

Education Policy Implementation Research: A Call for New Approaches

Chad R. Lochmiller and Samantha L. Hedges

INTRODUCTION

Within this chapter, we argue that education policy research has experienced a somewhat fragmented expansion over the last few decades, particularly in relation to the use of varying and, at times, disparate methodological and theoretical perspectives. Specifically, we suggest that scholars from various methodological traditions have drawn the field in at least three distinct directions. In one direction, education policy researchers have increasingly advocated for the use of quantitative research approaches, particularly sophisticated econometric approaches (Brewer et al. 2008; McEwan 2008). This seems fueled, in part, by growing interest in school choice, teacher evaluation, performance-based compensation models, and other market-driven approaches to education reform as key policy issues. In another direction, scholars appear to be pulling the field toward the use of critical qualitative approaches to examine the inherent inequities, power differentials, and biases found within existing education policy arrangements (Young and Diem 2014). Of particular concern, scholars seem intent

C.R. Lochmiller (✉) • S.L. Hedges
Indiana University, Bloomington, IN, USA

© The Author(s) 2017
J.N. Lester et al. (eds.), *Discursive Perspectives on Education Policy and Implementation*, DOI 10.1007/978-3-319-58984-8_2

17

on unpacking inequities tied to educational opportunities for economically disadvantaged students, students of color, English-language learners, Lesbian, Gay, Bisexual, Transgender, Questionning (LGBTQ) students, and students with disabilities, among others. And, in still another direction, there are increasing calls by leading policy scholars to make salient connections between policymaking and evidence (Lubienski et al. 2014; The Pew-MacArthur Results First Initiative 2014). These scholars appear to be advocating for the use of mixed methods research approaches in order to make research more accessible to policymakers (Burch and Heinrich 2016).

Although these tensions are certainly shaping the field, there also appears to be some agreement that issues related to education policy implementation, which is the focus of this chapter, is best studied using qualitative research methods. For example, two well-known volumes discussing education policy implementation research have both highlighted the value of qualitative approaches by presenting examples of qualitative studies in their examination of education policy implementation issues (Honig 2006; Odden 1991). This reflects the recognition that contextual factors often influence how local policy actors take up policy issues and ideas (Weatherly and Lipsky 1977). Such a recognition necessitates the adoption of qualitative approaches. Indeed, as Denzin and Lincoln (2011) noted, "qualitative research is a situated activity that locates the observer in the world" and effectively "consists of a set of interpretive, material practices that make the world visible" (p. 3). Further, as Yanow (2007) stated,

> The use of qualitative methods in policy research is not new. Academic scholars and policy analysts have for some years been venturing out into the "field" as ethnographers or participant-observers to study first-hand the experiences of legislators, implementers, agency clients, community members, and other policy-relevant stakeholders. Others have based qualitative studies on in-depth interviews with various policy actors; and still others draw on legislative, agency, and other documents. (p. 405)

In short, qualitative research studies people, places, practices, and other elements found within a particular context, and this is certainly the case in the field of education policy. Thus, within this chapter, we do not attempt to resolve the vastly different directions pulling at the study of education policy. Rather, we take the view that differing methodological approaches have inherent value in a field as diverse as education policy and see the introduction of new methodological approaches as potentially beneficial.

Specifically, in this chapter, we argued for the use of language-based methods, such as conversation analysis, critical discourse analysis (CDA), and discursive psychology, among others, and note that such approaches may contribute to a further expansion of qualitative endeavors that aim to study education policy, particularly the study of policy implementation. In particular, we suggest that these approaches enable policy scholars to examine the linguistic and behavioral aspects of policy implementation at the level of text and talk, noting key implementation considerations such as sensemaking (Weick 1996; Spillane et al. 2002), which prior approaches have attended to at a more remote level.

More particularly, this chapter includes three sections. First, we present an overview of recent policy implementation research, beginning with a general summary and then offering more detailed discussion of the literature base. We use the first section both to highlight the scope of current policy research and to illustrate the methodological similarities across the literature. Indeed, in our review of this work, we found that qualitative policy scholars have generally employed some variation of case study methodology. We thus use this review as an opportunity to develop a rationale for new approaches to the study of policy implementation, particularly those which enable scholars to attend to the meaning and understanding of policy at the level of talk and text. Second, we offer a rationale for the application of language-based methods to the study of policy implementation issues and provide an abbreviate review of policy literature that has employed a language-based approach to research. In doing so, we highlight the benefits of such approaches in light of recent shifts toward the application of both cognitive and sociocultural learning perspectives on implementation of education policy. Finally, we offer recommendations for the field as they begin taking up language-based approaches.

RESEARCH ON POLICY IMPLEMENTATION

Within the field of education policy, implementation research has expanded considerably in recent years. Policy scholars have shown increasing interest in exploring the local nature of policy implementation as well as the experiences of key policy actors. Despite significant growth in the field, the field tends to lack widespread "agreement on the goals or methods of policy research" (Heck 2004, p. xviii). Indeed, the field has yet to identify seminal research studies, agreed upon theoretical perspectives, or even generated a significant number of basic textbooks with which to inform the training of aspiring education policy scholars. A cursory review of leading education policy journals (e.g., *Educational Administration Quarterly, Education Finance & Policy, Educational Policy, Educational Evaluation & Policy Analysis, Education Policy Analysis Archives*) appears to support this view. Scholars have recently examined a variety of topics within these journals using a wide range of quantitative and qualitative research methodologies. It does not appear that scholars have adopted a single methodological approach.

At the macro level, and owing much to the influx of interest in educational issues from economists (Brewer et al. 2008), the field has increasingly employed sophisticated quantitative research designs and statistical techniques to examine key policy issues. McEwan (2008) noted the widespread application of causal research methods (e.g., experimental and quasi-experimental designs). This application should not be surprising, however, as education policy research has historically been closely associated with quantitative research traditions and program evaluation methods (Berliner 2002; Heck 2004; Sadovnik 2007). Indeed, this reflects the implicit connections between education policy research and the more traditionally recognized fields of economics, political science, and public affairs. Further, it reflects a need among policy scholars to determine whether policy changes effect individuals, organizations, and communities.

Under the No Child Left Behind Act of 2001, federal education policy research has shifted dramatically toward "evidence-based practice" and "scientific research". As Berliner (2002) noted, such terms are simply "code words for randomized experiments" (p. 18). Indeed, in recent years, federal education funding has sought to undertake research studies that draw heavily on both experimental and quasi-experimental designs (Berliner 2002; Lather 2004a, b). In particular, federal education research funding has increasingly supported randomized control trials as the "gold standard" for education research (Shavelson and Towne 2002). These studies seek to determine whether interventions "work" in particular district and school contexts, with specific student populations, and given specific programmatic configurations. As such, they reflect the field's interest in associating policy designs and implementation choices with specific outcomes.

At the same time, the policy field has expressed considerable interest in qualitative research approaches (Herriott and Firestone 1983; Yanow 2003). These studies often adopt a localized perspective and rely heavily on the use of in-depth examination of policy issues and implementation experiences (Honig 2006). In many cases, these studies describe how actors implement policies under a narrow set of circumstances. For example, researchers have examined how classroom teachers and principals implement policy-driven reforms within elementary, middle, and high schools. One important aspect of these studies has been their tendency to highlight the implicit connections between policy implementation issues and broader social justice considerations. One of the emerging trends in the broader policy research literature has been the adoption of critical perspectives to study policy issues (Young and Diem 2014). These perspectives often employ qualitative methods and focus on unpacking issues of power, privilege, and (in)justice within the context of localized experiences.

Thus, there are variable approaches to which scholars have approaches the study of policy implementation. To offer a more detailed overview of these varying perspectives, we next offer a discussion of illustrative research studies focused on policy implementation.

Illustrative Research on Policy Implementation

A general review of recent literature suggests that scholars have conducted a significant amount of policy implementation research related to public education within the United States (e.g., Honig 2006; McLaughlin 1987; Odden 1991). This research has examined a variety of policy issues, including the implementation of state school reconstitution policies (Malen et al. 2002); comprehensive school reform models (Datnow et al. 2003); career ladder policies (Timar 1989); peer assistance and review (PAR) for the purposes of teacher evaluation (Goldstein 2004); student learning and graduation requirements (Sipple et al. 2004); school-based bonus policies for classroom teachers (Marsh 2012); and most recently the implementation of the Common Core State Standards (Coburn et al. 2016). Throughout this period, scholars have also studied the role of external actors within the policy implementation process (Coburn 2005a; Glazer 2009; Honig 2004) and sought to describe the behaviors of specific types of policy implementers, such as street-level bureaucrats within the context of school district central offices (Honig 2006). Collectively, these studies have promoted the importance of local policy actors within the context of implementation research. Indeed, as Odden (1991) noted, early policy implementation research suggested that many policy initiatives were "doomed to failure" because of "local implementation resistance" (p. 1). More recently, scholars have posited that such resistance might reflect localized sensemaking activities (Spillane et al. 2002), which refers to the process of reconciling a policy actors' understanding of policy with their practice. This view of policy research suggests that contextual influences heavily shape policy implementation. Thus, perhaps unsurprisingly, districts and schools have been particularly ripe settings for this research, given the confluence of federal, state, and local policy directives, as well as the historical tendency to view educational matters as an issue of local control.

We conducted a cursory review of articles focused on policy implementation published in *Educational Evaluation and Policy Analysis* since 2001. We found a number of qualitative studies, most of which described the implementation of policy in particular states, cities, districts, and schools. For example, Malen et al. (2002) conducted a two-year qualitative study of schools targeted for state-driven school reconstitution. Their analysis pointed to the powerful role that local factors have on policy implementation, in particular the conflict that arises when policy actors adopt positions that run counter to the intent of the policy. Their research highlight the power that such conditions have on the implementation process as well as the extent to which local policy actors' choices influence how policy will be implemented. Other studies we reviewed seemed to emphasize a similar understanding of the policy implementation process.

A core issue within the implementation research relates to the degree of alignment between a policy and various state, district, and school needs. Studies suggest that misalignment between goals often undermines the effectiveness of a policy's implementation (Glazer 2009; McDonnell 1991). For example, Glazer (2009) studied how an instructional reform program (e.g., America's Choice) fits with the broader policy goals of a district and state. He found that when implementing a new instructional reform program in a school, the congruence of the policy environment and the design of the program potentially predict whether implementation will be successful. When a program aligned with policy objectives, the state and district were more likely to support implementation. At the local level, such support increases the possibility that key resources (e.g., textbooks, professional development, funding) will be provided. Plus, state involvement in a particular reform program minimizes the number of competing programs, increases funding for staff and leaders, mandates texts that work well with the program, and better coordinates professional development efforts (Glazer 2009). Across these studies, we noted the importance of aligning policy goals with the institutional contexts surrounding the policy's implementation.

Policy scholars have also studied the influence that policy has on local policy actors' professional practice, which includes classroom instruction and school administration. Scholars have discerned that successful education policy implementation depends on the degree to which teachers and administrators have sufficient knowledge about policy to comply with and thus align their practice to the policy's primary goals (Coburn et al. 2016; Knapp et al. 1991). For example, Louis et al. (2005) conducted a case study of three schools and found that successful implementation and acceptance of state-mandated accountability standards depended on how well the standards related to what the teachers were already doing in the classroom, how the school leaders interpreted the standards, and whether the leadership and teachers felt the standards were a state overreach. If teachers felt the policy challenged their professionalism, the researchers concluded that implementation was unlikely to succeed. Moreover, Louis et al. (2005) discovered that negativity among school leaders affected interpretation of the policy. Implementation proceeded successfully if the state standards were borne out of school practices that were occurring in schools prior to development of the standards, and if teachers saw the standards as promoting better teaching and the facilitation of content coverage. In some cases, to foster effortless implementation within an educational structure, and to gain support from all stakeholders, new policies may be presented as somewhat ambiguous to a school environment. However, this top-down approach to policy implementation may lead to confusion during the implementation process. Through a qualitative study of the Peer Assistance and Review (PAR) approach to teacher evaluation, Goldstein (2004) learned that the ambiguity of the policy led to disagreement among policy implementers, which led to varying interpretations of leadership and staff roles in the implementation process. Across these studies, scholars highlighted the important association that must exist between policy, practice, and the local understanding of a policy's core messages or signals.

Not surprisingly, research has positioned teachers as playing a central role in the successful implementation of education policy and thus scholars have invested considerable effort exploring and understanding teachers' roles as policy actors. Indeed, a key assumption in the policy literature is that teachers serve as an important link between federal and state policy mandates and local implementation success. For instance, when examining school reform in culturally and linguistically diverse contexts, Datnow et al. (2003) discovered that reform implementation was often successful at the school level if teachers saw value in the reforms and could see how the reform meshed with their teaching and complemented the bilingual education program. Their longitudinal study of 13 schools concluded that reforms were successful if the teachers saw them as affirming student's cultural background and promoting multiculturalism in their school. Teachers' interpretation of policy appears critical to successful implementation. In some cases, teachers used their social networks to interpret policy (Coburn and Russell 2008). Policy messages were passed through teachers' social networks, with these messages often determining the effectiveness and level of policy implementation (Coburn and Russell). However, policy messages were only found to positively affect policy implementation when there was trust among teachers. Through an exploratory comparative case study of two school districts, Coburn and Russell determined that teachers were most likely to trust colleagues with whom they have had prior professional relationships and colleagues who were close in proximity to them in the school building. The authors also learned that the influence of social networks on policy implementation depends on the structure of the network, access to expertise, and the depth of interaction within the network.

Relatedly, scholars have argued that school leaders influence the success of policy implementation and found that leaders, particularly principals, occupy an important role in determining how policy implementation proceeds within local school sites. For instance, Jabbar (2015a, b) examined how school leaders responded to competition in New Orleans, a city that includes both a state-run Recovery School District and the Orleans Parish School Board, which operates traditional public schools and charter schools. In this context, parents choose which school to send their children and so school leaders must construct a means to attract and retain students. Through interviews, Jabbar (2015b) discovered that school leaders have responded to this competition by taking one or more of the following approaches: improving school quality and functioning; differentiating from others; "glossification" or marketing existing school offerings; and "creaming" and "cropping" or actively selecting or excluding particular types of students (p. 644). The localized interpretation of policy and the use of varying implementation mechanisms allow local leaders to match the policy to the context and the goals of their institution. An embedded case study conducted by Sipple et al. (2004) offered further evidence of school leaders' maneuvering during the implementation process. Through their examination of an organizational response to standards-based reforms, they learned that school leaders took advantage of internal mechanisms at their disposal to graduate students. The school leaders responded to the implementation of high-stakes testing and the need to increase graduation rates by creating a flexible school schedule to provide remedial courses and by transferring students to General Education Diploma (GED) programs or alternative schools to keep them from being reported as dropping out.

The emphasis on the teacher and principal role in the implementation process reflects an underlying recognition of the importance of "street-level bureaucracy", a term coined by Weatherly and Lipsky (1977) to describe the policy implementation process. Street-level bureaucrats can play a critical role in bridging relationships between bureaucracy and community. For example, Honig (2006) used the concept of street-level bureaucrats to examine how the frontline staff of public school bureaucracy, referred to as boundary spanners, broker relationships with community organizations to implement collaborative education policies. Similarly, Marsh (2012) examined the relationship between the New York City Department of Education (NYCDOE) and the United Federation of Teachers (UFT) through a two-year case study. She discovered that when a voluntary school-based bonus policy was introduced at the district level in New York City, the NYCDOE and the UFT worked together to form Compensation Committees (CC) at each school to determine how bonus compensation would be decided. The CCs helped the city to gain buy-in to the policy, bridge competing values of the UFT and NYCDOE and strengthen negotiations, and ensure that there was a democratic process for deciding how to distribute the bonuses within each school. Other studies that examined how street-level bureaucrats broker relationships with collaborators have shown that even when there is strong agreement on a policy, participants implementing the policy may view their roles disparately and act in ways that are divergent from the intent. For example, in a single case design, Goldstein (2004) analyzed the role of a consulting teacher, principal, and evaluation panel in the PAR evaluation method and how they negotiate distributed leadership at the implementation level. The researcher found that distributive leadership can have varying interpretations depending on the policy actor: that is, the consulting teachers viewed the processes as collaborative or task sharing; superintendents did not support (consulting) teachers evaluating (participating) teachers; and principals saw the collaboration as task division.

Further, an emerging line of research explores the role of external partners in shaping the implementation of policies within specific organizational settings. Honig (2004), for instance, considered the unique role that four intermediary organizations—defined as "organizations that operate between policymakers and implementers to affect changes in roles and practices for both parties" (p. 65)—played in the implementation of policies in Oakland, California. She found that intermediary organizations influenced the implementation process by providing the resources, knowledge, and infrastructure needed by local actors. External partners have also been referred to as "nonsystem actors" and may include for-profit firms, membership organizations, and nonprofit organizations (Coburn 2005b, p. 23). In a case study of two elementary schools, Coburn (2005b) interviewed three focal teachers and learned that nonsystem actors operated in the education arena to help mediate policy messages entering the schools and discovered nonsystem actors influenced teachers' policy implementation in the classroom more than system messengers (i.e., municipality, district). Nonsystem messengers were the key mediators between policy and practice, providing guidance to the teachers through information, professional development, technical assistance, and curricular material. Coburn (2005b) determined that teachers were more likely to respond to nonsystem actors when their message directly applied to the teacher's classroom, pedagogical practices, or afforded flexibility to implement the policy. Additionally, research refers to external partners as interveners (Glazer 2009). Interveners may offer curriculum-based programs, subject-specific innovations, school leadership models, and comprehensive school reform programs. Through qualitative methods, Glazer (2009) studied an intervener offering a comprehensive school reform program that targeted efforts at the school level and found that the interaction between the design, environment, and reform organization was more manageable when the design focused on the schools rather than on the district or municipal level. Glazer (2009) found that when key tasks of supporting schools and monitoring implementation began to shift away from the school-based reform program implementers to the district and state, the program design weakened and the goals of the program shifted, which led to inconsistencies in interpretation and implementation of the design. Overall, studies point to the value of external partners at the school level; however, to gain implementation success beyond the school level, external partners often need to focus their efforts on elaborate designs aimed at enhancing the knowledge and capabilities of district and state personnel (Glazer 2009).

Looking across these studies, it becomes clear that scholars have primarily relied upon various applications of the *qualitative case study* as their methodological approach. Indeed, as shown in Table 2.1, of the six policy implementation studies published in *Educational Evaluation & Policy Analysis* since 2001, all have used some form of a case study design.

Goldstein (2004) and Sipple et al. (2004) both conducted a case study of a state policy. Datnow et al. (2003) and Malen et al. (2002) both conducted a case study of a school district's response to a particular policy. Finally, Honig (2004) and Marsh (2012) both studied policy activities within the context of particular cities. Probing further, we also note that most of these studies have involved similar forms of data collection. For example, all of the studies carried out semi-structured interviews as the primary data collection technique. Four integrated observations of selected activities and three retrieved documents and other policy-relevant artifacts, such as news releases, technical reports, and internal memos. Two used participant surveys to augment interviews and observational data. While our review is not exhaustive, it does provide important insights about the current status of the case study, which we suggest is perhaps the signature qualitative research methodology used by the field.

QUALITATIVE APPROACHES TO THE STUDY OF POLICY

The methods literature appears to support the view that policy research often depends, at least in part, on case study applications to investigate the contextual influences on policy implementation. For example, Goertz (2006) offered a qualitative case study as the leading example of a policy analysis in the American Education Research Association's *Handbook of Complementary Methods in Education Research*. Further, Honig (2006) acknowledged that:

> qualitative research designs and methods have become important sources of knowledge for implementation researchers. In particular, strategic qualitative cases – cases that provide special opportunities to build knowledge about little understood and often complex phenomena – have long informed implementation in other fields and seem to be becoming more standard fare within education. Such methods and research designs, especially when well grounded in theory, have allowed contemporary researchers to elaborate the dimensions of and interactions among policy, people, and places that comprise implementation in the contemporary educational systems. (p. 22)

Such "strategic qualitative cases" have afforded policy scholars the opportunity to examine particular "cases" of implementation. Some scholars have advocated for the use of multiple cases to study the implementation of policy (Herriott and Firestone 1983). Other policy scholars have expanded

Table 2.1 Illustrative qualitative research studies focused on the implementation of education policy in Educational Evaluation Policy Analysis (EEPA) since 2001

Study authors	Year published	Policy level	Qualitative methodology	Primary data sources	Policy issues
Malen et al.	2002	District	Case study	Semi-structured interviews, extensive observations, document collection	School turnaround and reconstitution
Datnow et al.	2003	District and school	Case study	Semi-structured interviews, observations, document collection	Comprehensive school reform
Goldstein	2004	State	Case study	Observations, semi-structured interviews, multi-wave surveys	Teacher evaluation policy, accountability
Sipple et al.	2004	State	Case study	Semi-structured interviews	State standards, end-of-course exams (i.e., regents exams)
Honig	2004	City	Case study	Semi-structured interviews, observations	External support for policy implementation
Marsh	2012	City	Case study	Semi-structured interviews, surveys	Voluntary school-based bonus policy

on the list of possible qualitative methodologies. For instance, Sadovnik's (2007) chapter on qualitative policy research in the *Handbook of Public Policy Analysis* broadened the list of key qualitative methodologies to include ethnography (Hammersley and Atkinson 2007), action research (Stringer 2013), case study (Herriott and Firestone 1983; Yin 2014), and grounded theory research (Corbin and Strauss 1990; Glaser and Strauss 1967).

Given the widespread use of case study methodology in policy implementation research, it is important to examine why the case study has garnered such support from policy researchers. First, a case study's bounded nature affords opportunities for policy researchers to examine policy issues in-depth and to describe implementation experiences in a holistic manner. Likewise, the opportunity to integrate both qualitative and quantitative data appeals to many researchers who are seeking more pragmatic approaches, particularly those advocating the use of mixed methods research to understand the inherent complexity of policy issues (Burch and Heinrich 2016). Further, case study methodology offers policy researchers the ability to adopt multiple theoretical perspectives to explain various aspects of the policy process or to pursue grounded approaches wherein the scholars derive theoretical explanations from the experiences of those involved in the implementation of the policy (Corbin and Strauss 1990). Collectively, these strengths position the case study as a flexible methodological approach that affords policy researchers the ability to examine policy implementation experiences in-depth. With these strengths, it is perhaps unsurprising that policy scholars have relied so heavily on the case study as a dominant methodology.

While the case study represents an appealing approach, we note that it is not the only approach that policy researchers might consider employing. Further, there are limitations to what such an approach can afford. While the education policy and policy implementation literatures do not discuss such limitations, the broader qualitative methods literature has raised this point. Stoecker (1991), for example, outlined the criticisms of the case study approach, particularly those related to external and internal validity, and noted that the approach requires more work before considering it a rigorous approach. With respect to policy implementation research, the case study suffers from several limitations. First, by its nature, the case can present a somewhat superficial and highly interpreted understanding of policy as the analyst envisions it. Policy implementation thus becomes what the analyst "sees" as opposed to what the participants' experience. The analyst might place his or her interpretation on the policy actors as opposed to using the policy actor's own words or policy texts. Of course, a research can take measures to address this concern, and many scholars have. Second, the construction of particular cases can effectively extract policy actors from the communities within which the meaning(s) of policy exist. As such, the analyst decontextualizes the study of policy implementation from those who are engaged in the implementation process directly. Such an approach may be "naïve"; however, as Ball (2006) noted, "research is thoroughly enmeshed in the social and in the political" (p. 15). Thus, it is critical that a researcher be careful not to extract interpretations of policy from a given context, which case studies may risk doing. Finally, case study research has mostly relied upon policy actors "telling" the analyst about their experiences with the policy. Such an emphasis may neglect as a potentially valuable source of data the actors' own talk or social actions. Their talk or everyday actions, we suggest, incorporates both the actor's own understanding policy and their efforts to influence the understanding of others.

Emergent Approaches to the Study of Education Policy Implementation

While the preceding sections outline the dominance of the case study methodology for the study of education policy, we view this methodology as one of the many possible approaches. Indeed, given increasing interest, particularly in education, about the cognitive (Spillane et al. 2002, 2006) and sociocultural (Coburn and Stein 2006; Gallucci 2003; Rogoff 1994) aspects of policy implementation, we assert that language-based methods might offer alternative approaches for scholars to address both the complexity of the policy implementation process and the particular meanings that policy actors convey when engaging with policy issues. For the purposes of this chapter, we define language-based methods broadly and include within them conversation analysis (Psathas 1995), CDA (van Dijk 1993), and discursive psychology (Edwards and Potter 1992), among others. Conversation analysis "studies the order/organization/orderliness of social action, particularly those social actions that are located in everyday interaction, in discursive practices, in the sayings/tellings/doings of members of society" (Psathas 1995, p. 2), which is further discussed in Chaps. 3 and 5 of this volume. CDA is principally concerned with "the role of discourse in the (re)production and challenge dominance" (van Dijk 1993, p. 249). As such, CDA examines how issues of power, inequity, and injustice are manifest within the context of discourse and how discourse itself potentially reifies these concepts. This is exemplified in Chap. 9 of this volume. Discursive psychology focuses on the "action orientation of talk and writing. For both participants and analysts, the primary issue is the social actions, or interactional work, being done in the discourse" (Edwards and Potter 1992, p. 2). This perspective assumes that language itself accomplishes something. For example, within the context of policy implementation, an analyst might examine how individual actors use statements about a particular policy to promote support for or undermine the overarching objectives of the policy. Chapters 10 and 11 in this volume illustrate this orientation well. And, of course, there are many other language-based methods that we could note as potentially fruitful. Indeed, those approaches included within the umbrella of discourse analysis are principally concerned with studying "how language gets recruited 'on site' to enact specific social activities and social identities" where identities refer to "different ways of participating in different sorts of social groups, cultures, and institutions" (Gee 2005, p. 1). Thus, discourse analysis, and language-based methods more generally, might serve to support an analysis of how policy actors invoke particular statements, phrases, or words to identify themselves to other policy actors within the policy arena.

A cursory review of the policy literature reveals that language-based approaches, particularly CDA (Taylor 2004), have been used fairly broadly in the study of policy implementation. For example, a special issue of *Education Policy Analysis Archives* (Lester et al. 2016) recently presented a series of articles employing CDA to examine current policy issues, some of which were directly related to policy implementation. Lenhoff and Ulmer (2016) used CDA to examine how the language of educational reformers intersected with and informed the implementation of a twenty-first-century skills program. Emery (2016) investigated the discourses of policymakers in England and Wales as it relates to social-emotional learning. Jimenez-Silva, Bernstein, and Baca (2016) examined how school districts interpret state education policy using public statements posted on state and district websites. Their central finding was that policy is both a product of and produced by discourses.

A further review of the policy literature in leading journals pointed to studies using discourse analysis when studying policy meaning and implementation. To examine the meaning of policy, Little and Cohen-Vogel (2016) studied how policy organizations framed their views of kindergarten, while Adams (2016) employed positioning theory to understand the interplay between discourse and discursive acts when examining "policy-explanation", "policy-framing", and "policy-forming". As another example, Taylor (2004) used CDA to explain how language "works" in policy literature in order to understand in what ways "policy texts are read, implemented, and how they may be used in emancipatory ways by teachers and policy activists" (p. 445). Heineke and Cameron (2011) used discourse analysis to understand the situated meaning of Teach for America (TFA) alumni utilized to characterize and make sense of their interpretation of Arizona's English-only language policy and how to appropriate the policy. In a later, related study, Heineke (2015) employed discourse analysis to examine English-language development (ELD) teachers' engagement in an ongoing study group designed to share expertise and interpret and negotiate English-only policy implementation.

Computer-media discourse analysis (CDMA) and Fairclough's (1992, 2010, 2013) three-dimensional framework of discourse analysis, which includes the examination of governmental artifacts, discursive practices, and social practices, have also been applied to the study of policy implementation. CDMA was used by Scriven Berry and Herrington (2012) to examine community responses to a school district's newly adopted Differentiated Accountability (DA) system. Through the study of article comments published on the website of a major newspaper, the authors analyzed how social media was used to deliberate and organize against policy implementation. Drawing upon Fairclough's three-dimensional framework of CDA in conjunction with a qualitative thematic approach to data analysis, Hemmer et al. (2013) studied how alternative school leaders maintained their innovative mission while implementing an authoritative accountability policy.

When viewed through the lens of language-based methods, policy implementation research offers new and potentially valuable questions. Indeed, recognizing that policy implementation occurs within particular contexts elevates the need to understand how an actor's understanding(s) of policy come into existence. Such context likely plays an important role in the shaping of education policy goals during the legislative process as well as during the implementation of policy at the local level. Much as prior research has highlighted the frontline implementer's role in shaping policy understanding (Honig 2006; Weatherly and Lipsky 1977), more recent research has emphasized the importance of both the influence of communities on policy implementation and policy actor's sensemaking of new policy directives.

Given recent shifts in the field toward understanding the cognitive and sociocultural aspects of the policy implementation process (Ball 1994; Cohen and Hill 2001; Lin 1998; Spillane 2004; Spillane et al. 2002), the use of language-based methods to the study of education policy implementation may be particularly valuable. Indeed, much of the discussion about policy implementation has focused on sensemaking (Spillane et al. 2002; Weick 1996), which refers to the cognitive process that policy actors engage in when responding to policy-based stimuli. As Spillane et al. (2006) aptly noted:

> Considering the role of human cognition in policy implementation underscores the importance of unintentional failures of implementation. What is paramount is not simply *that* implementing agents choose to respond to policy but also *what* they understand themselves to be responding to. The "what" of policy begins with the policy texts such as directions, goals, and regulations. Individuals must use their prior knowledge and experience to notice, make sense of, interpret, and react to incoming stimuli. (p. 49)

Thus, talk and text both play an instrumental role in the sensemaking process and yet most studies of sensemaking in implementation have focused more broadly on higher level cases. The field of educational policy has not (widely) employed methodologies to examine and/or unpack how these everyday and institutional interactions may influence policy implementation or, more important, how policy actors use such interactions may shape the ways in which particular policies come to be known or taken up. Our contention is not that approaches such as case study methodology have been unhelpful but rather that language-based methods enable policy scholars to examine sensemaking at a macro and micro level. We suggest that through a close examination of talk and text, policy scholars may be better able to explore how nuanced understandings of policy are elevated within various individual, communal, and institutional discourses during the implementation process. These understandings are important in implementation, as they describe not only how actors make sense of the policy but also how actors position the policy in relation to their own role and work.

CONCLUSIONS AND POSSIBLE DIRECTIONS

Qualitative approaches to research have been widely used in the study of education policy implementation and will likely continue to be as the field continues to embrace such approaches. While case study methodology continues to be the dominant approach and there is ample support for such in the policy literature (Honig 2006), the opportunity to introduce other approaches to this work is both timely and worthwhile. Indeed, we conclude that language-based methods might be particularly valuable to the study of education policy implementation. These variable methods have the potential to illuminate new understandings regarding the policy actors' constructions and interpretations of policy as well as the ways in which such interpretations are made visible in talk and text. While such language-based methods have not been widely used in the study of education policy implementation, there is evidence that these approaches may be increasingly popular and applicable to the study of policy more broadly (e.g., Ball 1990; Emery 2016; Jimenez-Silva et al. 2016; Lenhoff and Ulmer 2016; O'Laughlin and Lindle 2014; Taylor 2004; Taylor et al. 1997).

The question that remains to be addressed is which issues language-based methods might examine in relation to policy implementation. We surmise, based on the literature that we have reviewed, that there are at least three specific issues that such approaches might be useful for studying. First, we see these methods as being useful for examining how policy actors' formulate responses to policy-specific goals, directives, or mandates. We envision that such responses are often formulated for the purposes of supporting and/or blocking the policy's implementation. Second, given increasing interest in the sociocultural aspects of policy implementation, we see the application of language-based methods as providing new ways to delve deeply into issues related to culture, learning, and social interaction as potential influences on policy. Indeed, while sensemaking has largely been studied using case study approaches, we see the opportunity to apply language-based methods as an important extension to this work by allowing scholars to probe deeply into images, arguments, and positions articulated by policy actors relative to their understanding of the policy. Finally, given the opportunity to look closely at talk and text, we see these methodologies as potentially useful tools for exploring how policy actors take up policy ideas and introduce said ideas within particular organizational settings. For example, we envision such approaches as being useful for understanding how principals and teachers discuss issues of reform, how teachers communicate state learning objectives to students, and how students identify and make sense of these standards in their own conversations with other students.

Summary

In this chapter, we first discussed tensions influencing the field of educational policy and shaping the methodological choices that policy scholars make. We then reviewed policy implementation research, highlighting across this review the ways in which localized understandings of policy shapes its implementation. After this review, we noted the methodological similarities of the research. In particular, we highlighted the dominance of the qualitative case study as the default methodology in policy research. We argued that this methodological approach has served the field well but the introduction and use of new approaches would expand the field. Finally, we advocated for the adoption of language-based methods in the study of policy implementation. We contend that such approaches provide scholars with the ability to study both the sociocultural and sensemaking aspects of policy implementation.

Key Connections to Policy Research

1. Much of the existing research on education policy implementation employs qualitative research designs used to unpack the experiences of implementing agents at various levels of the policy system.

2. The dominant research methodology used to investigate issues related to policy implementation is the qualitative case study, with interviews, observations, documents, and surveys being among the most common methods of data collection used.

3. Given the potential for case study research to decontextualize the policy implementation process from its institutional and community setting, other methodologies may be valuable in producing a more embedded interpretation of policy actors' understanding of and orientations to policy issues. Such methodologies may include language-based methods, including conversation analysis, CDA, and discursive psychology, among others.

References

Adams, P. (2016). Education policy: Explaining, framing and forming. *Journal of Education Policy, 31*(3), 290–307.

Ball, S. J. (1990). *Politics and policymaking in education: Explorations in policy sociology*. London: Routledge.

Ball, S. (1994). *Education reform*. Philadelphia: Open University Press.

Ball, S. J. (2006). *Education policy and social class: The selected works of Stephen J. Ball*. New York: Routledge.

Berliner, D. C. (2002). Comment: Educational research: The hardest science of all. *Educational Researcher, 31*(8), 18–20.

Brewer, D. J., Hentschke, G. C., & Eide, E. R. (2008). The role of economics in education policy research. In H. F. Ladd & E. B. Fiske (Eds.), *Handbook of research in education finance and policy* (pp. 23–41). New York: Routledge.

Burch, P., & Heinrich, C. J. (2016). *Mixed methods for policy research and program evaluation*. Thousand Oaks: SAGE.

Coburn, C. E. (2005a). Shaping teacher sensemaking: School leaders and the enactment of reading policy. *Educational Policy, 19*(3), 476–509.

Coburn, C. E. (2005b). The role of nonsystem actors in the relationship between policy and practice: The case of reading instruction in California. *Educational Evaluation and Policy Analysis, 27*(1), 23–52.

Coburn, C. E., & Russell, J. L. (2008). District policy and teachers' social networks. *Educational Evaluation and Policy Analysis, 30*(3), 203–235.

Coburn, C. E., & Stein, M. K. (2006). Communities of practice theory and the role of teacher professional community in policy implementation. In M. I. Honig (Ed.), *New directions in education policy implementation: Confronting complexity* (pp. 25–46). Albany: SUNY Press.

Coburn, C. E., Hill, H. C., & Spillane, J. P. (2016). Alignment and accountability in policy design and implementation the common core state standards and implementation research. *Educational Researcher.* doi:10.3102/0013189X16651080

Cohen, D. K., & Hill, H. C. (2001). *Learning policy: When state education reform works.* New Haven: Yale University Press.

Corbin, J. M., & Strauss, A. (1990). Grounded theory research: Procedures, canons, and evaluative criteria. *Qualitative Sociology, 13*(1), 3–21.

Datnow, A., Borman, G. D., Stringfield, S., Overman, L. T., & Castellano, M. (2003). Comprehensive school reform in culturally and linguistically diverse contexts: Implementation and outcomes from a four-year study. *Educational Evaluation and Policy Analysis, 25*(2), 143–170.

Denzin, N. K., & Lincoln, Y. S. (2011). Introduction: The disciplined practice of qualitative research. In N. K. Denzin & Y. S. Lincoln (Eds.), *The SAGE handbook of qualitative research* (4th ed.). Thousand Oaks: SAGE.

Edwards, D., & Potter, J. (1992). *Discursive psychology.* Thousand Oaks: SAGE.

Emery, C. (2016). A critical discourse analysis of New Labour discourse of social and emotional learning (SEL) across schools in England and Wales: Conversations with policymakers. *Education Policy Analysis Archives, 24*(104). doi:10.14507/epaa.24.2236

Fairclough, N. (1992). *Discourse and social change.* Cambridge: Polity Press.

Fairclough, N. (2010). *Critical discourse analysis: The critical study of language* (2nd ed.). New York: Routledge.

Fairclough, N. (2013). *Language and power* (2nd ed.). New York: Routledge.

Gallucci, C. (2003). Communities of practice and the mediation of teachers' responses to standards-based reform. *Education Policy Analysis Archives, 11*, 35.

Gee, J. P. (2005). *An introduction to discourse analysis: Theory and method* (2nd ed.). New York: Routledge.

Glaser, B. G., & Strauss, A. L. (1967). *The discovery of grounded theory: Strategies for qualitative research.* Piscataway: Transaction.

Glazer, J. L. (2009). How external interveners leverage large-scale change: The case of America's choice, 1998–2003. *Educational Evaluation and Policy Analysis, 31*(3), 269–297.

Goertz, M. E. (2006). Policy analysis: Studying policy implementation. In J. L. Green, G. Camilli, & P. B. Elmore (Eds.), *Handbook of complementary methods in education research* (pp. 701–710). New York: Routledge.

Goldstein, J. (2004). Making sense of distributed leadership: The case of peer assistance and review. *Educational Evaluation and Policy Analysis, 26*(2), 173–197.

Hammersley, M., & Atkinson, P. (2007). *Ethnography: Principals in practice* (3rd ed.). New York: Routledge.

Heck, R. H. (2004). *Studying educational and social policy: Theoretical concepts and research methods.* Mahwah: Lawrence Erlbaum.

Heineke, A. J. (2015). Negotiating language policy and practice: Teachers of English learners in an Arizona study group. *Educational Policy, 29*(6), 843–878.

Heineke, A. J., & Cameron, Q. (2011). Closing the classroom door and the achievement gap: Teach for America alumni teachers' appropriation of Arizona language policy. *Education and Urban Society, 45*(4), 483–505.

Hemmer, L. M., Madsen, J., & Torres, M. S. (2013). Critical analysis of accountability policy in alternative schools: Implications for school leaders. *Journal of Educational Administration, 51*(5), 655–679.

Herriott, R. E., & Firestone, W. A. (1983). Multisite qualitative policy research: Optimizing description and generalizability. *Educational Researcher, 12*(2), 14–19.

Honig, M. I. (2004). The new middle management: Intermediary organizations in education policy implementation. *Educational Evaluation and Policy Analysis, 26*(1), 65–87.

Honig, M. I. (2006). Street-level bureaucracy revisited: Frontline district central-office administrators as boundary spanners in education policy implementation. *Educational Evaluation and Policy Analysis, 28*(4), 357–383.

Jabbar, H. (2015a). 'Drenched in the past': The evolution of market-oriented reforms in New Orleans. *Journal of Education Policy, 30*(6), 751–772.

Jabbar, H. (2015b). "Every kid is money": Market-like competition and school leader strategies in New Orleans. *Educational Evaluation and Policy Analysis, 37*(4), 638–659.

Jimenez-Silva, M., Bernstein, K., & Baca, E. (2016). An analysis of how restrictive language policies are interpreted by Arizona's Department of Education and three individual school districts' website. *Education Policy Analysis Archives, 24*(105). doi:10.14507/epaa.24.2291

Knapp, M. S., Stearns, M. S., Turnbull, B. J., David, J. L., & Peterson, S. M. (1991). Cumulative effects of federal education policies at the local level. In A. R. Odden (Ed.), *Policy implementation* (pp. 105–124). Albany: SUNY Press.

Lather, P. (2004a). This is your father's paradigm: Government intrusion and the case of qualitative research in education. *Qualitative Inquiry, 10*(1), 15–34.

Lather, P. (2004b). Scientific research in education: A critical perspective. *British Educational Research Journal, 30*(6), 759–772.

Lenhoff, S. W., & Ulmer, J. B. (2016). Reforming for "all" or for "some": Misalignment in the discourses of education reformers and implementers. *Education Policy Analysis Archives, 24*(108). doi:10.14507/epaa.24.2273

Lester, J. N., Lochmiller, C. R., & Gabriel, R. (2016). Locating and applying critical discourse analysis within education policy. *Education Policy Analysis Archives, 24* (102). doi:10.14507/epaa.24.2768

Lin, A. C. (1998). Bridging positivist and interpretivist approaches to qualitative methods. *Policy Studies Journal, 26*(1), 162–180.

Little, M. H., & Cohen-Vogel, L. (2016). Too much too soon? An analysis of the discourses used by policy advocates in the debate over kindergarten. *Education Policy Analysis Archives, 23*(106). Retrieved from http://epaa.asu.edu

Louis, K. S., Febey, K., & Schroeder, R. (2005). State-mandated accountability in high schools: Teachers' interpretations of a new era. *Educational Evaluation and Policy Analysis, 27*(2), 177–204.

Lubienski, C., Scott, J., & DeBray, E. (2014). The politics of research production, promotion, and utilization in educational policy. *Educational Policy, 28*(2), 131–144.

Malen, B., Croninger, R., Muncey, D., & Redmond-Jones, D. (2002). Reconstituting schools: "Testing" the "theory of action". *Educational Evaluation and Policy Analysis, 24*(2), 113–132.

Marsh, J. (2012). The micropolitics of implementing a school-based bonus policy: The case of New York City's compensation committees. *Educational Evaluation and Policy Analysis, 34*(3), 164–184.

McDonnell, L. M. (1991). Ideas and values in implementation analysis: The case of teacher policy. In A. R. Odden (Ed.), *Policy implementation* (pp. 241–258). Albany: SUNY Press.

McEwan, P. J. (2008). Quantitative research methods in education finance and policy. In H. F. Ladd & E. B. Fiske (Eds.), *Handbook of research in education finance and policy* (pp. 87–104). New York: Routledge.

McLaughlin, M. W. (1987). Learning from experience: Lessons from policy implementation. *Educational Evaluation and Policy Analysis, 9*(2), 171–178.

O'Laughlin, L. O., & Lindle, J. C. (2014). Principals as political agents in the implementation of IDEA's least restrictive environment mandate. *Educational Policy, 29*(1), 140–161.

Odden, A. R. (1991). The evolution of education policy implementation. In A. R. Odden (Ed.), *Education policy implementation* (pp. 1–12). Albany: SUNY Press.

Psathas, G. (1995). *Conversation analysis: The study of talk-in-interaction.* Thousand Oaks: SAGE.

Rogoff, B. (1994). Developing understanding of the idea of communities of learners. *Mind, Culture, and Activity, 1*(4), 209–229.

Sadovnik, A. R. (2007). Qualitative research and public policy. In F. Fischer, G. J. Miller, & M. S. Sidney (Eds.), *Handbook of public policy analysis: Theory, politics, and methods* (pp. 417–428). Boca Raton: CRC Press.

Scriven Berry, K., & Herrington, C. D. (2012). Tensions across federalism, localism, and professional autonomy: Social media and stakeholder response to increased accountability. *Educational Policy, 27*(2), 390–409.

Shavelson, R. J., & Towne, L. (2002). *Scientific research in education.* Washington, DC: National Academy Press.

Sipple, J. W., Killeen, K., & Monk, D. H. (2004). Adoption and adaptation: School district responses to state imposed learning and graduation requirements. *Educational Evaluation and Policy Analysis, 26*(2), 143–168.

Spillane, J. P. (2004). *Standards deviation.* Cambridge, MA: Harvard University Press.

Spillane, J. P., Reiser, B. J., & Reimer, T. (2002). Policy implementation and cognition: Reframing and refocusing implementation research. *Review of Educational Research, 72*(3), 387–431.

Spillane, J. P., Reiser, B. J., & Gomez, L. M. (2006). Policy implementation and cognition. In *New directions in educational policy implementation: Confronting complexity* (pp. 47–64). New York: State University of New York Press.

Stoecker, R. (1991). Evaluating and rethinking the case study. *The Sociological Review, 39*(1), 88–112.

Stringer, E. T. (2013). *Action research.* Thousand Oaks: Sage.

Taylor, S. (2004). Researching educational policy and change in 'new times': Using critical discourse analysis. *Journal of Education Policy, 19*(4), 433–451.

Taylor, S., Lingard, B., Rizvi, F., & Henry, M. (1997). *Education policy and the politics of change.* London: Routledge.

The Pew-MacArthur Results First Initiative. (2014). *Evidence-based policymaking: A guide for effective government.* Washington, DC: The Pew Charitable Trusts. Retrieved from http://www.pewtrusts.org

Timar, T. B. (1989). A theoretical framework for local responses to state policy: Implementing Utah's career ladder program. *Educational Evaluation and Policy Analysis, 11*(4), 329–341.

van Dijk, T. A. (1993). Principles of critical discourse analysis. *Discourse & Society, 4*(2), 249–283.

Weatherly, R., & Lipsky, M. (1977). Street-level bureaucrats and institutional innovation: Implementing special-education reform. *Harvard Educational Review, 47*(2), 171–197.

Weick, K. E. (1996). *Sensemaking in organizations.* Thousand Oaks: SAGE.

Yanow, D. (2003). Interpretive empirical political science: What makes this not a subfield of qualitative methods. *Qualitative Methods, 1*(2), 9–13.

Yanow, D. (2007). Qualitative-interpretive methods in policy research. In F. Fischer, G. J. Miller, & M. S. Sidney (Eds.), *Handbook of public policy analysis: Theory, politics, and methods* (pp. 405–416). Boca Raton: CRC Press.

Yin, R. K. (2014). *Case study research: Design and methods* (5th ed.). Thousand Oaks: SAGE.

Young, M. D., & Diem, S. (2014). Putting critical theoretical perspectives to work in educational policy. *International Journal of Qualitative Studies in Education, 27*(9), 1063–1067.

Chad R. Lochmiller is Assistant Professor of Educational Leadership in the Department of Educational Leadership & Policy Studies in the School of Education at Indiana University. His current research focuses on education policy issues, particularly those related to school finance, human resource management, and leadership development. Lochmiller's research has been published in *Educational Administration Quarterly, Journal of Educational Administration, Journal of School Leadership, Education Policy Analysis Archives, Leadership and Policy in Schools,* and edited volumes.

Samantha L. Hedges is a doctoral student in Educational Leadership & Policy Studies at Indiana University, Bloomington. Her research interests include education policy design and implementation, philanthropic giving to K-12 education, and equity in education. Formerly, she taught at the elementary level and was a public policy advocate for a nonprofit organization.

CHAPTER 3

Language-Based Approaches to the Study of Education Policy

Jessica Nina Lester, Francesca A. White, and Chad R. Lochmiller

INTRODUCTION

Over the last few decades, there has been a growing acceptance of the place of qualitative methodologies and methods across many disciplines. Within education writ large, there has been an increasing emphasis on the ways in which qualitative evidence can and should inform practice. At the same time, qualitative evidence has often, and perhaps inappropriately, been placed at the bottom level of evidence in applied fields, including education (Lester and O'Reilly 2015). Regardless, there is a growing acceptance that qualitative approaches to research offer insight to scholars interested in understanding and/or exploring social phenomena of interest. This qualitative focus on local knowledges, everyday and institutional social activities, and context offers researchers a nuanced and situated understanding of a given research site. Indeed, such a qualitative focus has been of importance for education policy and practice, as highlighted in Chap. 2 of this volume. More particularly, language-based methodologies, such as conversation analysis (CA) (Sacks 1992) and discourse analytic approaches (Wood and

J.N. Lester (✉) • F.A. White • C.R. Lochmiller
Indiana University, Bloomington, IN, USA

© The Author(s) 2017   41
J.N. Lester et al. (eds.), *Discursive Perspectives on Education Policy and Implementation*, DOI 10.1007/978-3-319-58984-8_3

Kroger 2000), have the added benefit of entailing a close examination of everyday and institutionalized practices wherein policy is (re)constructed and enacted. There is great variety in conceptualizing and applying the various methodological approaches to discourse analysis (Jørgensen and Phillips 2002), with CA typically conceived of as being a single methodology that is distinct from discourse analytic approaches; hence, our use of the more encompassing term "language-based methodologies".

In this chapter, we provide a general background to some of the methodological perspectives taken up in this volume, with a particular focus on approaches to discourse analysis as well as CA. Specifically, we provide an overview to two discourse analytic perspectives—both of which are employed by some of the contributing authors included in this volume—as well as an overview of CA. First, we offer a general discussion of the landscape of discourse analysis and then briefly introduce the two selected approaches (critical discourse analysis [CDA] and discursive psychology [DP]) with an abbreviated overview of how discourse analysis is carried out within each perspective. While this chapter is focused on the methodological practices of discourse analysis and CA, throughout the chapter we incorporate empirical examples to illustrate how these methodological perspectives "play out" in the context of education policy studies. Further, we also aim to offer concrete suggestions for scholars new to the study and application of discourse analytic perspectives and CA. We conclude the chapter by discussing the implications of these approaches for education policy research.

An Abbreviated Overview of Discourse Analysis

Notably, there is not a single definition of discourse analysis; instead, discourse analysis is perhaps best understood as an umbrella term that includes within it a multitude of qualitative approaches that are broadly focused on the study of language as it relates to social practice (Potter 2004). While many of the foundational ideas that underpin discourse analytic perspectives can be traced back to linguistic philosophers (see Lester 2011, for a discussion of the historical influences of discourse analysis), it was not until the 1980s that a proliferation of discourse analytic approaches occurred, along with subsequent specializations within particular disciplines (e.g., DP initially grew out of social psychology and is now considered an approach used across many disciplines).

Across the many discourse analytic approaches, there are several common assumptions. First, it is typically assumed that language is performative

(Jørgensen and Phillips 2002), meaning that it is in and through language that the social world is ordered and people accomplish things. For example, through language an individual offers a complaint or compliment, engages in debate, negotiates peace, provides an account, and so on. Second and closely related to the assumption related to the performativity of language, it is typically assumed that it is in and through language that the social world is built; that is, a social constructionist orientation to knowledge and reality construction is assumed (Burr 2003). Closely related to this idea is the assumption that language is constitutive and not simply a reflection of inner mental workings—a claim that was offered by linguistic philosophers such as Wittgenstein (1958) and Winch (1967), among others. In other words, language is not understood as being directly correlated to mental schema or to a given social reality. This particular view is one that came to the fore during the early part of the twentieth century and is often referred to as the linguistic turn (see Rorty 1989, for a more detailed discussion). Finally, while varying perspectives to the meaning of criticality are taken up across discourse analytic perspectives, there is a general commitment to critiquing taken-for-granted knowledge, with knowledge presumed to be historically and culturally specific. Lester and O'Reilly (2016) provided further explication of the commonalities across discourse analytic perspective, noting a shared focus on (1) language, (2) how accounts of the world are constructed, and (3) the variability by which people account for the world.

Despite these common assumptions, the variability across discourse analytic approaches is striking, with some approaches focused more on the content of language use and others attending to the structure of language—to name but a few of the differences. Potter and Wetherell (1987) noted that the diversity of discourse analytic perspectives can be explained by the varying disciplines that contributed to the development of the individual approaches. Thus, perhaps unsurprisingly, it is not possible to offer a shared, step-wise description of the procedures used for carrying out a discourse analysis study. Rather, individual approaches to discourse analysis bring with them particular assumptions about the meaning of discourse, the types of data most appropriate to use, and guidelines for how analysis should proceed (O'Reilly et al. 2009).

While many approaches to discourse analysis exist, we discuss only two here: CDA and DP (along with the related critical approach to DP). We discuss these particular discourse analytic approaches because they offer variety in terms of how often they have been employed in education policy research (e.g., CDA has been used far more than DP), as well as the ways in which discourse is defined and thereby studied. Nonetheless, we acknowledge that what we offer here is necessarily brief and thereby results in a less than complete discussion of these particular approaches. We note, however, that other chapters included in this volume provide additional insights about other approaches to discourse analysis (e.g., see Chap. 4 for a discussion of Foucauldian discourse analysis, Chap. 5 for a discussion of membership categorization analysis, Chap. 6 for a discussion of policy discourse analysis, and Chap. 7 offers an empirical example of a Bakhtian discourse analysis). Further, we certainly encourage readers interested in these and other discourse analytic perspectives to use this chapter as a starting point—one which we hope leads to further and more detailed study.

What Is Critical Discourse Analysis?

CDA comprises a multidisciplinary approach, along with various theories and methods, to the study of language and sociopolitical problems. This discourse analytic tradition gives particular attention to power, inequality, and dominance within political and social realms (re)produced in talk and text (van Dijk 2001). While this approach cannot be easily traced back to one, unified origin (Jørgensen and Phillips 2002, p. 60), many of the CDA approaches are informed by ideas from critical theories (e.g., Marxism) and Foucault's notion of power as generative and productive, which produces subjects, rather than a view of power as property owned by those in power. For Foucault (1990), "discourse transmits and produces power; it reinforces it, but also undermines and exposes it, renders it fragile and makes it possible to thwart it" (p. 101). Further, along with this explicit focus on power and sociopolitical conditions, the critical discourse analyst, according to van Dijk (2001), is situated as a social actor within and part of the discourse produced. Scholars in this tradition reject notions of "value-free" and "objective" research and instead describe its adherents as engaged, committed, intervention-oriented, and on the side of the oppressed (Fairclough et al. 2011, p. 358). As such, critical discourse analysts are committed to exposing power and inequalities that are assumed to be produced and maintained in discursive practices and aim to increase critical awareness in order to promote "social change" (Jørgensen and Phillips 2002, p. 64).

In the sections that follow, we describe key features of CDA and provide exemplars of this work in the field of education policy.

Key Features

As described above, CDA represents a diverse set of approaches to studying language with explicit emphasis on sociopolitical concerns. Fairclough et al. (2011) identified six key developments and approaches in CDA, along with their key contributors: critical linguistics, Fairclough's approach (see Fairclough 1992), a discourse-historical approach (see Wodak 2001), socio-cognitive studies (see van Dijk 2001), argumentation and rhetoric, and corpus-based or computer-mediated approaches (for a detailed discussion, see Fairclough et al. 2011). Taylor (2004) has also written about the usefulness of using CDA in critical policy research projects.

Here, we provide a brief overview of common features of CDA and encourage readers interested in this approach to study the cited sources in more detail. First, it is perhaps important to note that each language-based analytical approach described in this chapter defines discourse in specific and particular ways. Fairclough et al. (2011) described CDA's definition of discourse (used synonymously with semiosis) in at least three ways: (1) as an analytical category describing resources for meaning-making; (2) inclusive of words, pictures, symbols, gestures, and so on; and (3) as a form of social practice. Further, within this tradition discourse is considered to be "socially *constitutive* and socially shaped" (Fairclough et al. 2011, p. 358, emphasis in original) and situated within historical contexts "in a dialectical relationship with other aspects of the social" (Jørgensen and Phillips 2002, p. 62). As such, close analysis of talk and text in context while attending to the social, cultural, and political contexts form the basis for understanding social phenomenon (Benwell and Stokoe 2006).

In addition, of particular interest in CDA are ideologies; that is, how society is represented in ways that power and inequality are maintained by discursive practices (Fairclough et al. 2011, p. 371). Analysis of the ideological nature of text, for example, may take the form of identifying policies presented as neutral that promote anti-homophobic discourses (Barrett and Bound 2015). Thus, analysis serves to interpret and deconstruct talk and texts in order to illustrate unequal power relations as well as "reveal the social implications of various reading" (Fairclough et al. 2011, p. 373). In that regard, CDA is both interpretive and explanatory critique, linking the micro practices (local discourse) with the macro (broader discourse of the historical sociopolitical context). Thus, it is common for critical discourse analysts to describe both micro and macro discourses in their analysis. To summarize, Fairclough et al. (2011) and van Dijk (2001) identified common features across CDA work:

- focus on social problems
- power relations as discursive
- discourse functions ideologically
- discourse is historical
- discourse analysis is interpretive and explanatory
- discourse is a form of social action

Now, we turn to a discussion of the methods of CDA.

For critical discourse analysts, research begins with topics (e.g., education policy reform, state accountability metrics, inequity and educational opportunity gaps, etc.) rather than "a fixed theoretical or methodological stance" (Fairclough et al. 2011, p. 358; see also van Dijk 2001). The analyst's approach is informed by, for example, literature related to education policy reform and historical and theoretical issues surrounding the topic. Proponents of CDA describe methodology as "the process during which, informed by theory, the topic is refined so as to construct the object of research" (Fairclough et al. 2011, p. 359). Analysts thus choose methods and data (e.g., historical texts, audio recordings, multimodal, etc.) best suited for the topic of study. This methodological flexibility, perhaps, contributes to the diversity within CDA. This "top down" approach, however, is not without critique. For example, CDA has been critiqued for the use of a priori categories (e.g., "race", "gender"), which are made relevant by analysts rather than the individuals involved (Benwell and Stokoe 2006). However, CDA takes the stance of positioning analysts as social actors and reflectively considers the role of scholars in the discourse produced in analysis (van Dijk 2001).

To summarize, we have thus far described CDA, a discourse analytic approach to the study of language, power, and social problems. We noted common features across the various types of CDA as well as its flexible stance on methodology. Next, we describe three empirical examples in education policy that draw upon various perspectives with CDA.

Critical Discourse Analysis and Education Policy: Empirical Examples

CDA has been widely used in the fields of education and education policy and could perhaps be considered the dominant language-based methodology used in education policy (see Rogers et al. 2005, 2016, for a comprehensive review of education and CDA-related literature). For instance, keyword searches using "critical discourse analysis" in *Education Policy Analysis Archives* and *Education Policy* journals returned over 30 articles; "education policy" in discourse analysis journals (*Discourse Studies* and *Discourse & Society*) returned 19 articles. The articles represented a broad range of emphases, including historical analysis of education policy (e.g., Mulderrig 2012), analysis of education reform texts (Anderson et al. 2015), and higher education policy (Patton 2014; Saarinen 2008), for instance. As another example, in 2016, a special issue published in *Education Policy Analysis Archives* and *Education Policy* focused on CDA and education policy (Lester et al. 2016), with the six included articles offering varying empirical examples of its application and relevance to education policy. Indeed, there is a fairly substantial body of education policy literature that has drawn upon CDA.

We highlight next three different examples from the literature, which illustrate the variety of ways in which CDA has been taken up.

Corpus-Based Analysis of Education Policy Discourse (Mulderrig 2012)
In this research, Mulderrig (2012) took to task the use of "we" in historical education documents from 1972 to 2005. The researcher used a *corpus-based approach*, which describes the systematic, "replicable" use of computer software to analyze large bodies of data (500,000 words) (p. 702; also see Fairclough et al. 2011, p. 366). Drawing on political economic theory and CDA, Mulderrig sought to interpret the rhetorical and ideological significance of deixis usage as well as to explain the sociopolitical implications. To situate the study, the author provided a detailed discussion of the historical, social, and political context of education policy in the UK and the positions of political parties (i.e., New Labour). Context, in this case, was described as both "pre-established" and "emergent", referring to the social, political, historical, and interactional landscape within which the discourse occurs (Mulderrig, p. 709). The author identified three types of uses of "we"—exclusive, inclusive, and ambivalent—and discussed their functions. As an example, Mulderrig described inclusive phrasings such as "we all know that" as common occurrences in the beginning sections of policy documents. The author asserted that these types of phrases allow "the government to make privileged claims about shared attitudes and belief", especially when presented as "uncontroversial" (p. 716). The author concluded by describing the use of deixis as rhetorically strategic, which

ultimately serves to support the sociopolitical aims of proponents of New Labor's neoliberalism.

Media Coverage of Education Policy (Piazza 2014)

In an article published in *Education Policy Analysis Archives*, Piazza (2014) argued that "the examination of new media can provide an indication of the dominant values and beliefs shaping public perception of key players in the policy process" (p. 3). Primarily drawing on Fairclough's CDA approach, the author sought to identify themes and framing within media coverage of state-level policy changes and representations of key political actors. Data for this study included several forms of media coverage (e.g., news articles, op-eds, online blog posts, letters to the editor) and interviews with local stakeholders involved in Massachusetts Teacher Association and Stand for Children groups. In the analysis, the author compared and contrasted media representations on stances on local education policy with the views of stakeholders, noting throughout claims that "the media flatly got it wrong" (p. 15). Piazza explained that these "wrong" portrayals may "force the broad and sensational social narratives that cannot adequately capture local-level political realities" (p. 18). That is, sensationalism and inaccurate representations of stances on education policy are shown to have real consequences and shape local legislature.

Respectability Politics and Historically Black Colleges and Universities' Attire Policies (Patton 2014)

Drawing on van Dijk's socio-cognitive approach to CDA and intersectionality (e.g., Crenshaw 1989), Patton (2014) analyzed the Morehouse College' Appropriate Attire Policy (MCAAP). The author noted that "CDA has not been widely used in higher education research" (p. 731). In this study, Patton aimed to link "micro" practices (e.g., attire policy discourse) with "macro issues" (e.g., power, hegemonic masculinity, and intersectionality). Central in this work was the notion of power as control (van Dijk 2003) in institutions of higher education. In the analysis, the author attended to the discursive work of the institution to "maintain what it perceives to be a positive and respectable image", while working to constrain the identities of students within societal norms for black men (pp. 736–739).

What Is Discursive Psychology?

DP represents a diverse field of study that examines talk and text as both topic and resources, focusing on the ways in which psychological matters are on display and made accountable by participants (Potter 2012). From this view, matters of states, such as "beliefs", "identities", and "emotions", are conceived of as being produced in and through interaction, with language understood as the medium for human action (Potter and Hepburn 2008). This perspective moves away from traditional understandings of language, which position talk as providing direct access to inner minds or mental schema (Benwell and Stokoe 2006). Thus, rather than giving accounts of people's psychological, cognitive, or emotional states or assuming that an explanation for why people speak and think as they do exists, DP scholars argue that thoughts, emotional states, motives, and so on are features situated in and made visible through language (Potter 2005). In their foundational text, *Discourse and social psychology: Beyond attitudes and behaviour*, Potter and Wetherell (1987) drew attention to the centrality of language as a medium human action and focused on questioning the taken-for-granted assumptions involved in the study of constructs (e.g., attitudes) in the field of social psychology. Their early ideas were developed further in the Discourse and Rhetoric Group at Loughborough University in the UK, wherein DP was influenced by multiple disciplines, including sociology of scientific knowledge (e.g., Gilbert and Mulkay 1984), rhetorical psychology (Billig 1991), ethnomethodology (Garfinkel 1967), and CA (Sacks 1992). In Edwards and Potter's (1992) seminal text, *Discursive psychology*, the authors further articulated an alternative approach to studying psychological matters. As such, one of the initial aims of DP was to respecify psychological matters as actions negotiated, resisted, and managed in interaction (Edwards and Potter 2001). Since these early and seminal publications, DP has flourished and its proponents have homes in a broad range of fields, including psychology, education, linguistics, health-related fields, and so on, with research focused on various everyday and institutional contexts (Tileagă and Stokoe 2015). In the sections that follow, we describe key features of DP and provide exemplars of empirical work related to education policy.

Key Features

Tileagă and Stokoe (2015) described at least two strands of work within DP: one that is closely aligned with (and perhaps blurring) with ethnomethodology and CA, and another named "critical discursive psychology", a more synthetic approach which combines a micro-interactional focus and (macro) broader social-cultural contexts and concerns. Critical DP generally includes an analytic focus on subject positions, ideological dilemmas, and interpretative repertoires, while maintaining close ties to post-structuralism (Wetherell 1998). Margaret Wetherell has been a key scholar in the development of critical DP (see Wetherell and Edley 1999, for an example of critical DP study).

The two strands of DP described by Tileagă and Stokoe (2015) can also be situated within Potter's (2012) description of three historical trends or developments in DP, which included (1) the analysis of interviews and interpretive repertoires drawing primarily on Potter and Wetherell's (1987) early discourse analysis work, (2) defining the type of social constructionism—named discursive constructionism—which focused on the ways in which talk and text construct accountable versions of the world, and (3) increased focus on the sequential features of interaction informed by works in CA (see Wooffitt 2005, for a more detailed discussion of CA). With the shift away from the early work of Potter and Wetherell (1987), a new focus on naturalistic interactions rather than interviews or "contrived" data emerged for DP scholars (see Potter and Hepburn 2005; Goodman and Speer 2015, for a discussion of the debated distinction between "naturalistic" and "contrived" data). Nonetheless, common across the various strands of DP, discourse is generally defined as *action-oriented*, *constructed* and *constructive*, and *situated*. First, DP scholars presume that whenever people interact, they are engaged in some form of social action or activity. Second, discourse is *constructed* in that people draw on resources (e.g., words, categories) available to them, and *constructive* in that the words and categories used produce accountable versions of the social world (Potter 1996). Third, the *situated* nature of talk and text is another feature of discourse in DP. That is, discourse is situated *sequentially* within unfolding interactions; *institutionally* as according to identities and actions relevant to the local context; and *rhetorically* wherein the versions of the social world are managed as reasonable and defensible against possible alternative versions (Potter 2012).

Given DP's emphasis on the ways in which activities are managed in talk or text, methods of analysis in DP often begin with close engagement with talk or text and draw on some of the tools of conversations analysis (see below for a more detailed discussion of CA). Common forms of data include audio and video recordings, computer-mediated communications, documents, and interviews, with a growing emphasis on naturally occurring data (rather than researcher-generated data). Upon collection of data, audio and/or video data, recordings are generally transcribed using Jefferson's transcription method (2004), which results in detailed transcription. This detailed transcription process is informed by CA and it is one that emphasizes both *what* is said and *how* it is said. See Table 3.1 for common transcription symbols used in Jefferson's transcription method. Indeed, transcription is assumed to be interpretative and a central aspect of the analysis process in a DP study, and the degree to which DP scholars draw upon the transcription symbols varies.

Next, analysts engage in unmotivated looking or noting what they notice, privileging the participants' orientations in interactions (Sacks 1992).

Table 3.1 Transcription symbols common in Jefferson transcription method (Jefferson 2004)

Symbol	Explanation
(.)	A period within parentheses denotes a micro pause: that is, a hearable pause but not long enough to measure
(0.2)	A number placed inside parentheses denotes a hearable and measurable pause
[ ]	Square brackets denote overlapping speech
> <	A greater than-less than symbol denotes that the pace of the speech quickened
< >	A less than-greater than symbol denotes that the pace of the speech slowed
( )	A blank space within parentheses denotes that spoken words were unclear and therefore unable to be transcribed
(( ))	A double parentheses with a description of contextual information within it occurs when no other symbol is available
Under	Underlining a word or part of a word denotes a rise in volume or emphasis
↑	An upward arrow denotes a rise in intonation
↓	A downward arrow denotes a drop in intonation
CAPITALS	Capital letters denote that something was said loudly or shouted
Hum(h)our	A bracketed "h" denotes that there is laughter in the talk
=	An equal sign denotes latched speech: that is, a continuation of talk
:::	Colons denote an elongated or stretched sound
hhh or .hh	To denote outbreaths or inbreaths, "hhh" or ".hh" are used

Unlike many other approaches to research, the formulation of research questions takes place after unmotivated looking in order to "mak [e] broader sense of the setting as a whole" (Potter 2012, p. 21). Patterns are identified using basic discourse analytic questions: "What is the discourse doing? How is the discourse constructed to make this happen? What resources are presented and being used to perform the activity?" (Potter 2004. p. 369). Analysts then engage in line-by-line analysis, providing representative segments of talk to demonstrate patterns. These claims are warranted by pointing to specific practices. This micro-analysis is available for reader evaluation and alternative interpretations (Antaki et al. 2003; Potter 2012). To summarize, we offer a list of some of the key features of DP identified my major contributors to the development of DP (Potter 2012; Tileagă and Stokoe 2015):

- Discourse is defined as:
  - action-oriented,
  - constructed and constructive, and
  - situated.
- DP affords an alternative approach to studying psychological matters as actions made visible in and through language.
- DP has been significantly influenced by ethnomethodology and CA.
- Similar to CA, DP scholars foreground participants' orientations as made visible in talk.

Broadly, DP can be considered a discourse analytic approach that takes a more micro-oriented orientation to the study of language-in-use.

Thus far, we have offered a general overview of DP, highlighting some of its key features. In the next section, we review two examples of DP research and one example of critical DP research in education policy research.

Education Policy Research and Discursive Psychology

Relatively few studies have explicitly described using DP as an approach to studying topics in education policy. For example, a search of *Education Policy Analysis Archives* for "discursive psychology" resulted in only two returns (Gabriel and Lester 2013; Hurst 2017). Despite its underuse, we argue that this particular approach offers a useful way to examine more micro-specific concerns. We next review two key studies covering both strands within DP.

Race and Affirmative Action in Focus Groups (Augoustinos et al.
2005)
This study, aligned with the critical discursive psychology DP strand, investigated the discursive construction of race relations with regard to affirmative action programs in Australia. In keeping with the "synthetic" approach advocated for by Wetherell (1998), Augoustinos et al. (2005) attended to the micro-features of the talk, such as rhetorical devices, while also linking these practices to the sociopolitical context and race relations between Indigenous and non-Indigenous groups more broadly. Data in this analysis included two focus group interview sessions with undergraduate students about a wide range of topics regarding racism in Australia and affirmative action. In their analysis, the authors identified the varied ways in which affirmative action was constructed as problematic and the resources drawn upon to do so. For example, the authors demonstrated participants' use of affect to problematize how affirmative action might negatively affect recipients ("imagined subjectivity"), particularly their self-esteem and feelings, compared to the presumed positive impact of merit-based acceptance to a university (p. 326). The authors highlighted how this construction would constrain or minimize potential arguments about the benefits of the policy (p. 331). Discursive practices such as these were linked to a broader "meritocratic discourse" surrounding affirmative action, which the authors argued works to maintain majority group privilege and the marginalization of minorities. This study demonstrates an approach that can connect the micro-social practices to broader sociopolitical consequences.

Consultants and Constructing Education Policy (Gabriel and Paulus
2015)
Published in *Education Policy*, this study examined the construction of education policy and decision-making with particular focus on talk of education consultants. Gabriel and Paulus (2015) argued that despite the fact that external parties, such as education consultants, do not have voting rights, their talk can influence decision-making and establish priorities often presumed to be the sole authority of policy committees. Data for this study comprised audio recordings of meetings and a conference call held by the Tennessee Teacher Evaluation Advisory Committee regarding the Race to the Top teacher evaluation policy. The analysis focused on the ways in

which talk around committee decisions and controversy were managed, negotiated, and facilitated in talk. Two patterns were identified across the consultant talk in these meetings: (1) "making decisions through validation" and (2) "deferring and redirecting decisions" (p. 994). To demonstrate these findings, Gabriel and Paulus provided extracts and line-by-line analyses of stretches of talk. For the first pattern, the authors demonstrated how revoicing and validating an initial request were used by consultants to make decisions informally, as an example (p. 996). In summary, this work made visible how participants in policy meetings oriented to the talk of all parties involved to make decisions regardless of their voting privileges. Studies of this sort build a case for pursuing methodological approaches that highlight the centrality of talk as a medium for action.

An Abbreviated Overview of Conversation Analysis

CA is the qualitative study of talk-in-interaction in everyday or institutional settings (ten Have 2007), with a particular focus on the orderly and sequential nature of talk. Arising from the field of sociology, CA has had multiple influences, including ethnomethodology, linguistic philosophy, and ethnography (Maynard 2013). Garfinkel's (1967) ethnomethodological work in particular has shaped the underlying assumptions of CA, with its focus on the study of peoples' methods for managing everyday affairs. Harvey Sacks (1992) is generally credited as the founder of CA, with his seminal work, *Lectures on conversation*, offering insights on how to understand and analyze social interactions. The premise of this approach is that "we produce utterances which perform actions, which invite particular next kinds of actions" (Wooffitt 2005, p. 8). Sacks and collaborators Emanuel Schegloff and Gail Jefferson, thus developed analytical methods to describe the structure of social interactions. Using Jefferson's (2004) specialized transcription system, conversation analysts attend to the details of turn-taking and the sequential organization of talk, focusing on how they function in interactions. Scholars using CA typically focus on how participants in a given interaction negotiate meanings on a turn-by-turn basis (Hutchby and Wooffitt 2008; McCabe 2006). Further, scholars in this tradition generally analyze naturally occurring data in a variety of settings, such as meetings, doctor appointments, and classroom interactions.

There are some similarities between CA and discourse analysis, particularly for those discourse analytic approaches that draw upon the principles of CA (such as DP). Yet, key differences exist. Most notably, CA takes up a micro-orientation to the study of interaction, attending explicitly to how participants manage or negotiate an interaction via the sequential structuring. While many approaches to DA emphasize the action-oriented nature of language, this is often done at a much broader level. For instance, a DA approach focused on sequential organization may also attend to the organization as it relates to broader social conditions or structures.

To further explicate CA's central ideas, we next highlight four key features of CA.

Key Features

First, the primary focus of CA is to study how talk is organized and more particularly how participants in an interaction make sense of or orient to the interaction. Thus, patterns in a given interaction are identified through studying the sequential organization of a given interaction, resulting in a focus on conversational structures such as turn-taking, repair, and turn design (McCabe 2006).

Second, in that CA focuses on the sequentiality of talk, it is generally described as studying "talk-in-interaction" (rather than "discourse" or simply "talk") (Drew and Heritage 1992). The term "talk-in-interaction" conveys the conversation analyst's focus on what talk is *doing* rather than what the talk is *about* (Schegloff 1999).

Third, CA favors naturally occurring data rather than data dependent upon a researcher's presence (e.g., interviews, focus groups). This particular emphasis aligns with Sack's (1992) argument that

> If we are to understand and analyze participants' own concepts and accounts, then we have to find and analyze them not in response to our research questions, but in the places they ordinarily and functionally occur...in the activities in which they're employed. (p. 27)

As such, rather than asking people to talk about or reflect on their practices, CA scholars generally collect video or audio recording of people going about their everyday or institutional activities. This, then, becomes the basis for a detailed study of social interaction.

Fourth, the analysis of data in CA is generally described as complex and specialized and is thus best pursued with the support of colleagues trained in CA and/or CA-specific training (Lester and O'Reilly 2016). As a general guide, however, Seedhouse (2004) overviewed five general stages of the analytic process of a CA study, including:

1. The analyst begins with unmotivated looking wherein they remain open to identifying patterns in the interaction without allowing preconceptions to guide their "looking".
2. After a focus or key pattern has been identified, the analyst inductively searches the data corpus to identify a collection of interactional instances wherein this focus or key pattern is visible/present.
3. To deepen understanding, patterns in the dataset are established by considering how they are produced and oriented to by participants.
4. A line-by-line analysis of single instances of the pattern of focus is generated, while also considering deviant cases or instances.
5. The analyst interprets how the pattern relates to the larger interaction, thereby identifying the key social action being produced.

It is important to note that analysis within CA is inductive and thus it is not appropriate to view the process as linear or step-wise.

Education Policy Research and Conversation Analysis

Notably, there is relatively little education policy research that has employed CA. There are, however, some studies that draw upon the principles of CA and/or employ DP (which is heavily influenced by CA). Thus, we view the use of CA as fairly novel and full of methodological possibility for education policy scholars. In line with the fairly limited literature base using CA, we highlight next only one published article related to education policy and CA.

Language Policies and Conversation Analysis (Bonacina-Pugh 2012)

Bonacina-Pugh (2012) offered a conceptual, methodological, and empirical argument to propose how language policy can be understood as a practice, with CA employed to make this visible. The author argued that policy has been generally understood and studied as distinct from practice. More particularly, Bonacina-Pugh noted that there have been three primary ways that language policy has been conceptualized in the literature: policy as text (Ball 1993), policy as discourse (Ball 1993), and, what she proposed in her study as policy as practice. Notably, Spolsky (2004) also presented a model of language policy that included a focus on practice, with an emphasis on "the existence of a policy at the level of language use" (p. 218). Building upon Spolsky's propositions, Bonacina-Pugh suggested that CA was an "efficient tool for the study of practiced language policies" (p. 218). To illustrate her claims, Bonacina-Pugh drew upon data from a "project in an induction classroom for newly-arrived immigrant children in France" (p. 220), with a focus on France's withdrawal or pull-out policy. Through a close analysis of her interactional data, Bonacina-Pugh made visible how language policies were actually negotiated, resisted, and implemented. Significantly, with this work, the author provides a methodological basis for drawing upon CA to study policy as practice.

Recommended Starting Points

In that we hope this chapter can be used as a useful starting place for readers new to language-based approaches to the study of education policy, we offer in this section some recommended beginning points. Table 3.2 provides a listing of key readings related to language-based methodologies we introduced in this chapter. In preparing this list, we aimed to identify those readings that were both foundational and fairly accessible. Thus, we suggest that what is offered here is a useful starting point for those new to language-based methodologies.

Implications for Education Policy Scholars

Based on our discussion, we believe that there are two sets of implications. One set relates to the methodological possibilities that these perspectives have for the field of policy research. We see the application of language-based methodologies as an important and valuable extension to the field of education policy research, particularly research related to the implementation of education policy in different local contexts. Indeed, this extension builds on the already substantial research base that has used CDA. Much as this research highlights, the methodological approach affords policy scholars an opportunity to examine discourse-based constructions of key policy issues, including those related to (in)equity, the construction of targeted groups, articulation of political agendas, emergence conflict, and so on. This approach promotes a deeper examination of these issues and creates an opportunity to examine these issues using both talk and text. While CA and DP have been used less in policy research, we think these micro-analytic strategies are plush with possibilities for education policy

Table 3.2   Key readings related to particular language-based methodologies

Language-based methodology	Useful readings
Critical discourse analysis	• Fairclough, N. (2013). *Critical discourse analysis: The critical study of language*. Routledge. • Rogers, R. (Ed.). (2011). *An introduction to critical discourse analysis in education* (2nd edition). New York, NY: Routledge. • van Dijk, T. A. (1993). Principles of critical discourse analysis. *Discourse & Society, 4*(2), 249–283. • Weiss, G., & Wodak, R. (Eds.). (2007). *Critical discourse analysis*. New York: Palgrave Macmillan.
Discursive psychology	• Edwards, D. & Potter, J. (1992). *Discursive psychology*. Sage. • Potter, J. (2012). Discourse analysis and discursive psychology. In Cooper, H. (Editor-in-Chief). *APA handbook of research methods in psychology: Vol. 2. Quantitative, qualitative, neuropsychological, and biological* (pp. 111–130). Washington: American Psychological Association Press. • Potter, J. & Wetherell, M. (1987). *Discourse and social psychology: Beyond attitudes and behaviors*. Sage. • Wiggins, S. (2016). *Discursive psychology: Theory, method and applications*. London, UK: Sage.
Conversation analysis	• Jefferson, G. (2004). Glossary of transcript symbols with an introduction. In G. H. Lerner (Ed.). *Conversation analysis: Studies from the first generation* (pp. 13–31). Amsterdam: John Benjamins. • Sacks, H. (1992). *Lectures on conversation*. Oxford, UK: Blackwell. • ten Have (2007). *Doing conversation analysis: A practical guide* (2nd ed.) London, UK: Sage. • Wooffitt, R. (2005). *Conversation analysis and discourse analysis: A comparative and critical introduction*. London, UK: Sage.

scholars. These approaches enable policy scholars to focus on actual understandings of policy as opposed to reflections about the policy experience.

Another set of implications relates to the types of data these perspectives enable policy scholars to use to examine key policy issues. While case studies using interviews, observations, and documents have served as the primary vehicle for qualitative policy research (see Chap. 2 of this volume), language-based approaches open new possibilities to use a variety of qualitative data sources. Utilizing data drawn from multiple sources opens up new, potentially fruitful ways to examine how meaning of policy is constructed at the design, implementation, and evaluation levels. For instance, scholars could examine state board of education meeting tran-scripts to examine how institutionally derived governance norms influence the interactions between board members. Likewise, scholars might compare technical reports published by university-based think tanks and newspaper articles to determine how the media articulates research-based ideas about important policy issues, such as early childhood education or charter schools. Further, the possibility of focusing on naturally occurring data, rather than interviews or focus groups alone, is potentially useful. For example, the opportunity to review videos of principals and classroom teachers working together within the context of policy-driven teacher eval-uation systems would provide important insights about the ways in which these policies shape instructional discourses in schools. This would allow for a more nuanced understanding of how people go about in their everyday lives talking about policies as well as potentially attending to institutional contexts wherein policymaking is actualized.

SUMMARY

In this chapter, we have provided a general overview to some of the language-based methodologies, which we argue are useful for framing potential inquiries pursued by education policy scholars. Specifically, we briefly introduced discourse analysis and then more specifically discussed CDA and DP. We then provided a general overview of CA, discussed some of its key features, and offered an empirical example. Throughout our discussion of these varying approaches to the study of language, we pointed to policy-related empirical studies. Finally, we offered several suggestions for how these perspectives might inform policy scholars.

Key Connections to Policy Research

1. The chapter provides an introduction to three language-based methodologies which are suitable for education policy research, including CDA, DP, and CA. These approaches afford policy scholars a valuable tool to examine how policy ideas are taken up at the local level as well as how various understandings, positions, and identities emerge throughout the policy process.

(continued)

2. While CDA has been used extensively in policy research, we see the opportunity to apply other language-based approaches, particularly DP and CA, as potentially valuable extensions to the existing research base.

3. The opportunity to shift policy research to micro-analytic techniques creates opportunities to examine policy meaning at a more granular level. This shift also creates opportunities to draw upon new and potentially fruitful data sources (e.g., legislative documents, committee transcripts, videos of committee hearings, online posts, research reports, etc.), which have not been widely used in policy research.

References

Anderson, A., Aronson, B., Ellison, S., & Fairchild-Keyes, S. (2015). Pushing up against the limit-horizon of educational change: A critical discourse analysis of popular education reform texts. *Journal for Critical Education Policy Studies, 12* (3), 338–370.

Antaki, C., Billig, M. G., Edwards, D., & Potter, J. A. (2003). Discourse analysis means doing analysis: A critique of six analytic shortcomings. *Discourse Analysis Online, 1*. Retrieved from http://extra.shu.ac.uk/daol/articles/open/2002/002/antaki2002002-paper.html

Augoustinos, M., Tuffin, K., & Every, D. (2005). New racism, meritocracy and individualism: Constraining affirmative action in education. *Discourse & Society, 16*(3), 315–340. Retrieved from http://www.jstor.org/stable/42888940

Ball, S. J. (1993). What is policy? Texts, trajectories and toolboxes. *Discourse, 13*(2), 10–17.

Barrett, B., & Bound, A. M. (2015). A critical discourse analysis of 'no promo homo' policies in U.S. schools. *Educational Studies, 51*(4), 267–283. doi:10.1080/00131946.2015.1052445

Benwell, B., & Stokoe, E. (2006). *Discourse and identity.* Edinburgh: Edinburgh University Press.

Billig, M. (1991). *Ideology and opinions: Studies in rhetorical psychology.* London: Sage.

Bonacina-Pugh, F. (2012). Researching 'practiced language policies': Insights from conversation analysis. *Language Policy, 11*(3), 213–234.

Burr, V. (2003). *Social constructionism.* London: Psychology Press.

Crenshaw, K. (1989). Demarginalizing the interaction of race and sex: A black feminist critique of antidiscrimination doctrine, feminist theory, and antiracist politics. *University of Chicago Legal Forum, 139*, 139–167.

Drew, P., & Heritage, J. (1992). Analyzing talk at work: An introduction. In P. Drew & J. Heritage (Eds.), *Talk at work* (pp. 3–65). Cambridge: Cambridge University Press.

Edwards, D., & Potter, J. (1992). *Discursive psychology*. London: Sage.

Edwards, D., & Potter, J. (2001). Discursive psychology. In A. W. McHoul & M. Rapley (Eds.), *How to analyse talk in institutional settings: A casebook of methods* (pp. 12–24). London: Continuum International.

Fairclough, N. (1992). *Discourse and social change*. Cambridge, MA: Polity Press.

Fairclough, N., Mulderrig, J., & Wodak, R. (2011). Critical discourse analysis. In T. Van Dijk (Ed.), *Discourse studies: A multidisciplinary introduction* (pp. 357–378). London: Sage.

Foucault, M. (1990). *The history of sexuality—Volume 1: An introduction*. New York: Vintage.

Gabriel, R., & Lester, J. N. (2013). Sentinels guarding the grail: Value-added measurement and the quest for education reform. *Educational Policy Analysis Archives, 20*(9). Retrieved from http://epaa.asu.edu/ojs/article/view/1165

Gabriel, R., & Paulus, T. (2015). Committees and controversy consultants in the construction of education policy. *Educational Policy, 29*(7), 984–1011. doi:10.1177/0895904814531650

Garfinkel, H. (1967). *Studies in ethnomethodology*. Englewood Cliffs: Prentice-Hall Press.

Gilbert, G. N., & Mulkay, M. (1984). *Opening Pandora's box: A sociological analysis of scientists' discourse*. Nueva York: CUP Archive.

Goodman, S., & Speer, S. A. (2015). Natural and contrived data. In C. Tileagă & E. Stokoe (Eds.), *Discursive psychology: Classic and contemporary issues* (pp. 57–69). New York: Routledge.

Hurst, T. M. (2017). The discursive construction of superintendent statesmanship on Twitter. *Education Policy Analysis Archives, 25*, 29.

Hutchby, I., & Wooffitt, R. (2008). *Conversation analysis*. Cambridge: Polity.

Jefferson, G. (2004). Glossary of transcript symbols with an introduction. In G. H. Lerner (Ed.), *Conversation analysis: Studies from the first generation* (pp. 13–31). Amsterdam: John Benjamins.

Jørgensen, M. W., & Phillips, L. J. (2002). *Discourse analysis as theory and method*. London: Sage.

Lester, J. N. (2011). Exploring the borders of cognitive and discursive psychology: A methodological reconceptualization of cognition and discourse. *Journal of Cognitive Education and Psychology, 10*(3), 280–293.

Lester, J. N., & O'Reilly, M. (2015). Is evidence-based practice a threat to the progress of the qualitative community? Arguments from the bottom of the pyramid. *Qualitative Inquiry, 21*(7), 628–632.

Lester, J. N., & O'Reilly, M. (2016). The history and landscape of conversation and discourse analysis. In *The Palgrave handbook of adult mental health: Discourse and conversation studies* (pp. 23–44). London: Palgrave Macmillan.

Lester, J. N., Lochmiller, C. R., & Gabriel, R. (2016). Locating and applying critical discourse analysis within education policy: An introduction. *Education Policy Analysis Archives.* doi:10.14507/epaa.24.2768

Maynard, D. (2013). Everyone and no one to turn to: Intellectual roots and contexts for conversation analysis. In J. Sidnell & T. Stivers (Eds.), *The handbook of conversation analysis* (pp. 11–31). Malden: Blackwell Publishing.

McCabe, R. (2006). Conversation analysis. In M. Slade & S. Priebe (Eds.), *Choosing methods in mental health research: Mental health research from theory to practice* (pp. 24–46). Hove: Routledge.

Mulderrig, J. (2012). The hegemony of inclusion: A corpus-based critical discourse analysis of deixis in education policy. *Discourse & Society, 23*(6), 701–728. Retrieved from http://www.jstor.org/stable/43496421

O'Reilly, M., Dixon-Woods, M., Angell, E., Ashcroft, R., & Bryman, A. (2009). Doing accountability: A discourse analysis of research ethics committee letters. *Sociology of Health & Illness, 31*(2), 246–291.

Patton, L. D. (2014). Preserving respectability or blatant disrespect? A critical discourse analysis of the Morehouse Appropriate Attire Policy and implications for intersectional approaches to examining campus policies. *International Journal of Qualitative Studies in Education, 27*(6), 724–746. doi:10.1080/09518398.2014.901576

Piazza, P. (2014). The media got it wrong! A critical discourse analysis of changes to the educational policy making arena. *Education Policy Analysis Archives, 22*(36). doi:10.14507/epaa.v22n36.2014

Potter, J. (1996). *Representing reality: Discourse, rhetoric and social construction.* London: Sage.

Potter, J. (2004). Discourse analysis as a way of analysing naturally occurring talk. In D. Silverman (Ed.), *Qualitative research: Theory, method and practice* (2nd ed., pp. 200–221). London: Sage.

Potter, J. (2005). Making psychology relevant. *Discourse & Society, 16*(5), 739–747.

Potter, J. (2012). Discourse analysis and discursive psychology. In H. Cooper (Editor-in-Chief), *APA handbook of research methods in psychology. Vol. 2. Quantitative, qualitative, neuropsychological, and biological* (pp. 111–130). Washington, DC: American Psychological Association Press.

Potter, J., & Hepburn, A. (2005). Qualitative interviews in psychology: Problems and possibilities. *Qualitative Research in Psychology, 2*, 281–307.

Potter, J., & Hepburn, A. (2008). Discursive constructionism. In *Handbook of constructionist research* (pp. 275–293). New York: Guildford.

Potter, J., & Wetherell, M. (1987). *Discourse and social psychology: Beyond attitudes and behaviour*. London: Sage.

Rogers, R., Malancharuvil-Berkes, E., Mosley, M., Hui, D., & Joseph, G. O. G. (2005). Critical discourse analysis in education: A review of the literature. *Review of Educational Research, 75*(3), 365–416.

Rogers, R., Schaenen, I., Schott, C., O'Brien, K., Trigos-Carrillo, L., Starkey, K., & Chasteen, C. C. (2016). Critical discourse analysis in education: A review of the literature, 2004 to 2012. *Review of Educational Research, 86*(4), 1192–1226.

Rorty, R. (1989). *Contingency, irony, and solidarity*. Cambridge, MA: Cambridge University Press.

Saarinen, T. (2008). Persuasive presuppositions in OECD and EU higher education policy documents. *Discourse Studies, 10*(3), 341–359. Retrieved from http://www.jstor.org/stable/24049534

Sacks, H. (1992). *Lectures on conversation*. Oxford: Blackwell.

Schegloff, E. (1999). Discourse, pragmatics, conversation, analysis. *Discourse Studies, 1*(4), 405–435.

Seedhouse, P. (2004). Conversation analysis methodology. *Language Learning, 54* (s1), 1–54.

Spolsky, B. (2004). *Language policy*. Cambridge: Cambridge University press.

Taylor, S. (2004). Researching educational policy and change in 'new times': Using critical discourse analysis. *Journal of Education Policy, 19*(4), 433–451.

ten Have, P. (2007). *Doing conversation analysis: A practical guide* (2nd ed.). London: Sage.

Tileagă, C., & Stokoe, E. (2015). *Discursive psychology: Classic and contemporary issues*. New York: Routledge.

van Dijk, T. A. (2001). Critical discourse analysis. In *The handbook of discourse analysis* (pp. 349–371). Oxford: Blackwell.

van Dijk, T. A. (2003). Introduction: What is critical discourse analysis? In D. Schiffrin, D. Tannen, & H. E. Hamilton (Eds.), *The handbook of discourse analysis* (pp. 352–371). Malden: Blackwell.

Wetherell, M. (1998). Positioning and interpretative repertoires: Conversation analysis and post-structuralism in dialogue. *Discourse & Society, 9*(3), 387–412.

Wetherell, M., & Edley, N. (1999). Negotiating hegemonic masculinity: Imaginary positions and psycho-discursive practices. *Feminism & Psychology, 9*(3), 335–356.

Winch, P. (1967). *The idea of a social science and its relation to philosophy*. London: Routledge & Kegan Paul.

Wittgenstein, L. (1958). *Philosophical investigations* (2nd ed.) (trans: Anscombe, G. E. M.). Oxford: Basil Blackwell.

Wodak, R. (2001). The discourse-historical approach. In R. Wodak & M. Myers (Eds.), *Methods of critical discourse analysis* (pp. 63–94). London: Sage.

Wood, L. A., & Kroger, R. O. (2000). *Doing discourse analysis: Methods for studying action in talk and text.* London: Sage.

Wooffitt, R. (2005). *Conversation analysis and discourse analysis: A comparative and critical introduction.* London: Sage.

Jessica Nina Lester is Assistant Professor of Inquiry Methodology in the Department of Counseling & Educational Psychology in the School of Education at Indiana University. Much of her research is positioned at the intersection of discourse studies and disability studies. Lester recently co-edited a book focused on performance ethnographies and co-authored a book focused on the use of digital tools across the qualitative research process. She also co-authored a research methods textbook and is the co-editor of *The Palgrave Handbook of Child Mental Health: Discourse and Conversation Studies* and *The Palgrave Handbook of Adult Mental Health: Discourse and Conversation Studies.* Her most recent article has appeared in journals such as *Qualitative Inquiry, Qualitative Research,* and *Discourse Studies.*

Francesca A. White is a doctoral candidate at Indiana University, Bloomington, in the Science Education and Inquiry Methodology Programs in the School of Education. Her current research interests include methodological approaches to studying identity and discourse, validity in qualitative research, postsecondary STEM education in out-of-class settings, and diversity and equity in higher education.

Chad R. Lochmiller is Assistant Professor of Educational Leadership in the Department of Educational Leadership and Policy Studies in the School of Education at Indiana University. His current research focuses on education policy issues, particularly those related to school finance, human resource management, and leadership development. Lochmiller's research has been published in *Educational Administration Quarterly, Journal of Educational Administration, Journal of School Leadership, Education Policy Analysis Archives, Leadership and Policy in Schools,* and edited volumes. Lochmiller is also a co-author of a research methods textbook, *An Introduction to Education Research: Connecting Methods to Practice,* designed for practitioner-scholars.

From Subjectification to Subjectivity in Education Policy Research Relationships

Erica Burman

INTRODUCTION

This chapter evaluates what a Foucauldian discursive approach can bring to analysis of educational policy-related material in highlighting how institutional practices—in this case of state welfare benefit reductions—produce particular forms of 'subject position', or experience and relationships. While there are many discursive approaches, a Foucauldian-informed analysis shows the connections between social structure and subjectivity, enabling attention to not only how educational policies are enacted in a wide range of social practices but also how these both constrain and produce—albeit in non-determining ways—specific forms of experience. Analysis here is focused on a specific textual example drawn from a local, UK-based study of educational impacts of welfare reforms on poor families. It is spoken by a parent of three children in the context of a research interview. Her statement 'Tell your professor we are good mothers' is discussed in relation to four features: first, the range of subject positions elaborated and, second, the

E. Burman (✉)
Manchester Institute of Education, School of Environment, Education and Development, University of Manchester, Manchester, UK

© The Author(s) 2017
J.N. Lester et al. (eds.), *Discursive Perspectives on Education Policy and Implementation*, DOI 10.1007/978-3-319-58984-8_4

incitement to 'confession' and investments indicated around being (or not being) seen as 'good mothers' and how these investments are interpellated (hailed or called into being) even when not explicitly topicalized within an educational research study. These two discursive aspects occur alongside but are also countered by, third, the articulation of a collective subjectivity that repudiates the surveillance and regulation of working-class communities, as well as, fourth, an ethical-political demand made by the participant that the researchers challenge the dominant discourses to which this mother and others like her are subject. From this analysis, which is also informed by feminist and antiracist perspectives, distinct practical-policy contributions of Foucauldian discourse analysis are identified, including indications of discursive shifts (elaborated from the analysis of how, when and what is spoken) and possibilities of resistance.

KEY LITERATURE

This chapter frames its methodological discussion around an extract generated from a research study exploring the impacts on children and families of a current UK policy concerned with a reduction in housing-related welfare support, called the 'Removal of the Spare Room Subsidy' policy (which is more colloquially known as 'the bedroom tax'). This policy was introduced in April 2013 as part of a wider programme of welfare reforms (DWP 2012). Our project, the first specifically investigating connections between welfare, education and well-being in relation to this new 'tax' (or welfare cut), was conducted in our locality (Manchester, UK)[1] and documented material and emotional effects of these cuts in welfare support (which are financially quite significant)[2] on parents and children. While the financial penalties arising from this 'tax' were accompanied by other welfare cuts affecting the same groups (see Bragg et al. 2015), our particular focus was on exploring impacts on children's educational engagement, so also thereby highlighting continuities between educational and wider social policies.[3]

As its more common or popular designation as the 'bedroom tax' suggests, this policy directly intervenes in the structure and composition of domestic space, in terms of specifying age, gender and generational relations governing allocation and entitlement to space within the household (Gibb 2015; Gibb et al. 2016). Through these policies, the 'bedroom tax' works both to normalize particular family forms and ties and, in this sense, can be read as going beyond mere economic considerations (of cutting welfare costs) to intensify a regulatory psychological gaze upon families (see Greenstein et al. 2016). This point is important to our analysis here, as such presuppositions are at play in particular within the example discussed below, while it may also account for why the 'bedroom tax' is generally understood as both indicative of, and perhaps the most despised example of, current welfare reforms.

It should be noted that this policy participates in the neoconservative political narrative that portrays the global economic crisis of 2008 as arising from the moral/characterological deficits of the poor, and too much public spending on welfare, rather than the mismanagement of the banks (Clark et al. 2014). As with other welfare 'reforms' associated with 'austerity' economic measures, such policies discursively rely upon and also configure certain types of individuals and families: 'classed Others are produced and symbolically shamed for not being austere enough' (Jensen 2012, p. 15). Nevertheless, the 'bedroom tax' is merely one of the many cuts in welfare reflecting economic reforms that have restructured the labour market (worldwide and also in the UK)—which include cuts in both state and third-sector provision and the undermining of employment conditions, all of which reduce household income and make work low-paid, precarious, fragile and often short term (Bailey 2016). Relevant also is how, contrary to the public discourse of poverty as a matter of unemployment or chronic unemployment, the most common situation is of in-work poverty (Rosso et al. 2015; Shildrick et al. 2010), whereby periods of temporary, low-paid employment generate incomes below minimum thresholds. This context has been shown to particularly affect single parents and households with children (Padley and Hirsh 2016).

It is well known that neoliberal policy reforms construct poverty as a question of individual responsibility (Grabham and Smith 2010; Pantazis 2016), with a focus on 'activation'. Poverty is understood as the result of reckless behaviour, so that its alleviation becomes a matter of re-educating the poor out of state dependency. That is, the neoliberal state, apparently marketized but exercising further central control through its promotion of individual choice and responsibility, wants its citizens to be entrepreneurial and self-sufficient. Such policies then have gendered and racialized, as well as classed, consequences (Bhattacharyya 2015; Lister 2006, 2011). Questions of unemployment are transformed into discussions about strate-gies addressed to individuals to increase 'employability' or to counter 'worklessness', both portrayed as intrinsic traits of individuals rather than socio-political conditions, and so configured as questions of personal responsibility. In relation to the 'bedroom tax', and its impacts on parents of school-age children, the focus is on economic mobility, rather than on inequality, which occludes the role of structural changes to global markets in the creation and maintenance of poverty, in and out of work (Jensen and Tyler 2012).

These pedagogical and psychoeducational imperatives, that operate outside explicit schooling institutions, need to be understood as a key arena for the elaboration of educational discourse and policy. Indeed the prevailing pedagogical discourse of responsibilization configures poverty as an educational issue in three ways. First, the poor should be 'educated' to find work via policies that penalize poverty, thereby supposedly 'incentivising' people into finding (and keeping) paid work (Jones et al. 2013), with policies emphasizing parent training rather than infrastructural or service investment. Second, through the (false) portrayal of intergenerational worklessness (see Shildrick et al. 2012), mobilizing the discourse of 'cycles of disadvantage' and 'cultural deprivation', these policies espouse claims to social mobility, supposedly by working as an educational measure preventing the spread of this 'culture' to future generations. Third, policies focus on how mothers should nurture resilient children who can withstand and even maximize their 'human capital' in face of poverty (Henderson and Denny 2015), so giving further legitimacy to prevailing policies of early intervention.

Alongside the Foucauldian framework mobilized here, the analysis in this chapter builds on feminist critiques of the individualization of poverty which highlight its gendered aspects (e.g. Lister 2006; Morini 2007), alongside covert racializations (Bhattacharyya 2013) and disproportionately unequal impacts on disabled people (e.g. Duffy 2013; Power et al. 2014). Not only is unwaged care and reproductive work mainly carried out by women, this is made invisible through rendering entitlement to many benefits conditional on actively seeking and gaining waged work and prioritizing it over other commitments (Grabham and Smith 2010; Pykett 2012a). Moreover, cuts to social and educational services actually increase demands for this unpaid care (Abramovitz 2012; Harrison 2012; Roberts 2014).

While the 'bedroom tax' coexists with and accompanies other welfare cuts under neoliberal state policies, then, it is of particular interest in relation to policy analyses concerned with gender and class (and their intersections with racialization and disability status), which it both presumes and intensifies. Attention to this performativity, as Murray (2014) recently noted, indicates that the feminization of poverty through welfare cutbacks may be better understood as feminization *through* poverty. In particular, not only does the 'bedroom tax' incite further state surveillance of the domestic sphere (in the name of neoliberal responsibilization), it also *performs*—in the example analysed below, particularly gendered and classed—acts of reification, or fixing of positions and identities. There are methodological implications of this conceptual-political point, in terms of how to analyse policy narratives of its impacts.

METHODOLOGICAL AND THEORETICAL PERSPECTIVE

A focus of this analysis is how, whether and when speakers do more than reproduce the dominant discourse. This question combines conceptual and methodological as well as policy concerns. I draw on Foucauldian discourse analysis to attend to an instance encountered within a speaker's narrative where she narrates herself as *subject of*, as well as *subject to*, policy discourse (s). From a Foucauldian perspective, as participants located within particular historical and cultural-political contexts, it may be impossible not to be *subject to* (and so being rendered the object of) those dominant discourses Butler (1997). Nevertheless, policy discourses are not entirely coherent and shift in specific contexts of practice (Ball 2005). In this analysis, a participant's narrative reformulates, comments upon and even offers alternative framings of the dominant policy discourse, and, in this sense, the speaker becomes the *subject of* discourse.

This analysis mobilizes a more activist reading of Foucault, in particular as elaborated by both recent and contemporaneous theorists. This reading suggests that, even though policy may speak through us as subjects, sometimes we also speak back to it. Through close attention to particular accounts, or narratives of the practice of policy arising from and situated within particular contexts, the play and interplay of repetition/reproduction, reflection and re-formulation can be attended to. This—as I illustrate below—can sometimes offer more indications of resistance that predominating (governmentality) readings of Foucault allow.

The relevance of Foucauldian ideas here is not only as a tool to analyse participant accounts of the educational impacts of welfare reforms but also as a method to interpret the ways educational discourse circulates and functions. Educational discourses have become a key feature of current neoliberal political practice, in the sense of designing policy interventions that focus on promoting better teaching or guiding the performance of good citizens. This pedagogical state (Jones et al. 2013) positions citizens as in need of learning (the correct political) lessons (of how to behave, work, live, etc.), while it also promotes the regulation and scrutiny of some social groups over others—in particular welfare recipients who form the focus of significant moral and scientific policy discourse. Thus policy mobilizes educational discourses (of teaching and learning) to produce particular forms of subject position (Davies and Harré 1990) or subjectivity (Henriques et al. 1984/1998) or, in the terms I use here, subjectify (Patton 1996; Davies 2006) particular groups of citizens as teachers, students or learners. As will become clear below, not only are children addressed as educational subjects but also are parents, according to the particular conceptions of the social that are correspondingly being enacted.

Many authors claim that discursive approaches are helpful to identify and evaluate the elements and positions brought into focus by contemporary policy (Ball 2015; Ball and Olmedo 2013). Neoliberal subjects are active, and increasingly agile (Gillies 2011) subjects, who are exhorted to maximize themselves amid fluctuating markets and a retrenched state. Alongside this, there is a move towards responsibilization, that is, the making responsible of citizens for functions and activities previously undertaken by and guaranteed by the state. In particular, the shift from discussion of 'unemployment' (a structural condition) to 'worklessness' (portrayed as an individual attribute or state) highlights the work of psychologization (De Vos 2012, 2014). This not only occludes global and local structural explanations for deprivation and poverty but also—as a correlate of responsibilization—privileges individual activation. Hence the pedagogical state works to promote the psychologized subject by extending schooling outside classrooms as a matter of guiding and educating parents and families to make better choices, rather than fund resources (Pykett 2012b; Jones et al. 2013).

Method/Analytic Approach

Rationale for Selecting This Text

As already indicated, the analysis is focused on a small fragment of material generated from a local study of educational impacts of welfare reforms on poor families, specifically analysing a statement made by a mother of three children in a research interview, recruited as a parent of school-aged children affected by the 'bedroom tax'. Her comment was made late in a (second) interview, conducted six months after the first and with the same interviewer. (To assess and discuss with participants the range and viability of their coping strategies for dealing with the extra financial burden imposed by the 'bedroom tax', a key feature of the design of the study was to interview 'bedroom tax'-affected parents twice, six months apart.)

In terms of the rationale for selecting this, it should be noted that this is by no means a 'representative' example, in the sense of being typical or frequently occurring. Rather, drawing on the different criteria and foci warranted by a qualitative, discursive (in this case specifically Foucauldian) approach, its exceptional character is precisely what makes it interesting, in the sense that it not only departed from the canonical, self-regulated and confessional narratives documented in our other interviews but also differed from other sociological research documenting subjective responses to current policy stigmatization of poverty (Shildrick and MacDonald 2013).

Various discursive approaches have been applied to social and educational policy that range from the sociolinguistic (Fairclough 2013; Fairclough and Fairclough 2013) to the macrosociological and ideological (Laclau and Mouffe 2001). As Parker (2013) outlines, all of these can be useful but each approach works best at particular levels of analysis and with particular kinds or genres of text: that is, with distinctive spatial and temporal textual specifications. Each is also oriented to particular epistemological commitments that in turn link to methodological conditions. Hence, the research questions under investigation—in this case about the forms of subjectivity and subjectification discernible from this mother's statement—reflect a Foucauldian concern with the forms and conditions of possibility for the articulation of subject positions and identifications.

A (But Not 'the') Foucauldian Approach

My analysis here draws on Foucault's analyses of the institutions structuring modern states as disciplinary practices and the corresponding subject positions they enable or ward off (Foucault 1980, 1981, 1988a, b): that is, the way people are disciplined by the organization of discourse as elaborated by modern institutions governing the family and individual-state relations. I mobilize a Foucauldian model of subjectification or subject formation (Foucault 1970, 1983a; Ball 1990, 2005, 2015; Bourke and Lidstone 2015; Olssen 2006) to focus on modalities of subjectivity (or forms of experience) produced, promoted or proscribed by particular discourses as much as on the forms of regulation and control, and so does not fall foul of the criticisms made by Scheurich and McKenzie (2005). This emphasis perhaps arises from my disciplinary background in critical psychology, where the reception of Foucault was oriented to challenging the 'psy complex' (Ingleby 1985; Rose 1985) with its production of forms of normalization and pathologization. While influenced by, my analysis here also departs from, some governmentality approaches (e.g. Rose 1990; Rose et al. 2006), which I read as offering too deterministic a reading of power relations. Instead, reflecting the activist—antiracist feminist—stance that informed the design and conduct as well as analysis of this study, I prefer to align with new engagements of Foucault's earlier work emerging within educational research, that motivate both more for political engagement and understanding of counterpractices of power (Allen and Goddard 2014; Ball 2005; Pêcheux 2014). Importantly, then (and contrary to some criticisms of discursive perspectives as disconnecting language from material or power relations), while this approach destabilizes the humanist subject (that underlies notions of 'agency' or 'empowerment', e.g.), it is not relativist or apolitical. As Foucault put it:

> my position leads not to apathy but to a hyper- and pessimistic activism. I think that the ethico-political choice we have to make every day is to determine which is the main danger. (1983b, p. 356)

Indeed Foucault himself was politically engaged, with his activism—conducted in alliance with prisoners' rights campaigns—animating his analyses of the carceral state elaborated in *Discipline and Punish* (Foucault 1977), a text which also connects his discussion of surveillance with schooling and schools with other institutions of hierarchization, standardization and normalization. Similarly Allen and Goddard (2014) promote a reading of Foucault's work as less concerned with governmentality (or the ways state practices shape forms of mental life) and more with resistance. Hence, discourses are always multiple and contested, with practices of power producing counterdiscourses and counterpractices. As Foucault (1981) pointed out, '[t]here is not, on the one side, a discourse of power, and opposite it, another discourse that runs counter to it. Discourses are tactical elements or blocks operating in the field of force relations' (pp. 101–102).

Discourse, Power, Regulation and Resistance

According to this framework, then, discourses are structurally elaborated and situationally reiterated frameworks of meaning, which carry possibilities of shifts and renegotiations of positioning within specific local practices (Burman et al. 1996; Parker 1992, 2016). Foucault's model of power as relationship 'exercised from innumerable points' (Foucault 1981, p. 94), highlights the complex networks of relations across, between and within bodies and minds, and so also between the psychic and the political. While discursive frameworks may define and delimit what can be spoken and, in particular, elaborate positions and relationships between elements and parties within each discourse, still there are also counterdiscourses—suppressed or subordinated ways of speaking or perspectives. These counterdiscourses are present even if (or perhaps precisely because) there are predominating or hegemonic discourses. A Foucauldian discourse analyst notices the gaps and shifts within and between discourses, using these as routes to explicate suppressed or subaltern voices (Spivak 1988) or hidden transcripts of power (Scott 1990). Foucault's student and interpreter, philosopher Michel Pêcheux (in a recently re-translated paper) commented: 'The object of discourse analysis, as it actually developed on the basis described, is precisely to explain and describe the construction and socio-historical ordering of constellations of utterances' (Pêcheux 2014, p. 95, fn6). Hence, Foucault's claim, 'Where there is power, there is resistance' (1981, p. 95), highlights how attending to the relational character of power enables us to see that resistance takes many forms.

In using the term *subjectification*, then, I am referring to 'those forms of conscious and unconscious relation to the self which make us subjects of a certain kind' (Patton 1996, p. 24). As transindividual frameworks of meaning, therefore, discourses are both symbolic and material in effect (Burman 1991; Burman et al. 1996; Parker 2014). This approach helps to identify how participants are both *subject to* prevailing political and practice-oriented discourses (of educational 'problems') and—at times—how they become the *subject of*—in the sense of reformulating—these in accounts of their everyday activities. This enables attention to how policies do not merely either produce or regulate people as subjects but also how those policies are engaged with and reconfigured. In this sense, a Foucauldian discursive approach underlies the policy analysis methodological shift towards attending to the enactment of policy, as performed rather than passively transmitted (see Webb and Gulson 2015).

Analysis: 'Tell Your Professor We Are Good Mothers'

As discussed above, this statement was spoken by a mother of three children in the context of a second research interview. I will suggest that this example addresses not only the production and regulation of subjectivity via social and educational policy implementation but also indications of resistance to this as expressed by one of its primary subjects. As previously indicated, discourses of marketization currently structure those of parenting, especially mothering. Recent analyses highlight parents' own subscription to discourses of entrepreneurialization (Edwards et al. 2015; Lupton 2012; Thornton 2011) as well as other forms of governmentality through pedagogy promoted within wider policies (Pykett 2012b). For some time, UK Parliament initiatives have preferred to focus on educating (and regulating) parents instead of increasing investment in public services (including education). Recent British research has documented and tried to explain how and why people in poor communities seem to accept dominant psychologized definitions of poverty/inequality (Shildrick and MacDonald 2013). It is in relation to this policy research picture that the discussion below of a discursive example of resistance is of particular interest. As explored below, these indications of resistance included: (1) refusing an individualized model that positions particular individuals or families as subject to the welfare cuts, in favour of (2) claiming wider collective impacts.

To the extent that this is a familiar example, this, first, shows how discursive analysis of everyday, assumed descriptions offers ways to explicate and interrogate the socio-political context they imply, since the mother's statement not only indicates how she understands how she is positioned within the dominant discourse but also offers a counterdiscourse to it. Second, this example highlights how such common cultural-linguistic resources combine with the specific and current case of welfare 'reform'/ cuts to both inscribe and intensify anew particular vilified subject positions for children and families from poor communities, subject positions that this participant both subscribes to and resists. Third, this example also brings to the fore the relational processes of this study, where the researchers were directly addressed in terms of subject positions assumed, attributed and re-negotiated in the interview—hence contesting prevailing power/knowledge relations inscribing academic research as a performance of practices of normalization and pathologization. Beyond merely 'giving voice' to the participant's perspective (as in the humanist model of qualitative research), I interpret this statement as working performatively to set an alternative discourse in circulation about her, and others' like her, competence and resourcefulness in dealing with adverse circumstances, and, in particular, fourth, in line with Foucault's later discussion of ethics as action rather than identity, to make an ethical-political demand of the researchers to use our authority to promote this discourse.

Subject Positions

Foucauldian analysis focuses on the conditions for the emergence of, and effects of, specific forms of subjectivity, including attending to shifts and contestations of identifications and subject positions. In evaluating this statement, 'Tell your professor we are good mothers', it is important to recall that the study did not explicitly concern parenting, or mothering, but rather its focus was on educational impacts of the 'bedroom tax' as a current reduction in welfare support, and so with likely implications for family income and well-being. So, it is all the more significant that a subject position of regulation and evaluation as a mother was inferred by this participant and interpellated (or hailed into being and identified with). Perhaps this interpellation (Althusser 1971) is not surprising, given the ways wider discourses around women and children entangle and even conflate their positions (Burman 2008, in press). Moreover (as already indicated), this likely arises due to the ways the 'bedroom tax' reiterates and consolidates particular forms of aged, generational and gendered identities through specifying space allocations.

To situate this statement in its conversational context, here is what immediately preceded it: 'these council houses women they are the most loving to their families it is the external environment which is causing because they want to change the family dynamic'. Next she said:

> We are good mothers (.) tell your professor we are good mothers (.) we are poor we live in council houses we have life skills (.) uff because we have suffered not because we are dummy ...you're constantly battling they will reduce this they send this they will stop this eviction letters this and that bills coming left right centre.

Here various subject positions can be identified. These include 'professor' and 'mothers', as well as the variously specified 'you' and 'your' (which in English can indicate both a specific and general subject, so the 'you' of 'your professor' is of course specifically addressed to the interviewer, while the 'you' of 'you're constantly battling' is general). An exclusive 'we' specifies mothers, or perhaps researched mothers; that is, it does not include 'you' (here specified as the researchers). The question of who comes under the policy/research gaze is implicitly topicalized, in particular indicating that not all mothers, but only poor, benefit-receiving mothers are subject to scrutiny and evaluation. Significantly, a field of discourse is elaborated, organized around the binary between 'good' mothers and an implied figuration of 'bad' mothers.

Moreover, in terms of both the number and gendering of the subject positions topicalized, it is worth noting that an elision is implied between parents and mothers in her account. That is, the roles and responsibilities of men as fathers do not arise. At play is a dominant discourse that aligns responsibility for children with women as mothers. (This is despite the fact that in our study fathers who had shared custodial arrangements emerged as specifically negatively impacted.)

Confession

Alongside, or as a corollary of, the shift from direct exercise of authoritarian control to the production of the self-regulating subject, Foucault (1981) described how forms of reflexivity have emerged that—corresponding with the modern state—include secular (rather than only religious) forms of confession. A notable feature indicated by this statement is the investment, or emotional importance, for women as mothers in being seen as 'good'. If this seems obvious, then this banality itself should be understood as revealing a key social norm. Subscribing to this norm imports other features, extending also to anxieties about regulatory or disciplinary surveillance about children being taken away and put into institutional care if they are considered not to be 'good' mothers.

There is clearly a classed as well as gendered intersection at play here, with poor, working class disproportionately scrutinized, evaluated and positioned by current social and educational policies as responsible not only for their children's welfare and current (educational and social) achievements but also for the children's future well-being, adjustment, health and wealth. However, there are also self-disciplining features, in the sense that women's identities remain powerfully oriented around the perceived adequacy of their caring and relational capacities (Burman 2012; Walkerdine and Lucey 1989). It is worth reflecting here on how the demand to be a 'good' mother has not only entered into the subjectivity of the speaker (so showing how dominant discourses produce subjectivities), that adopting the position of not being a good mother appears unthinkable.

Further reflection highlights not only present subject positions but also those that are absent. For there is an implied binary between 'good' and not 'good'/'bad' mother. Missing here is the discourse of the 'good enough' mother, circulating in post-World War Two parenting advice discourse (as formulated by the psychoanalyst, Donald Winnicott 1965) precisely to reassure women that they did not need to be perfect, only 'good enough'. Its absence could be read as highlighting how high stakes currently surround not only children's school achievement but also parenting (Blum and Fenton 2016).

Collective Subjectivity

Foucault's analyses highlight the discursive production of forms of individualization arising as a consequence of normalization. Perhaps most noteworthy about this text is how the speaker names a collective subject ('we', not 'I') as being 'good mothers', that is also later generalized to the inclusive 'you/your' (of *'you're constantly battling'*). This is significant in particular as it challenges the usual, 'confessional' genre of one-to-one interviews (Freund 2014), which in turn presumes a stable interiority to be excavated and scrutinized (Alldred and Gillies 2002). This alerts us to subject positions that are refused, or at least warded off, by this utterance. First, there is an explicit repudiation of the position of not being good mothers. But, alongside, and precisely because of this, there is a refusal to subscribe to a current discourse that aligns the position of being 'poor' with shame (Youngmie 2012; Chase and Walker 2012). Third, this speaker is also refusing to identify as the canonical uncertain, doubtful, confessional mother/parent (Geinger et al. 2014), albeit that this may be because expressing uncertainty in this context would warrant further unwanted scrutiny/intervention and pathologization of 'family dynamics', especially since she has already talked of how (unspecified people, but presumably social service professionals) 'want to change' these.

Finally, in place of the singular (confessional, individual) voice (that would claim 'I am a good mother'), this participant uses the collective first person voice, 'we'. This works to resist the ways individualization functions as a dividing practice, by naming subjectivity as a singular, privatized interiority (which would be a key example of psychologization discussed above). In doing this, this participant departs from other recent documented accounts generated from welfare recipients in poor communities who refused to identify themselves with other poor people, so resisting the stigmatization of poverty that has been seen as limiting or even preventing solidarity (Shildrick and MacDonald 2013), and thereby also repudiating the surveillance and regulation of working-class communities.

Revealing Institutional Relations of Knowledge Production to Make an Ethical-Political Demand

Foucault's later work focused on ethics, but throughout he emphasized the ethical-political choices to be made by researchers. Hence, it is worth reflecting further on the relational refusals or resistant agencies at play in this utterance. Unlike the forms of prevarication or sly avoidance that have been regarded as the only available modes of resistance in circumscribed contexts (see Wagner 2012 for an overview and Hoy 2005), by this statement this participant not only claims an active, positive and collective subjectivity (for mothers) but also makes a demand, in fact three demands. First, she demands to be heard ('tell your professor...'); second, she makes a collective/political claim ('we are...') on practices of representation (for 'the professor' surely stands in for 'research'), and third, she asserts an ethical demand of the interviewer that she (for the interviewer was indeed a woman) should use her authority, and the wider institutional relations of knowledge production that she participates in (with and via 'the professor'), to challenge unjust state stigmatization and blame of poor people for their poverty. That is, a claim made by the participant of the researchers to challenge the dominant discourses to which this mother and others like her are subject—which, it should be admitted, is precisely the ethical demand that prompted our study in the first place (see also Bragg et al. 2015).

The analysis of this statement is an example of the performativity of discourse that links dominant systems of power and knowledge. Its implications therefore not only engage current debates on the intensification of regulation of mothering under neoliberal, so-called active citizenship regimes. It also highlights the importance of recognizing speech as action: that is, how the act of speaking can make a claim to harness authority. By this example, we are invited to attend to the event of the interview, as an act of speaking to a researcher that is connected to the act of reporting research, and this in turn can generate an ethical appeal to the researchers to intervene to counter a current or incipient injustice. The statement, 'Tell your professor we are good mothers', makes a moral-political claim on what we as researchers (should) do, and on what research is and does. In so doing, it links the micropolitics of the dyadic interview to the institutional power relations that prevail and determinate it from outside, whilst equivalently harnessing a collective voice, as one political constituency addressing another.

SUMMARY

This example, from an educational research project on *The Impacts of the Bedroom Tax on Children and Their Education* (Bragg et al. 2015), indicates how a Foucauldian-informed discursive approach can contribute and extend policy analysis. In particular, this approach can document and highlight how prevailing neoliberal policies position poor children and families, with implications also for the positioning of the professionals and practitioners who work with them. One key consequence of this model of analysis is that it helps ward off deterministic and fatalistic models that threaten to overstate the reach of neoliberal discourse. Instead, the example I have discussed suggests how a discursive analysis can help identify the forms and varieties of subjectivities created by social/educational policies (of welfare reform) and their consequences, alongside documenting how some ways of speaking open up spaces for negotiation and resistance.

This analysis has worked to 'chip away at bits of the social, always looking for joins and patterns but equally aware of fractures and discontinuities' (Ball 2005, p. 2). The example discussed is of significance by virtue of its refusal of prevailing configurations of mothering and of the subject positioning of research participant. It also offers an important reassertion of or claim to collective subjectivity and solidarity. Following Pêcheux (2014), we can therefore see the interview as an event that elaborates, rather than merely rehearses or repeats, discourse. Indeed, Foucault (1981) himself pointed out that '[t]here is not, on the one side, a discourse of power, and opposite it, another discourse that runs counter to it. Discourses are tactical elements or blocks operating in the field of force relations' (pp. 101–102).

More generally, what this example indicates is how policy discourse, in this case a housing-related welfare reform that has widespread impacts on family and children's well-being and their education (Winter et al. 2016), is both reproduced and transformed by the various subjects who are both subjectified by, but also become subjects of, these discourses. Yet via this discourse analysis, the story here is not only one of co-option or ineluctable subscription to these dominant framings. Rather, this example highlights adept manoeuvring within, negotiation, and even contestation of, prevailing discursive arrangements that exemplify Foucault's (1981) claim that 'Discourse transmits and produces power; it reinforces it, but also undermines and exposes it, renders it fragile and makes it possible to thwart it' (p. 100).

So we see that research not only documents discourse, it also produces it. Policy is formulated and also enacted and re-enacted through practices of subjectification. From this example, I have offered a specific Foucauldian reading that also intervenes in prevailing Foucauldian approaches, which emphasize governmentality, to attend instead to practices of resistance as well as regulation. The ethical-political project to document and enact such practice remains all too urgent. As Pêcheux's analysis highlights, what we do as generators and interpreters of this material puts into stark focus both our own understandings, as researchers, of the relations between policy and discourse but also how we respond to the claims made of us as producers of such discourse, to use this authority to change those policy discourses.

Key Connections to Policy Research
1. The example taken for analysis illustrates how policies produce and regulate subjects who, following a Foucauldian approach, are both subject to and subjects of those policies.
2. These subjects are, however, positioned within various discourses—in this case as a mother of three children affected by welfare cuts, that both limit her capacity to provide for her children but also extend the state surveillance of her as a poor working-class woman claiming welfare benefits.
3. Foucauldian discourse analysis highlights how, as socially shared frameworks of meaning, discourses are multiple and contested, here analysed in terms of the various attributions and investments associated with the claim of being a 'good mother'.
4. A Foucauldian analysis highlights how power is relational: it is regulatory, self-regulatory, and also, under certain conditions, can be documented as sometimes resisted; hence, this participant claimed as unquestionable the position of being a good mother and demanded that the research study promoted that claim.
5. Research produces as well as analyses discourse; therefore, as researchers, we need to reflect critically on what discourses our research practice contributes to, and how we can document and even promote resistance to dominant policy discourses.

(continued)

6. A Foucauldian analysis does more than describe or analyse language, but documents conflicts produced between and within dominant discourses as forms of institutional relations, and from this can support the making of policy interventions. The discursive objects who are also embodied and psychic *subjects* of policy research speak of and make claims of us as researchers to make socio-political change.

NOTES

1. The project was funded by the University of Manchester Humanities Strategic Investment Fund under the title 'Investigating the social and educational implications of reforms to housing welfare in Manchester' from January 2014 to July 2015.
2. Affected households have had their housing benefits cut by an average sum of £10–25 per week.
3. The sample of participants was drawn from key geographical areas of the city affected by the welfare changes with high populations in social housing and comprised: 14 parents of (in total 24) school-aged children (9 women, 5 men), 10 of whom were interviewed twice with a six-month interval to document their changing situations and perspectives as the policy took force, 39 service support providers, including 12 community support and service providers (3 housing, 3 social support—specializing in work with children and young people—and 3 from faith-based organizations, and 2 from health-related organizations, one of which provided a food bank), 20 school-based professionals were interviewed drawn from 8 schools (4 primary, 4 secondary) in the two areas.

REFERENCES

Abramovitz, M. (2012). The feminization of austerity. *New Labor Forum, 21*(1), 30–39.

Alldred, P., & Gillies, V. (2002). Eliciting research accounts: Re/producing modern subjects. In M. Mauthner, M. Birch, J. Jessop, & T. Miller (Eds.), *Ethics in qualitative research* (pp. 146–165). London: Sage.

Allen, A., & Goddard, R. (2014). The domestication of Foucault: Government, critique, war. *History of the Human Sciences, 27*(5), 26–63.

Althusser, L. (1971). Ideology and ideological state apparatus. In *Lenin and philosophy and other essays* (pp. 1–60). London: New Left Books.

Bailey, N. (2016). Exclusionary employment in Britain's broken labour market. *Critical Social Policy, 36*(1), 82–103.

Ball, S. J. (Ed.). (1990). *Foucault and education: Disciplines and knowledges.* London: Routledge.

Ball, S. J. (2005). *Education policy and social class: The selected works of Stephen J. Ball.* London: Routledge.

Ball, S. J. (2015). What is policy? 21 years later: Reflections on the possibilities of policy research. *Discourse: Studies in the Cultural Politics of Education, 36*(3), 306–313.

Ball, S. J., & Olmedo, A. (2013). Care of the self, resistance and subjectivity under neoliberal governmentalities. *Critical Studies in Education, 54*(1), 85–96.

Bhattacharyya, G. (2013). Racial neoliberal Britain? In N. Kapoor, V. S. Kalra, & J. Rhodes (Eds.), *The state of race* (pp. 31–49). Basingstoke: Palgrave.

Bhattacharyya, G. (2015). *Crisis, austerity, and everyday life: Living in a time of diminishing expectations.* London: Palgrave Macmillan.

Blum, L. M., & Fenton, E. R. (2016). Mothering with neuroscience in a neoliberal age: Child disorders and embodied brains. In L. Folkmarson Käll (Ed.), *Bodies, boundaries and vulnerabilities* (pp. 99–118). New York: Springer International Publishing.

Bourke, T., & Lidstone, J. (2015). What is Plan B? Using Foucault's archaeology to enhance policy analysis. *Discourse: Studies in the Cultural Politics of Education, 36* (6), 833–853.

Bragg, J., Burman, E., Greenstein, A., Hanley, T., Kalambouka, A., Lupton, R., McCoy, L., Sapin, K., Winter, L. (2015). *The impact of the 'bedroom tax' on children and their education: A study in the city of Manchester.* Manchester Institute of Education: The University of Manchester. http://www.seed.manchester.ac.uk/medialibrary/research/Bedroom_Tax-Final-Report.pdf

Burman, E. (1991). What discourse is not. *Philosophical Psychology, 4*(3), 325–341.

Burman, E. (2008). Beyond "women vs. children" or "womenandchildren": Engendering childhood and reformulating motherhood. *International Journal of Children's Rights, 16*(2), 177–194.

Burman, E. (2012). Deconstructing neoliberal childhood: Towards a feminist antipsychological approach. *Childhood: A Global Journal of Child Research, 19* (4), 423–438.

Burman, E. (in press). A necessary struggle-in-relation? Three current frameworks for addressing practical-political problems. In B. Mayall, R. Rosen, K. Twarmley, & A. Varley (Eds.), *Feminism and the politics of childhood: Friends or foes?* London: UCL Press.

Burman, E., Aitken, G., Alldred, A., Allwood, R., Billington, T., Goldberg, B., Gordo Lopez, A., Heenan, C., Marks, D., & Warner, S. (1996). *Psychology discourse practice: From regulation to resistance.* London: Taylor & Francis.

Butler, J. (1997). *The psychic life of power: Theories in subjection.* London: Routledge.

Chase, E., & Walker, R. (2012). The co-construction of shame in the context of poverty: Beyond a threat to the social bond. *Sociology, 47*(4), 739–754.

Clarke, A., Hill, L., Marshall, B., Monk, S., Pereira, I., Thomson, E., Whitehead, C., & Williams, P. (2014). *Evaluation of removal of the spare room subsidy: Interim report, Research report 882.* London: Department for Work and Pensions.

Davies, B. (2006). Subjectification: The relevance of Butler's analysis for education. *British Journal of Sociology of Education, 27*(4), 425–438.

Davies, B., & Harré, R. (1990). Positioning: The discursive production of selves. *Journal for the Theory of Social Behaviour, 20*(1), 43–63.

De Vos, J. (2012). *Psychologisation in times of globalization.* London: Routledge.

De Vos, J. (2014). *Psychologization and the subject of late modernity.* London: Palgrave.

Duffy, S. (2013). A fair society? Sheffield: The Centre for Welfare Reform. http://www.centreforwelfarereform.org/uploads/attachment/261/a-fair-society-and-thelimits-of-personalisation.pdf

DWP. (2012). Housing benefit: Size criteria for people renting in the social rented sector. *Equality Impact Assessment,* updated, June. https://www.gov.uk/government/uploads/system/uploads/attachment_data/file/220154/eia-social-sector-housing-under-occupation-wr2011.pdf

Edwards, R., Gillies, V., & Horsley, N. (2015). Brain science and early years policy: Hopeful ethos or 'cruel optimism'? *Critical Social Policy, 35*(2), 167–187.

Fairclough, N. (2013). Critical discourse analysis and critical policy studies. *Critical Policy Studies, 7*(2), 177–197.

Fairclough, I., & Fairclough, N. (2013). *Political discourse analysis: A method for advanced students.* London: Routledge.

Foucault, M. (1970). The order of discourse. In I. Parker (Ed.). (2011). Critical psychology: Critical concepts in psychology, Volume 4, dominant models of psychology and their limits (pp. 190–220). London/New York: Routledge.

Foucault, M. (1977). *Discipline and punish: The birth of the prison.* Harmondsworth: Penguin.

Foucault, M. (1980). Prison talk. In C. Gordon (Ed.), *Power/knowledge: Selected interviews and other writings, 1972–1977* (pp. 37–54). Brighton: Harvester.

Foucault, M. (1981). *History of sexuality, Vol 1: An introduction.* Harmondsworth: Pelican.

Foucault, M. (1983a). The subject and power. Afterward to H. Dreyfus & P. Rabinow (Eds.), *Michel Foucault: Beyond structuralism and hermeneutics* (pp. 208–264). Chicago: University of Chicago Press.

Foucault, M. (1983b). On the genealogy of ethics: An overview of work in progress. In P. Rabinow (Ed.), *The Foucault reader: An introduction to Foucault's thought* (pp. 340–372). London: Penguin.

Foucault, M. (1988a). Technologies of the self. In L. Martin, H. Gutman, & P. Hutton (Eds.), *Technologies of the self: A seminar with Michel Foucault* (pp. 16–49). London: Tavistock.

Foucault, M. (1988b). The political technology of individuals. In L. Martin, H. Gutman, & P. Hutton (Eds.), *Technologies of the self: A seminar with Michel Foucault* (pp. 145–162). London: Tavistock.

Freund, A. (2014). "Confessing animals": Toward a longue durée history of the oral history interview. *The Oral History Review, 41*(1), 1–26.

Geinger, F., Vandenbroeck, M., & Roets, G. (2014). Parenting as a performance: Parents as consumers and (de)constructors of mythic parenting and childhood ideals. *Childhood, 21*(4), 488–501.

Gibb, K. (2015). The multiple policy failures of the UK bedroom tax. *International Journal of Housing Policy, 15*(2), 148–166.

Gibb, K., Stephens, M., Reuschke, D., Wright, S., Besemer, K., & Sosenko, F. (2016). *How does housing affect work incentives for people in poverty.* York: Joseph Rowntree Foundation. https://www.jrf.org.uk/report/how-does-housing-affect-work-incentives-people-poverty. Posted 22 Feb.

Gillies, D. (2011). Agile bodies: A new imperative in neoliberal governance. *Journal of Educational Policy, 26*(3), 207–223.

Grabham, E., & Smith, J. (2010). From social security to individual responsibility (part two): Writing off poor women's work in the Welfare Reform Act 2009. *Journal of Social Welfare and Family Law, 32*(1), 81–93.

Greenstein, A., Burman, E., Kalambouka, A., & Sapin, K. (2016). Constructing and deconstructing 'family' through the 'bedroom tax'. *British Politics, 11*(4), 508–525.

Harrison, E. (2012). Bouncing back? Recession, resilience and everyday lives. *Critical Social Policy, 33*(1), 97–113.

Henderson, J., & Denny, K. (2015). The resilient child, human development and the "postdemocracy". *BioSocieties, 10*(3), 352–378.

Henriques, J., Hollway, W., Urwin, C., Venn, C., & Walkerdine, V. (1984/1998). *Changing the subject: Psychology, social regulation and subjectivity.* London: Methuen.

Hoy, D. C. (2005). *Critical resistance: From poststructuralism to post-critique.* Cambridge: MIT Press.

Ingleby, D. (1985). Professionalizers as socializers: The "psy complex". *Research in Law, Deviance and Social Control, 7,* 79–109.

Jensen, T. (2012). Tough love in tough times. *Studies in the Maternal, 4*(2). http://www.mamsie.bbk.ac.uk/articles/abstract/10.16995/sim.35/

Jensen, T., & Tyler, I. (2012). Austerity parenting: New economies of parent-citizenship (editorial). *Studies in the Maternal, 4*(2). http://www.mamsie.bbk.ac.uk/article/10.16995/sim.34/

Jones, R., Pykett, J., & Whitehead, M. (2013). *Changing behaviours: On the rise of the psychological state.* Cheltenham/Northampton: Edward Elgar.

Laclau, E., & Mouffe, C. (2001). *Hegemony and socialist strategy: Towards a radical democratic politics.* London: Verso.

Lister, R. (2006). Children (but not women) first: New Labour, child welfare and gender. *Critical Social Policy, 26*(2), 315–355.

Lister, R. (2011). The age of responsibility: Social policy and citizenship in the early 21st century. In C. Hoden, M. Kilky, & G. Ramia (Eds.), *Social policy review* (pp. 63–84). Bristol: The Policy Press.

Lupton, D. (2012). 'Precious cargo': Foetal subjects, risk and reproductive citizenship. *Critical Public Health, 22*(3), 329–340.

Morini, C. (2007). The feminisation of labour in cognitive capitalism. *Feminist Review, 88*, 40–59.

Murray, K.B. (2014). Feminization through poverty. *Politics and Culture.* http://politicsandculture.org/2014/03/10/feminization-through-poverty-by-karen-bridget-murray/

Olssen, M. (2006). *Michel Foucault: Materialism and education.* Boulder/London: Paradigm.

Padley, M., & Hirsh, D. (2016). Families below a minimum income standard, 2008/9–2013/14, Joseph Rowntree Foundation, February. https://www.jrf.org.uk/report/households-below-minimum-income-standard-200809-201314

Pantazis, C. (2016). Policies and discourses of poverty during a time of recession and austerity. *Critical Social Policy, 36*(1), 1–18.

Parker, I. (1992, 2016). *Discourse dynamics.* London: Routledge

Parker, I. (2013). Discourse analysis: Dimensions of critique in psychology. *Qualitative Research in Psychology, 10*(3), 223–239.

Parker, I. (2014). *Discourse dynamics.* London: Routledge.

Patton, P. (1996). Deleuze and Guattari: Ethics and post-modernity. *Intervention, 20*, 24–34.

Pêcheux, M. (2014). Discourse: Structure or event? In I. Parker & D. Pavón-Cuéllar (Eds.), *Lacan, discourse, event: New psychoanalytic approaches to textual indeterminacy* (pp. 77–98). London: Routledge.

Power, A., Provan, B., Herden, E., & Serle, N. (2014). *The impact of welfare reform on social landlords and tenants.* York: Joseph Rowntree Foundation. http://www.jrf.org.uk/sites/files/jrf/Welfare-reform-impack-FULL.pdf. Accessed 14 Apr 2015.

Pykett, J. (2012a). The new maternal state: The gendered politics of governing through behaviour change. *Antipode, 44*(1), 217–238.

Pykett, J. (Ed.). (2012b). *Governing through pedagogy.* London: Routledge.

Roberts, A. (2014). Gender, financial deepening and the production of embodied finance: Towards a critical feminist analysis. *Global Society*. doi:10.1080/13600826.975189

Rose, N. (1985). *The psychological complex: Psychology, politics and society in England 1869–1939*. London: Routledge.

Rose, N. (1990). *Governing the soul*. London: Routledge.

Rose, N., O'Malley, P., & Valverde, M. (2006). Governmentality. *Annual Review of Law and Social Science, 2*, 83–104.

Rosso, A., Gaffney, D., & Portes, J. (2015). What explains the growth in 'never-worked' households? https://www.jrf.org.uk/report/what-explains-growth-never-worked-households. Posted 25 Sept 2015.

Scheurich, J., & McKenzie, K. (2005). Foucault's methodologies: Archaeology and genealogy. In N. Denzin & Y. Lincoln (Eds.), *The SAGE handbook of qualitative research* (pp. 141–169). Thousand Oaks: Sage.

Scott, J. C. (1990). *Domination and the arts of resistance: Hidden transcripts*. New Haven: Yale University Press.

Shildrick, T., & MacDonald, R. (2013). Poverty talk: How people experiencing poverty deny their poverty and why they blame 'the poor'. *The Sociological Review, 61*, 385–303.

Shildrick, T., Macdonald, R., Webster, C., & Garthwaite, K. (2010). *The low-pay, no-pay cycle: Understanding recurrent poverty*. York: Joseph Rowntree Foundation.

Shildrick, T., MacDonald, R., Furlong, A., Roden, J., & Crow, R. (2012). *Are 'cultures of worklessness' passed down the generations?* York: Joseph Rowntree Foundation.

Spivak, G. C. (1988). Can the subaltern speak? In C. Nelson & L. Grossman (Eds.), *Marxism and the interpretation of culture* (pp. 217–313). Urbana: University of Illinois Press.

Thornton, D. J. (2011). Neuroscience, affect and the entrepreneurialization of motherhood. *Communication and Critical/Cultural Studies, 8*(4), 399–424.

Wagner, R. (2012). Silence as resistance before the subject, or could the subaltern remain silent? *Theory, Culture & Society, 29*(6), 99–124.

Walkerdine, V., & Lucey, H. (1989). *Democracy in the kitchen: Regulating mothers and socialising daughters*. London: Virago.

Webb, P. T., & Gulson, K. N. (2015). Policy scientificity 3.0: Theory and policy analysis in-and-for this world and other-worlds. *Critical Studies in Education, 56* (1), 161–174.

Winnicott, D. W. (1965). The theory of the parenting relationship. In D. W. Winnicott (Ed.), *The maturational processes and the facilitating environment: Studies in the theory of emotional development* (pp. 37–55). London: Hogarth Press.

Winter, L., Burman, E., Hanley, T., Kalambouka, A., & McCoy, L. (2016). Education, welfare reform and psychological wellbeing: A critical psychology perspective. *British Journal of Educational Studies, 64*(4), 467–483.

Youngmie, J. (2012). Psychosocial dimensions of poverty: When poverty becomes shameful. *Critical Social Policy, 33*(3), 514–531.

Erica Burman is Professor of Education at Manchester Institute of Education, University of Manchester, UK. She is the co-founder of the Discourse Unit (www.discourseunit.com), a transinstitutional, interdisciplinary research centre that focuses on language and subjectivity as sites for social reproduction and transformation. She uses discursive approaches and critical theory to inform methodological and theoretical debates and policy applications.

CHAPTER 5

Membership Categorization Analysis for Education Policy

Justin Paulsen

INTRODUCTION

This chapter presents the usefulness of Membership Categorization Analysis (MCA) as a methodological perspective for educational policy research. MCA is a language-based approach to deconstruct common categorizations (e.g. teachers, students, parents) present in any culture. This deconstruction allows researchers to better understand how a culture creates boundaries specifying the expected actions, characteristics, and relationships in a given category (e.g. "good teachers form partnerships with parents"). To demonstrate the usefulness of MCA, the chapter includes a case example examining the extent to which a preeminent global education reform discourse on teachers has been taken up by three different educational organizations in Bangladesh. The case example illustrates in depth how one might conduct an MCA study as well as the kinds of findings that are gained. Thus, the purpose of this chapter is to (a) present a review of MCA scholarship including its genesis and current uses in education policy research, and

J. Paulsen (✉)
Indiana University, Bloomington, IN, USA

© The Author(s) 2017
J.N. Lester et al. (eds.), *Discursive Perspectives on Education Policy and Implementation*, DOI 10.1007/978-3-319-58984-8_5

(b) illustrate the use of MCA in education policy research using the Bangladesh case study.

The chapter begins with a discussion of MCA and its origins with Harvey Sacks and Conversation Analysis (CA). This is followed by a review of the uses (current and prospective) of MCA in policy research. Thereafter, I draw on the MCA literature to indicate how researchers do MCA. The bulk of the chapter consists of the illustrative example using the Bangladesh-global education reform discourse example, followed by a summary and conclusion.

Overview of MCA

MCA was first developed in Harvey Sacks' well-known lectures. Sacks, considered one of the original developers of CA, took interest in the way that everyday language constructs the world and patterns interactions. Analysis of suicide line phone calls led to Sacks' research that contributed to the development CA methodology (Sacks 1992), a qualitative methodology that focuses on the structures and sequential nature of talk. CA differs from other language-based methodologies in a number of ways: the most important for the purposes of this chapter are the importance of sequential positioning for understanding language and CA's essentially emic approach. CA traditionally uses as its data recorded, naturally occurring conversations, and its analysis focuses on word-by-word and line-by-line interactions (Hutchby and Wooffitt 2008). Each part of the interaction is working to accomplish some action; activities achieved in conversation include requests, repair, proposals, accusations, and complaints, to name a few (Hutchby and Wooffitt 2008). CA adopts a somewhat radical approach to language-based methodologies in that it confines itself solely to the words in the interaction. Thus, analysis of the language itself does not look through a particular critical lens or theoretical background; however, findings from CA analyses can be used to inform social life (ten Have 2007). MCA similarly draws on these key ideas.

In the same lectures in which Sacks developed CA, he also identified membership categorization as an important resource used in structuring language. At its most basic form, MCA is concerned with identifying the terms speakers use to refer to others and the language attached to those references (Schegloff 2007). For Sacks, categories and the process of categorization is a key feature in conversation and bring organization to the interaction (Housley 2002). A common example to teach this principle is shown in the following excerpt, "The baby cried. The mommy picked it up" (Schegloff 2007). Without needing to ask a question, someone reading this will intuit that the activity of crying is natural to the baby, the mommy is the mother of that baby, and that picking up the baby is the responsibility of mommy. Sacks argued that language is built on categories that exist in a commonsense network to those inside the language culture. Critically examining the network surrounding categories gives insight into how a population defines that category.

While some scholars have suggested that Sacks' two offspring, CA and MCA, are distinctly separate or that MCA is the byproduct of initial thought and CA the more mature outcome, Housley and Fitzgerald (2002) described how Sacks emphasized both ideas in conjunction with each other. Thus, this chapter follows Stokoe's (2012) call for a "systematic analysis of membership categories" and "track[ing] categorial concerns in the same way that CA has pursued sequential practices" (279).

MCA in Education Policy

My search for literature leveraging the use of MCA in education found few studies employing this methodology. After searching through education policy databases, CA and discourse-specific journals, and broad search platforms like Google Scholar, I found that only four studies combined MCA and educational policy. Two of these studies assessed the operationalization of Spain's and France's language policies in primary classrooms receiving immigrant students (Dooly and Unamuno 2009; Bonacina-Pugh 2012). Dooly and Unamuno used MCA to determine that while the policy document established using Catalan as a means of social cohesion and plurilingualism as a threat to that, teachers in the classroom oriented to plurilingualism as a resource to achieve their educational goals. Bonacina-Pugh similarly differentiated between the policy as a text mandating monolingualism in the class and the policy in action where students did categorization work to decide which language to use with their peers (i.e. those with shared English background spoke English, while a mixed language background resulted in French interaction). Neither case made explicit recommendations for addressing the disconnect discovered between the language policies and the policies in action.

The other two studies addressed very different areas. Thomas et al. (2015) identified a trend in Australian policy documents to emphasize the responsibility of parents in students' academic achievement and analyzed parent-teacher interviews to see whether parents and teachers were constructing a similar parent category. They identified teachers and parents engaging in similar categorization and warned that accepting such categorization implicitly shifts accountability away from educational administrators and bureaucracies. (MacLure et al. 2012) considered the role early childhood education policy has on developing negative reputations among students. They argued that such policies as audits and baseline assessments, age-related statements and goals within policy frameworks, student case files, and collective instructional approaches ossifies categorization work relative to the "good child" rather than allowing further development. The authors recommended against early interventions, providing wider spectrums of developmental mapping and smaller group instruction to avoid prematurely establishing categorizations.

As these studies demonstrated, MCA provides a unique method of understanding the individual impact and lived experience of educational policies. Categorization work revealed how students and teachers circumvent language policy to achieve more pressing goals than those of the educational language policy. In the latter two cases (Thomas et al. 2015; MacLure et al. 2012), categorization work being done by policies was shown to be affecting how parents and students were being categorized on a local basis. In each case, the findings problematized the taken for granted, inviting policy makers to reflect on the goals of their policies and the various impacts they had on teachers and students.

As suggested above, MCA can identify the boundary within which a culture allows a category (e.g. teacher, student, parent) to act. These boundaries are the actions, characterizations, and relationships prescribed for a particular category. Schegloff (2007) described it in this way, "If an ostensible member of a category appears to contravene what is 'known' about members of that category, then people do not revise that knowledge, but see the person as 'an exception', 'different', or even a defective member" (469). This kind of information can be critical to policy makers and administrators. Attempts to develop a new policy may be in vain should a policy contravene the commonsense understanding of a key category. An example of this based on the data used below would be an international organization using financial aid leverage to pressure a local government to implement learner-centered policies without recognizing the boundaries of the teacher category defined by activities such as lecturing and testing. Thus, studying the categorization of teachers can provide useful insight to policy researchers.

Doing MCA

In regard to MCA, Sacks (1992) offered more general analytical under-standings and constructs but gave relatively little specific guidance on how one might conduct a MCA research study. Synthesizing Sacks' develop-ment of MCA and subsequent key analyses using MCA, Stokoe (2012) developed guiding principles and key concepts for doing MCA. These guiding principles provide novices to MCA or CA a means of pursuing such an analysis.

Stokoe (2012) identified ten key concepts in the membership categori-zation literature described below with examples drawn from the texts analyzed in the illustrative example. These are the constructs developed by Sacks and used by MCA scholars generally. All of these concepts may or may not always be used in a study, but they roughly form the universe from which to draw when doing an MCA study:

1. Membership categorization device: the collective category that binds categories together (e.g. the membership category device for principals, teachers, and teachers aids would be school employees).
2. Category-bound activities: activities that are linked in the text or interaction to categories (e.g. "The students (category) are supposed to follow (category-bound activity) their teachers").
3. Category-tied predicates: descriptor or characteristic tied to a par-ticular category (e.g. "Qualified (predicate) teachers (category) are essential (predicate)") (Ministry of Education 2010, 57).
4. Standardized relational pairs: categories linked together by expected duties or obligations (e.g. student-teacher, "The students are sup-posed to follow their teachers") (CAMPE 2011, 116).
5. Duplicative organization: categories bound together in a common purpose with set obligations like a team (e.g. parents and teachers in an "educator team").
6. Positioned categories: categories that are linked by a hierarchical relationship where one category being described by the lower or higher hierarchical category provides unique meaning (e.g. local teacher, qualified teacher).
7. Category-activity puzzles: categories linked in an unusual sequence (e.g. "student-teacher") to perform a particular action of setting the category apart or making jokes.

8. The economy rule: seeing a single category invoked is sufficient to understand the categorization work taking place (e.g. "the students follow their teachers") (CAMPE 2011, 116).

9. The consistency rule: if two or more categories are next to each other and can be understood as belonging to a common membership categorization device, then they should be.

10. Viewer's maxim: "if a member sees a category-bound activity being done, then, if one sees it being done by a member of a category to which the activity is bound, see it that way" (Sacks 1992, 221).

Stokoe (2012, 280) also provides practical guidance for how one might conduct an MCA study:

1. Collect discursive data. Data could be interactional, textual, or both (the case below exclusively uses textual data).

2. Build collections of explicit mentions of categories (e.g. teacher, student) and membership categorization devices (e.g. school employees).

3. Locate the sequential position of the category mentioned within the interaction or text.

4. Analyze the design and action orientation of the interaction or text surrounding the category mention.

5. Look for evidence of how parties orient to the category and build upon or resist the categorization.

Stokoe (2012) made a key point worth considering here: the key concepts invoked by the speaker or writer are made meaningful by the discursive act and not in a preconceived, decontextualized way. Thus, the MCA study should examine how the parties involved orient to categories and link them to particular activities, predicates, and relational pairs in the local context as opposed to the analyst's.

Illustrative Case of MCA in Education Policy: Bangladesh and the Global Teacher Construct

Background of the Case Example To illustrate the use of MCA in educational policy, I examine the extent to which a preeminent global discourse about teachers has penetrated different levels of the education system in Bangladesh. Over the past 10–20 years, one of the primary focuses of global education policy reform has been on the role of the teacher (Rotberg 2010; Paine et al. 2016). Paine et al. (2016) described a multifaceted discourse about teachers that has become particularly influential across the world:

1. Teachers are the fulcrum of the education system, the primary reason for inadequate results and the solution to any problem.
2. Teachers are defined in terms of deficits; they lack training, they lack accountability, they lack motivation, there aren't enough of them.
3. Teachers should lead child-centered instruction and should not primarily function as dispensers of information to students.
4. Teachers ultimately produce student learning that can be measured in achievement tests.

Paine et al. (2016) described some useful concepts for understanding how this global discourse could spread. The first is the idea of "global flows" (719). Ideas flow through a variety of mechanisms across the world, penetrating places and competing with local norms and traditions. Second, "flows occur through spaces, but not all spaces are the same" (Paine et al., 719). The degree to which global ideas and policies influence locales differs depending on the political relationships and networks at hand.

Many global education policy researchers have identified international organizations and international aid as one of the key levers by which education policy has become globalized (Verger et al. 2012; Stromquist and Monkman 2014; Rizvi 2004). This is generally accomplished by either making funding conditional on reform, using persuasion and expertise to implement certain policies, or establishing common objectives that require policy harmonization (Verger et al. 2012).

The case of Bangladesh is particularly useful to examine the theories of global flows in spaces and the role of international organizations. Bangladesh is one of the largest recipients of international aid for education. Additionally, its educational system has both governmental and non-governmental schools with a significant proportion of primary education offered by non-governmental organizations (NGOs). Thus, my analysis is able to examine a variety of Paine et al.'s "spaces". Specifically, this analysis considers the differential penetration of the preeminent global discourse in (a) Bangladesh's Ministry of Education (MoE), (b) the Campaign for Popular Education (CAMPE) (a network of 1300 NGOs providing educational services), and (c) Dhaka Ahsania Mission (DAM) (an individual large, local NGO) using the insights gained from MCA.

Primary Education in Bangladesh Around the time that the Bangladeshi Educational organizations indicated above produced these education sector strategy documents, primary education (classes 1–5) in Bangladesh continued to struggle. Bangladesh boasted one of the largest education systems in the world with 16.4 million primary-age children (all data from UNICEF 2009). While 90% of children were enrolled, only 51% of students completed primary education. Additionally, only 10% of schools reach the standard of 900 contact hours per year. Thus, many primary-age students drop out, and those who do remain receive relatively little instruction. Bangladesh does have a non-formal education sector that reaches out to youth who have dropped out to engage them in some amount of instruction.

The study posits that the selected organizations have different degrees of connection with the global education policy network which influences the degree to which they wittingly or not adopt the international teacher discourse described above. The MoE was the most connected because of its many direct interactions with international organizations and foreign aid agencies. In 2007, it partnered with over 20 different organizations on a variety of education system projects (Ministry of Primary and Mass Education 2007). CAMPE also connects with the international community but to a lesser extent than the MoE. It was founded after the 1990 Education for All declaration and defines its historical phases by its international partnerships (CAMPE 2014). CAMPE claimed key partnerships with three European foreign aid organizations during the timeframe in which the document included in this study were published, but previously had other international partners. DAM was founded in 1958 by a Bangladeshi Sufi. DAM engages in eight different primary education projects, two of which enjoy partnerships with an Asian foreign aid organization and an international organization, respectively. While these are only rough indicators of relative connection to international organizations, it seems reasonable to believe that organizations with more international partnerships would be more likely to engage with and potentially adopt global education trends than those that have fewer partnerships. Thus, I hypothesize that DAM was likely further removed from the global teacher discourse flow than CAMPE, CAMPE was likely more removed than the MoE, and that this will be apparent in the analyzed documents.

Case Example Data For my analysis, I selected documents that would provide insight into how these organizations discursively develop the category of teacher. Also, given my own language constraints, the documents needed to be in English. Additionally, I wanted to find documents from approximately the same timeframe to capture the flow of the global discourse of interest at a particular time in the country. Documents from the same timeframe would ostensibly be responding to the same educational issues in the country. Therefore, for the MoE I selected *National Education Policy 2010* (86 p.). This document outlines the policy priorities for the coming five years. For CAMPE, I chose *Education Watch 2009–10: Exploring Low Performance in Education* (121 p. excluding bibliography and appendices). CAMPE produces annual reports describing a particular issue or section in the Bangladesh education system. This particular report conducts an in-depth study of a particular region's challenges in primary education to gain insight into the country as a whole. For DAM, I chose *Education Sector Strategy 2009–2015* (37 p.). This is a straightforward document outlining its education sector strategy for the coming years. All of these documents build a teacher identity in the way they assign responsibilities and actions to teachers in their approach to the education sector.

These data contrast with the interactional or conversational data typically used in CA or MCA analysis. However, Stokoe's (2012) key concepts and guiding principles of MCA opens up the data to be analyzed to include text. Additionally, the analytical features and purposes of MCA differ from CA in that they do not seek to identify sequential patterns and the intricacies of talk that require conversational data. Rather MCA focuses on deconstructing categorization work that is a feature of any kind of discourse while using sequential analyses. Thus, I argue that using MCA to analyze textual data is not incongruent with its intent.

Methodological Approach For the purposes of this study, I focused on the following key constructs: membership categorization devices, membership categories, category-bound activities, category-tied predicates, standardized relational pairs, and the viewer's maxim. The other means of analysis in MCA do not occur or only occur infrequently in the current dataset and will not be considered.

Using the key concepts discussed above to identify the key aspects of the dataset, I employed Stokoe's five guiding principles. Thus, my dataset was built on the policy documents from the three organizations. I went through each text to build a collection of each instance of teacher. Each selection included the context surrounding the reference to capture the whole idea around the reference. Additionally, as I built collections, I erred on the side of over-including sequential exchanges to insure that all relevant initiating discussion was included. After building the collections and identifying the sequential positions of the categorial instances, I analyzed them based on the key concepts noted above. I read through the different selections of the data in each of the collections to identify common descriptions of category activities, predicates, and relational pairs, as well as highlighting divergent uses. I then analyzed each sequential segment to determine the policy document's orientation to the category of interest. By examining the lexical choices surrounding the teacher category in each of these documents, this study demonstrates to what extent the dominant global "teacher" discourse has flowed into all levels of the education sector in Bangladesh. Thus, the case study both assesses the theory of global flows and how they impact local education organizations, and it illustrates how different organizations develop different frames for establishing what a teacher is and does.

Findings To share my findings, I first share extracts from each of the education organizations and the line-by-line analysis that provides insights into how they've constructed "teacher". These analyses are compared to the global discourse, as defined above, individually. Thereafter, I analyze the similarities and differences among the three organizations' documents as well as document and compare the relative frequency of different categorical tools.

Ministry of Education Toward the end of the policy, the MoE took up the topic of teacher dignity. This brief excerpt captured many of the key ideas that the education policy presents throughout the document.

1   If the issue of the status of teachers is limited to rhetoric and the teachers do not enjoy a
2   respectable social status in real terms, the quality of education cannot be improved. The
3   teachers are to be trained up as self-confident, efficient and important persons in the
4   cause of education. This is an urgent task. So, opportunities of training for them at home
5   and abroad will be created and stipends and training courses in the overseas countries will
6   be made available to them. These steps can strengthen the education sector. A separate
7   pay scale will be introduced for teachers of all levels to enhance their financial benefits.
8   (Ministry of Education 2010, 60)

Line 1 immediately attached the predicate "status" to teachers as a quality that teachers possess and later "enjoy". However, ministry officials created a dichotomy of possible statuses teachers could possess or enjoy: a limited rhetorical status or a "respectable social status in real terms". This suggests that the MoE automatically presents teachers with a social status, a rhetorical, respectable status simply conferred by being a teacher. This further suggests a teacher is an important, respectable societal institution. However, this status may not actually be enjoyed by teachers in their day-to-day practice. This issue was then tied to improving the quality of education in both lines 2 and 5, that is, teachers' respectable social status is a necessary feature for education quality to improve. This first line indicated some features similar to Paine et al.'s construction of the teacher as the fulcrum of educational success. Teachers, through their status, were highlighted as a key element in improving quality education. However, the construction of teacher status linked to quality of education was not made as a necessary and sufficient condition which suggests that other factors may be critical in improving the quality of education.

The next sentence suggests that training is the remedy to teachers' status being rhetorical or in "real terms". Teachers currently lack training and are thus in need of it. The Ministry prescribed that the training is to make teachers "self-confident, efficient, and important persons in the cause of education". This construction suggests that the reason teachers do not "enjoy a respectable social status in real terms" is because they have not claimed it through the manner by which they carry themselves. Self-confidence and self-importance are essentially ways of seeing oneself, which assumedly would come through in the teachers' actions. Efficiency is ostensibly related to the way that the teachers conduct their work; however, this is not made explicit. Thus, the Ministry placed the responsibility on the teacher for the way in which the teacher is viewed in society and focuses primarily on self-belief rather than their skills or abilities. This construction builds upon the idea established in line 1 and strengthens the idea of teachers as the fulcrum of education. Considering a teacher's social status only in regard to the teachers' self-belief suggests a singular, even myopic focus on teachers that does not account for other stakeholders and conditions in the broader society. By not developing these broader considerations of social status, the MoE built a teacher construct similar in nature to the global teacher construct identified by Paine et al. and described at the beginning of the case study.

Additionally, lines 2 through 4 highlight the relative agency of teachers and the government in this training. The Ministry has constructed a problem where teachers lack social status due to their own incapacity in their person and their effort, and thus they prescribe training. Rather than allow teachers or local administrators the freedom to select the training most responsive to their needs, the government further prescribed what kind of training this must be. Line 4 provided an interesting construction saying that the opportunities for training "will be created" and stipends "will be made available". However, these activities were not tied to any particular party. While the "will be" verb phrase suggests the most confidence in an activity being conducted, the lack of an organization attached to this phrase raises questions as to who will take on these important tasks. This focus on training and teachers' deficits was the most common construction of teacher in the MoE document. This is also another aspect of the global teacher discourse, teachers defined by their lack of effective training.

Lines 5 and 6 are an interesting addendum to this discussion. After discussing teachers' status and immediately linking it to a lack of training that would be addressed by some party in the future, the ministry officials indicated in the document that a pay scale will be "introduced for teachers...to enhance their financial benefits". Since this sentence was included in a paragraph specifically focused on addressing teacher social status, using the viewer's maxim rule, my analysis treats it as an answer to the lack of social status. What is interesting about this idea is that, unlike the above implementation of training, the MoE made no explicit connection of the introduction of a pay scale to achieving a change in teachers' real status. It comes off as an afterthought, although it does address the relative social standing of the teacher in society.

In summary, the MoE developed a teacher construct that is deficient in training and status suggestive of the global teacher discourse. The Ministry began by describing a situation where teachers may enjoy a rhetorical or real respectable social status which is then confirmed as rhetorical. The responsibility for this was found in the teachers' deficiencies and not a broader, more systematic concern. This is a teacher as fulcrum-type situation. Similarly, the answer to this was training which again aligns with the global teacher discourse. This teacher training was to occur but the Ministry did not specify by whom or when.

Campaign for Popular Education The extract below came in CAMPE's 2009–2010 annual report analyzing the factors inhibiting a particular region from achieving success in primary education. In the final section of the report, the authors summarized their findings and made recommendations for improvements. This excerpt captured much of the key categorical work done throughout the document.

1	The students are supposed to follow their teachers. If the teachers do not come to school
2	regularly or not be punctual, the students may do the same. If the students attend
3	regularly this is of little use because proper teaching-learning cannot happen without
4	simultaneous presence of both in the classroom. Such an environment has potential
5	negative effect on students' attendance, teachers' care of the students, quality learning in
6	the classrooms leading to ultimate dropping out of students from the system. We scanned
7	the meeting minutes of the school managing committees and, sadly did not find any
8	record of discussion on the issues. (CAMPE 2011, 116)

The first sentence captured a key idea in CAMPE's construction of teacher, the critical relational pair between teacher and student. Students are bound to teachers by the expectation that they follow their teacher. This implicitly indicates that one of the teachers' bound activities is to set an example. The following sentence is built on this by describing how this should be accomplished. The teacher, defined by their absence and lack of punctuality, was implicitly leading the student to do the same because of the teacher-student relational expectation of example-follower. This is something of a departure from the global teacher discourse described above. Instead of describing "teacher" by the student's achievement outcomes, CAMPE discursively built "teacher" as successful in terms of the example set for the student.

The third sentence that runs from lines 2 to 3 returned to the categorial predicate frequently used by CAMPE of the teacher as not present. CAMPE often returned to the teachers' presence because, as this sentence indicated, teacher and student presence was associated with "proper teaching-learning". For CAMPE, when both parties were present, learning happened. However, when teachers were not present, teaching-learning could not happen. Teachers became a necessary cause for learning to take place, as did the student. This construction is interesting compared to the global discourse with which the study began. The teacher as fulcrum construction directs attention to the teacher, disregarding other parties. CAMPE's construction of the teacher above indicates that teacher and student are equally necessary for learning to take place. This relational pair is activity-bound by learning as it could not take place independent of both parties.

The fourth sentence in lines 3, 4, and 5 turned the focus back on the teachers' lack of presence and punctuality and ascribed negative consequences to the absent/late teacher. The subject of this sentence "such an environment" reached back to the previous sentence's "proper teaching-learning" which was linked to the teachers' hypothetical not showing up or showing up late. Thus, absent or late teachers were tied to decreasing student attendance, teachers' care for students, quality learning in the classroom, and student dropout. This echoes the earlier idea of the teacher and student bound by an example-follower relationship: as teachers disengage from their role, students follow suit. To some extent, this negates the construction of the teacher described in the previous paragraph where both teachers and students were responsible for learning. In this construction, the teacher is the foundational element for student presence, learning, and persistence. However, CAMPE's use of a distant chain to tie these predicates to the teacher seems to highlight their construction of a more networked teacher rather than a fulcrum-type teacher.

The final sentence spanning lines 5 through 7 indicated a new aspect of the CAMPE teacher as a teacher needing and lacking accountability. The School Managing Committee is a body of local community member and others responsible for the management and governance of the school (Al Mamun 2014). Part of their role is to ensure a functioning school environment. This sentence indicated that "the issues" of teacher presence and teacher punctuality were not addressed in any of the meetings. This is an obvious shortcoming, and its inclusion in this section establishes a link between the idea of teacher failure to fulfill responsibilities and the limited engagement of the school managing committee charged with governing the school's functions. This tacitly suggests that were the school managing committee to discuss "these issues" and establish accountability for the teachers, the teachers' actions would align with expectations. Thus,

CAMPE situated its construct of teacher similarly to the global discourse as it sees a lack of accountability for teachers as a key constraint to a successful educational system.

In summary, CAMPE created a teacher that is tightly bound to the student by setting up an example-follower dynamic. Additionally, learning cannot happen without both teacher and student being present. Thus, the teacher is not a fulcrum in this system but part of a dyad where both parties are equally important. This CAMPE construction suggests an outcome orientation that is broader than the global discourse including responsibility, school attendance, and quality learning. Finally, CAMPE aligns with the global discourse of teachers lacking and needing accountability. Thus, CAMPE finds some common constructs with the global discourse while emphasizing other aspects that differentiate their construct of teacher.

Dhaka Ahsania Mission Of all the education sector organization documents, DAM's was the shortest and had the fewest references to the category "teacher". Despite this, DAM developed a unique understanding of what it means to be "teacher". DAM outlined different areas of focus for their education strategy. The section below was one of the specific objectives for their primary education goal of "creating an enabling environment for the quality learning of all children".

1   Ensure community, local government institution members and teachers have
2   comprehensive understanding of issues of quality education in the target areas with
3   improved governance, accountability and capacity so that learning outcomes are
4   achieved. (DAM 2009, 26)

The first line develops a teacher relational pair that has not been encountered to this point. Teachers were bound to community and local government institution members. One of the categorical analytic tools developed by Sacks was the idea of a membership category device. A typical school category device groups teachers, principals, and students together. What DAM was constructing here is a school category device that link teachers, community members, and local government officials implicitly to students (whose learning outcomes were referred to) in the doing of education. Invoking the school category device, as opposed to other devices, seems clear due to the specific linking of these organizations to learning outcomes, one of the key purposes of schooling. This marks a clear difference from the global education discourse as described above. In that discourse, teachers were spotlighted as a party set apart from all others in its link to student learning. DAM however constructed a teacher bound to other parties, equally enlisted in the achievement of learning outcomes.

Some might argue that the collaboration DAM constructed here is part of a school governance device, rather than a school educational device, because of the discussion of governance and accountability in line 2. I dispute that because of the frequency with which DAM devises this idea of teachers, community members, local government institution members, and others being part of a collaboration that achieves learning outcomes. It seems clear from the document that DAM was intent on binding these to create a more holistic school device than is traditionally considered (i.e. teachers and students).

To ensure this collaboration achieved learning outcomes, DAM linked the collaboration to the need for "a comprehensive understanding of quality of education in the target areas with improved governance, accountability, and capacity". Traditionally, one might expect individual parties in this collaboration to be bound by one of these activities (e.g. community and local government institutions' members bound to teachers by governance, oversight, and accountability) or for teachers specifically to be singled out for developing capacity or needing accountability (as seen in the highlighted global teacher discourse and the MoE). However, DAM created a collaboration that collectively needed to have each of these category-bound predicates attached to them. Thus, governance, accountability, and capacity were shared responsibilities of the collaboration, each organization demanding it and providing it to the others in the collaboration. While this vocabulary of governance, accountability, and capacity suggests deficits similar to what Paine et al. describe in their review of the teacher discourse, DAM's construction altered this idea. This deficit was not that of teachers but of the whole education ecosystem. All parties involved were complicit in this deficit situation, and thus all parties needed to partner to address the issue. This is markedly different from a system that describes external authorities imposing governance and accountability on teachers, and teachers attempting to avoid these through union protection or tenure rights (Paine et al., 755).

A note must be made about DAM's tying of teachers, as part of a collaboration, to learning outcomes. As described above, the collaboration was repeatedly tied to this idea of learning outcomes. None of the instances specifically mentioned student-learning outcomes, but this may be assumed as the primary outcome of interest. This may initially appear to be synonymous with the global teacher discourse of tying teachers to student achievement measures. However, DAM never explicated how they operationalize the idea of learning outcomes. Additionally, leaning on the other Bangladesh education documents suggests a variety of possibilities of learning outcomes very different in nature than how the global discourse binds teachers and student achievement: student morality, student citizenship, student employment status. Thus, while the language may seem similar, the actual construct diverges significantly.

In summary, DAM discursively constructed a teacher as a part of a collaboration rather than as an individual. DAM described the collaboration as in need of governance, accountability, and capacity. This collaboration was responsible for learning outcomes, although it is not specified what these learning outcomes are. While these final two themes are reminiscent of the global teacher discourse, their development suggests significant differences. DAM attributed the lack of governance, accountability, and capacity to all of the parties in the collaboration, not only teachers. The possibility of learning outcomes meaning different things beyond the global discourse's preoccupation with student achievement was also a significant differentiator. Thus, DAM built a very different teacher construct from the global teacher construct.

Comparisons Across Educational Organizations Table 5.1 provides an initial sense of the different emphases, as measured by the number of times used, these educational organizations made on what it means to be a teacher. Listed under each organization are the top ten most frequently used predicates (i.e. descriptors attached to a category), activities (i.e. actions that categories do), or relational pairs (i.e. connections between the category and an external actor or object) connected to teacher. This table provides the opportunity to compare key ideas among the different organizations' constructs, while also giving readers a more complete sense of the data I used to draw my conclusions. While this is not a traditional analytic step in MCA, I use it to provide greater transparency and to help readers understand the source of the patterns referenced below.

The relative number of teacher categorical references is an interesting difference between the organizations' documents and their categorization of teachers. The ratio is a more telling data point given the relative sizes of the documents. As noted at the beginning of this case, the global construct of teacher identified here centralizes the role of teacher, linking most

Table 5.1   Teacher categorial references by organization

Ministry of Education (140 categorial references)	Campaign for Popular Education (203 categorial references)	Dhaka Ahsania Mission (23 categorial references)
Teachers are defined by training and qualifications (24%)	Teachers are bound to students (16%)	Teachers bound to community collaboration (35%)
Teachers are defined by their quantity (7%)	Teachers describe education system (10%)	Teacher-community groups achieve learning outcomes (22%)
Teachers are bound to students (7%)	Teachers physically, mentally abuse students (9%)	Teachers defined by training, qualifications (17%)
Teachers need accountability (5%)	Teachers are defined by presence in school (8%)	Teachers bound to students (9%)
Teachers need incentives, promotion (4%)	Teachers are defined by training qualifications (7%)	Teachers are defined by presence in school (4%)
Teachers are main force behind education (4%)	Teachers are defined by quantity (5%)	Teachers are defined by quantity (4%)
Teachers are appointed (4%)	Teachers are bound to parents (3%)	Teacher-community collaborations mobilize community (4%)
Teachers are defined by dignity (4%)	Teachers are defined by punctuality (3%)	Teacher-community collaborations create awareness (4%)
Teachers are defined by efficient use of training (4%)	Teachers need supervision and accountability (3%)	Teachers facilitate classes (4%)
Teachers are defined by teaching capacity (3%)	Teachers are defined by where they live (2%)	Teacher-student contact hours are very few (4%)

educational activities to the teacher. The relative rate of references and variety of constructs attached to the teacher category illustrate the degree to which these Bangladeshi organizations approximate the global construct of teacher. Thus, the MoE invoked the teacher category 1.6 times per page, CAMPE did so 1.7 times per page, and DAM did so 0.6 per page. This comparison point suggests the relative importance of the teacher category in the organization's education strategy as well as the complexity of the teacher category. So, DAM seems to formulate a less focal role for the teacher than the Ministry or CAMPE do. And, the complexity is vastly different as seen in the combined number of predicates, activities, and relational pairs found in each organization: MoE (53), CAMPE (64), DAM (18). These data suggest that CAMPE and MoE were closer in discourse to the global flow than DAM was.

The relative importance of relational pairs is another significant differentiator. While both CAMPE and DAM had relational pairs (teachers bound to students (16% of all the teacher category references in the CAMPE document) and teachers bound to community collaboration (35% of all the teacher category references in the DAM document) respectively) as their most frequent descriptor of teachers, that was less important for the MoE where their relational pair was the third most frequent descriptor (7% of all the teacher category references in the MoE document). This suggests that the teacher as constructed by the MoE is defined less by their interactions with others. This focus is reminiscent of the first indicator in Paine et al.'s description of the preeminent global discourse on teacher where the teacher is individually spotlighted as the primary party in education. The MoE deemphasized the role of other parties like students, parents, or community organizations in defining the teacher. In the same way, CAMPE and DAM departed from the global discourse by defining the teacher relative to others, diffusing the responsibility of education across many parties.

Another interesting difference relative to relational pairs is with whom the organization frequently tied their teacher. Both the MoE (7% of all teacher category references) and CAMPE (16% of all teacher category references) had teachers bound to students as the primary relational pair. DAM most frequent references included relational pairs with community collaborations (35% of all teacher category references) and students (9% of all teacher category references). As indicated above, DAM's teacher construct suggests a much more networked and system-wide, holistic construct of teacher than either of the other organizations. This again denotes the difference between DAM and the global discourse that does not focus attention on the teacher as it relates to the community or other public organizations.

A key aspect of CAMPE's construction of teacher as shown in the table above was that teachers are involved in the process of developing the teacher construct. Their report asked teachers questions and reported their answers, recommendations, and suggestions as seen in this example, "Teachers' diligent presence in the classroom was seen by the teachers as prerequisite." (96) Thus, teachers were established as agents sufficiently educated and aware as to provide insight. This was unique among the organization documents and the global discourse. In each of these other cases, teachers were not constructed as participants in developing the teacher discourse.

Data are gathered from them, papers are written about them, but their voice and agency is not as keenly present as it was in CAMPE's document.

An interesting observation is that with a few exceptions,[1] none of the most frequently cited teacher category predicates or activities address what teachers do in the classroom. At the same time, all organizations defined teachers by their quantity or presence in school. This combination suggests that these organizations equate learning with the presence of a teacher. While each organization mentioned the idea of teachers as facilitators or child-centered learning once, the weight of their constructive efforts favored the presence of the teacher being sufficient for constructing an in-class doing of "teacher". This rejects the global discourse of teacher above that defines teachers by their skill in making learning child-centered.

A counter-argument to this might suggest that the emphasis on training implicitly indicates a more robust in-class performance of "teacher". This may be the case for the MoE, where one of the references to training indicated that training would be for "learner-centered pedagogical approach". However, few of the other references tying teachers to training described what that training would look like. The few that did mention topics indicated training in self-confidence, information communication technology, or generic skills development.

Another significant absence from the organizations' formulation of teacher was the role of student achievement in defining "teacher". As indicated in the individual organization excerpts, some do mention the role of teachers in learning outcomes or quality education. However, in no instance were these ideas defined in terms of student academic achievement as measured through an assessment. This remains a teacher-bound predicate that has not been built into the Bangladesh education sector at this time, likely because Bangladesh had not participated in international achievement tests like Trends in International Mathematics and Science Study (TIMSS) or Programme for International Student Assessment (PISA) (and still has not). As Paine et al. described in their analysis, as countries engage in international student testing, their discourse around teachers begins to bind teachers to students in terms of a production function: teacher produce student learning as measured in achievement testing (2016). As indicated in Table 5.1, teachers were still defined in terms of inputs like teachers' training and qualifications and in-class presence. Paine et al. indicate this is an approach from previous discourses (2016, 755).

Conclusion

This study conducted MCA on three Bangladeshi organizational documents to assess the degree to which different levels of educational organizations aligned with a preeminent global discourse defining "teacher". These organizations differ in the extent to which they were connected to global organizations that might espouse this global discourse. Drawing on Paine et al.'s theories of global policy flows through spaces and networks, I hypothesized that organization documents from organizations with the most international organization and foreign aid agency partnerships would show the most evidence of a teacher construct similar to the global teacher discourse. The evidence presented above suggests that this is in fact the case.

In the example I provided in this chapter, MCA demonstrated distinct methodological insights to the question of global flows and local categorization. MCA indicated the extent to which categorization work done by the educational organization matched the preeminent global discourse around the teacher category. By using MCA, I was able to identify the different activities, attributes, and relationships that were expected of their teacher construct. While much of the categorization work used similar activities, attributes, and relationships, each organization emphasized different aspects, and these differences in emphases matched the global flows hypothesis. Of the three organizations, the MoE had the most international partnerships and aligned most with the global discourse on teacher. The Ministry showed a clear orientation toward an exclusive focus on the teacher as it deemphasized relational pairs with the teacher and, as shown in the excerpt, placed the onus on teachers for their social standing. Additionally, the most frequently used category description for the MoE focused on teachers' deficits in training, another common theme in the global teacher discourse as indicated above. While the MoE did not tightly bind teachers to any particular pedagogy, they were the only organization to explicitly indicate the need for learner-centered instruction training.

On the other extreme, DAM had the least international partnerships and constructed a teacher category that differed in substantive ways from the global teacher discourse assessed here. In general, DAM deemphasized the construct of teacher as seen in its limited usage in their strategy document. Relatedly, it established a teacher as a member of a collaborative force rather than an individual actor. Teachers were bound to community members and local government institution members in achieving learning outcomes. DAM even transformed the concepts of governance, accountability, and capacity to make them characteristics that bind the collaboration together rather than something to be imposed on teachers defined by deficits.

CAMPE was in the middle in terms of both the number of international partnerships and its relation to the global teacher discourse. CAMPE distinguished itself by foregrounding the teacher-student relational pair and the teacher as an agent of influence in defining the construct. On the other hand, the focus on the teacher and the emphasis on teacher accountability suggested some similarities with the global teacher construct.

A final interesting finding is the ways in which the educational system discursively resisted the global teacher discourse described above. While some language was used to tie teachers to broad learning outcomes, these constructs did not approach the global discourse's principal effort to tie teachers to students' academic achievement. Additionally, the organizations did little to define the teacher in terms of performing "teacher" in the classroom. Whereas the global discourse creates a teacher who is child-centered and not an information dispenser, Bangladeshi education organizations built a teacher who was mostly present at which point learning could occur.

Summary

This chapter began by describing the MCA methodology. Developed concurrently with CA, MCA draws on CA's attention to sequential positioning and emic perspective to analyze the component parts of commonsense categories occurring in discourse (e.g. teacher). This uncommon approach to educational policy analysis provides the possibility for researchers to understand how key categories of interest are bound by cultural category work and how this aligns with policy interests. The Bangladesh case illustrated how different levels of intercourse with global organizations was associated with differing degrees of global policy adoption as evidenced by common teacher attributes, activities, and relationships. Additionally, the absence of key attributes, activities, and relational pair characterizations demonstrated how local organizations resisted the global policy flow. Such findings could provide insights into the success of policy adoption and the ways policy can be adapted to effectively match local category boundaries.

Key Connections to Policy Research
1. Membership Categorization Analysis (MCA) is a novel method in educational policy research.
2. MCA can analyze key constructs in educational policy research using both interactional and textual data.
3. MCA deconstructs commonly used categories to identify the key activities, attributes, and relationships that define and bound the construct.
4. Understanding the construct's categorization network allows policy researchers to hypothesize policy effectiveness, adapt policies to be effective in particular cultural categories, and assess impact of policies.

NOTE

1. Exceptions include the Ministry of Education's "teaching capacity", CAMPE's "abuse students", and DAM's "facilitate class". The first and the last are generic terms that provide no detail, while teachers' physical and psychological abuse of students is a monstrous departure from actual teaching.

REFERENCES

Al Mamun, M. A. (2014). *Assessing the effectiveness of school management committees (SMCs) in improving governance of primary schools in Bangladesh: A case study of selective SMCs at Gouripur Upazila in Mymensingh district.* Master's thesis. Retrieved from BRAC University Institutional Repository.

Bonacina-Pugh, F. (2012). Researching 'practiced language policies': Insights from conversation analysis. *Language Policy, 11*(3), 213–234.

Campaign for Popular Education. (2011). *Education watch 2009–2010: Exploring low performance in education, the case of Sylhet division.* Dhaka: CAMPE.

Campaign for Popular Education. (2014, July 17). *Background.* Retrieved from http://www.campebd.org/page/Generic/0/3/1

Dhaka Ahsania Mission. (2009). *Education sector strategy [2009–15].* Dhaka: DAM.

Dooly, M., & Unamuno, V. (2009). Multiple languages in one society. *Journal of Education Policy, 24*(3), 217–236.

Housley, W., & Fitzgerald, R. (2002). The reconsidered model of membership categorization analysis. *Qualitative Research, 2*(1), 59–83.

Hutchby, I., & Wooffitt, R. (2008). *Conversation analysis.* Cambridge: Polity.

MacLure, M., Jones, L., Holmes, R., & MacRae, C. (2012). Becoming a problem: Behaviour and reputation in the early years classroom. *British Educational Research Journal, 38*(3), 447–471.

Ministry of Education. (2010). *National education policy 2010.* Dhaka: Government of the People's Republic of Bangladesh.

Ministry of Primary and Mass Education. (2007). *Learning for change: Education for all national plan of action (2003–2015).* Dhaka: Government of the People's Republic of Bangladesh.

Paine, L., Blomeke, S., & Aydarova, O. (2016). Teachers and teaching in the context of globalization. In D. Gitomer & C. Bell (Eds.), *Handbook of research on teaching.* Washington, DC: American Educational Research Association.

Rizvi, F. (2004). Theorizing the global convergence of education restructuring. In S. Lindblad & T. Popkewitz (Eds.), *Educational restructuring: International perspectives on traveling policies.* Greenwich: Information Age Pub.

Rotberg, I. (2010). *Balancing change and tradition in global education* (2nd ed.). Lanham: Rowman & Littlefield Education.

Sacks, H. (1992). *Lectures on conversation.* Oxford: Blackwell.

Schegloff, E. (2007). A tutorial on membership categorization. *Journal of Pragmatics, 39*, 462–482.

Stokoe, E. (2012). Moving forward with membership categorization analysis: Methods for systematic analysis. *Discourse Studies, 14*(3), 277–303.

Stromquist, N., & Monkman, K. (2014). Defining globalization and assessing its implications for knowledge and education, revisited. In N. Stromquist & K. Monkman (Eds.), *Globalization and education: Integration and contestation across cultures* (2nd ed.). Lanham: Rowman & Littlefield.

ten Have, P. (2007). *Doing conversation analysis.* London: Sage.

Thomas, S., Keogh, J., & Hay, S. (2015). Discourses of the good parent in attributing school success. *Discourse: Studies in the Cultural Politics of Education, 36*(3), 452–463.

UNICEF. (2009). *Quality primary education in Bangladesh.* Retrieved from UNICEF https://www.unicef.org/bangladesh/Quality_Primary_Education.pdf

Verger, A., Novelli, M., & Altinyelken, H. (2012). Global education policy and international development: An introductory framework. In A. Verger, M. Novelli, & H. Altinyelken (Eds.), *Global education policy and international development: New agendas, issues, and policies.* New York: Bloomsbury Academic.

Justin Paulsen is a doctoral student in Inquiry Methodology in the School of Education at Indiana University. Paulsen holds an MPA/MA in Russian Studies and International Development, and he uses a variety of methodologies in evaluation projects spanning a range of topics. He is also interested in adapting methodologies for use in novel, practical applications.

CHAPTER 6

A Mangled Educational Policy ~~Discourse~~ Analysis for the Anthropocene

Ryan Evely Gildersleeve and Katie Kleinhesselink

INTRODUCTION

All sectors of education today are called upon to do more and reach further into the social fabric of our post-modern lives than ever before. As social institutions reflective and productive of the contemporary zeitgeist, the contradictions and complexities of educational projects grow ever greater with each new crisis that education is called upon to help confront. From gun violence to climate change to hunger to terrorism to social mobility to civic responsibility to economic literacy, and on and on, educational institutions (pre-K, K-12 school systems, colleges and universities) are emplaced within, yet expected to act upon, the most compelling social imperatives of our time. Research about how to organize, govern, and lead the educational endeavors commanded by such challenging times—educational policy research—must review and perhaps reconfigure its fundamental assumptions about knowledge, being, purpose, and reality in order to accommodate the complexity of imperatives expected of education today.

R.E. Gildersleeve (✉) • K. Kleinhesselink
University of Denver, Denver, CO, USA

© The Author(s) 2017
J.N. Lester et al. (eds.), *Discursive Perspectives on Education Policy and Implementation*, DOI 10.1007/978-3-319-58984-8_6

In this chapter, we present the tradition of policy discourse analysis (PDA) as a method for critical policy studies in education. After reviewing key tenets, core principles, and a few exemplars of PDA, we suggest a post-humanist and post-qualitative addendum to the method, emplacing it within the Anthropocene—the current geological epoch which is marked by humankind's imprint on the Earth, and its attendant social implications. By post-humanist, we suggest incorporating non-anthropocentric ontologies that recognize the significance of non-human actants on the production of becoming-subjects (i.e., things and people). Decentering the human means recognizing the broader forces that co-constitute our realities, such as the power of *things* (Bennett 2009). By post-qualitative, we suggest that the post-humanist commitments directed from the Anthropocene are best operationalized in the emerging methodological tradition of post-qualitative research, which re-works, re-thinks, and un-does much of the taken-for-granted concepts in the traditional interpretive paradigms of qualitative inquiry (Lather and St. Pierre 2013). We pay closer attention to these conceptual territories later in the chapter.

We briefly illustrate our addendum using emergent analysis from Gildersleeve's broader project on the materialization of discourses of opportunity for Latino (im)migrants in higher education policy (Gildersleeve 2013; Gildersleeve 2017; Gildersleeve et al. 2015; Gildersleeve and Hernández 2012). We conclude by relating PDA for the Anthropocene to the methodological turn in policy research recognized as the third generation of policy research. In an essentialized understanding, third-generation policy research focuses on the "understanding of policy as demonstrated in educational discourses" (Lester et al. 2015, p. 1). Centering discourse as an organizing analytic, third-generation policy research explicitly engages in analyses of power to examine how policy mediates social opportunities (Fairclough 2013). In its attention to discourse, third-generation policy research also recognizes the partial, fractured, and produced qualities of policy truths (Kuntz et al. 2011). Third-generation policy research is more interested in how policy processes and outcomes come about as reflections and productions of society, rather than normative outcomes and measurements of policy practice (Lester et al. 2016). Our main objective in this chapter is to build upon the discursive commitments of third-generation policy research by insisting—and illustrating—how discourse and materiality are entangled in the production of realities. Thus, we claim it is incumbent on third-generation policy researchers to wrestle with the consequences of the Anthropocene as we seek to connect policy processes and outcomes to the production of societies.

Policy Discourse Analysis

Discourse, in a traditional sense, refers to the construct of language, both written and spoken, and its attendant social implications (Allan et al. 2010). PDA, however, employs post-structuralist notions of discourse. Foucault conceptualized discourses as historically and socially bound frameworks in which power and knowledge intersect to order what we conceive of as reality (2003). Mediated and reinforced through social institutions, discourse comprises not just language, but the rules, standards, and beliefs by which a society conducts itself (Ball 1994, 2015). We experience the knowledges produced through discourse as natural, static, and thus take them for granted. Understanding policy as discourse assumes that policy produces particular truths (albeit dynamic and unstable) and possible knowledges (albeit tentative and historically bound).

Policy as discourse both reflects and produces our understanding of the world around us and the ways that we behave within it (Ball 1994). Researchers typically treat policy and the truths and knowledges it produces as stable, unified, and self-evident. In approaching policy as discourse, the researcher seeks to understand "how a human being is envisaged in our present and the social practices that constitute this human being" (Ball 2015, p. 3). Attending to policy's discursive effects allows us to question the assumptions upon which policy is based, the realities it produces, and the ways in which it may further entrench rather than alleviate the problems it seeks to solve.

PDA has been used as a method for educational policy analysis for almost 30 years, though it is rooted in theories advanced by the post-structuralists including Michel Foucault, Jacques Derrida, Ernesto Laclau, and Chantal Mouffe, though in this chapter, we have chosen to focus specifically on theories advanced by Foucault. Fairclough (1992) began to develop critical discourse analysis (CDA), a three-dimensional framework for linguistic analysis that approaches text first as simple text, then as discursive practice, then as social practice during this same timeframe. Ball's (1994) work, *What Is Policy? Texts, Trajectories, and Toolboxes*, explicitly introduces the idea of treating policy as discourse as opposed to text, thus opening the door to applying post-structural tenets to policy analysis. Over the past two decades, feminist scholars have advanced feminist post-structural approaches to PDA that continue to shape the method (Allan 2010).

Pragmatically, PDA treats policy texts as sites of discursive production ripe for analysis. However, in order to do so, the text must be emplaced within a broader context—and context is mutable, dynamic, and always subjectively dependent and historical. That is to say, the context within which a policy text can be emplaced is tied to particular historicity—itself dynamic and subjective.

For example, in their study of Latina/o immigrant educational opportunity, Gildersleeve et al. (2015) analyzed policy texts associated with the Deferred Action for Childhood Arrivals (DACA) executive action crafted by Janet Napolitano as US Secretary of the Department of Homeland Security. DACA allows undocumented immigrants who entered the United States as juveniles and meet certain criteria a renewable two-year deferment of deportation. DACA does not infer legal status nor does it provide a path to citizenship. In order to draw out the discursive effects of DACA on Latina/o immigrant educational opportunity, Gildersleeve et al. emplaced this text within the broader context of Napolitano's leadership of the University of California (UC), of which she became President following her tenure as Secretary of the Department of Homeland Security. Gildersleeve et al. emplaced DACA within context provided by official speeches that Napolitano gave as UC President, as well as an on-air interview broadcast on public radio. This strategic contextualization by Gildersleeve et al. afforded their analyses to trace the discursive production of Latina/o immigrants in California higher education against the broader research literature about Latina/o educational opportunity. One implication from the intersection of immigration policy and post-secondary education leadership that Gildersleeve et al. derived was the production of Latina/o college students as a particularized caste of human capital, promoted chiefly in service to an American economy that by design benefits dominant subject positions (i.e., wealthy white men), while subjugating Latina/o educational achievement to the welfare of the marketplace.

Approaching policy as discourse requires that we abandon modernist notions of power. Foucault (1978) asserts that power cannot be divorced from knowledge, that they are bound together and expressed through discourse. A traditional understanding of power could be likened most closely to what Foucault (2008) describes as sovereign power. Here, power is located in an individual (or institution) and wielded over others. It binds and represses. Policy as discourse, on the other hand, operates through *biopower*. Where sovereign power is concerned with the individual body, Foucault (2003) conceives of biopower as a generative force that is wielded at the level of the population. Foucault introduces the term *biopolitics* to describe the framework through which biopower is expressed. Foucault instructs us:

> [Biopolitics'] purpose is not to modify any given phenomenon as such, or to modify a given individual insofar as he is an individual, but, essentially, to intervene at the level at which these general phenomena are determined, to intervene at the level of their generality. (p. 246)

Policy as discourse, as a biopolitical technology, expresses biopower in the ways it produces realities. Biopower and sovereign power are by no means mutually exclusive here—in fact, biopolitics requires that the individual self-surveils and monitors his/her own behaviors. Policy as discourse produces what we come to know and act within as reality.

Foucault (in Allan et al. 2010) describes the interaction of discourse and power/knowledge as the site in which "conditions of possibility" (p. 14) are produced, the framework within which we repeatedly construct ourselves and our world. Policy as discourse then, beyond creating reality, creates identities. Understanding the effects of policy requires us to deconstruct the subject positions that policy produces. Subjectivity—the space(s) wherein the self is made known—is a constant site of struggle, crafted and shaped by the conflicting subject positions made available from various discursive fields (Foucault 1978). Identity, in contrast to humanist thought, is neither static nor essential. Rather, produced by and through the interplay of discourse(s), identities are made plausible as tentative, contested, and conflicted subject positions. Identity, as constructed by policy, can be understood as a biopolitical technology for population control and an expression of biopower (Lemke 2011). Identity as an analytic technology must reconcile its populist notions of empowerment and its capitalist realities of inclusion/exclusion. These are the kind of concerns at stake and illuminated by using discursive analyses to interrogate policy in education.

PDA, in its challenge to static humanist notions of truth and knowledge, necessarily defies a singular definition. Allan (2010) conceptualizes PDA as a hybrid methodology building out significantly from feminism and post-structuralism, while employing methods associated with interpretive and critical theory. In contrast to other methodologies, PDA begins by questioning the assumptions underlying policy, the discursive framework in which policy is constructed (Allan et al. 2010). Specifically, PDA attends to how problems are identified, how identity constructs inform those problems and their possible solutions, and how policy as discourse both reflects and produces reality and subjectivity. PDA allows the researcher to pull from multiple traditions of critical inquiry to interrogate policy as discourse (and discourses by and through which policy is produced), as well as the subject identities it creates and informs (Allan 2010). In exposing and analyzing discourse(s), PDA shifts the starting point of policy analysis from a place of accepting the problems policy proposes to address to investigating the discursive production of the problem itself and the subject position(s) of those whom policy targets.

For example, in her interrogation of US Department of Education discourse regarding the role of higher education in economic advancement, Suspitsyna (2012) employs Fairclough's (2006) textually oriented discourse analysis (TODA) method to discursively analyze federal education policy. TODA involves the analysis of how power is expressed through spoken and written text. Suspitsyna engages in three levels of analysis: (1) analyzing the textual means through which realities are constructed; (2) investigating genre, audience, and authors as discursive practice; and (3) exploring the speeches' rhetoric as discursive social practice within the broader neoliberal regime. Through her analysis, Suspitsyna demonstrates how higher education's public purpose, through federal rhetoric, is co-opted by and subjugated to its role within the neoliberal regime as an engine for economic growth.

As Foucault (1978) writes, "discourse transmits and produces power; it reinforces it, but also undermines and exposes it, renders it fragile and makes it possible to thwart" (p. 101). In broadening the frame for policy analysis to interrogate policy discourse, PDA offers an important tool for exposing the systemic roots of perceived problems and, thus, a space in which to challenge systems and advocate for change.

However, PDA can be criticized for resting on critique as the sole outcome of analysis. Further, by treating policy texts as sites of *discursive* production, PDA runs a risk of ignoring the materiality of policy effects. By its definition of discourse, PDA relies on representational and interpretive ontologies, in which language reifies the real (Fairclough 2013). Education researchers working in the broad areas of post-humanism and post-qualitative inquiry point out that representation is a secondary intervention that creates static structures out of dynamic movements and difference (Massumi 2002; MacLure 2013). Scholars often point to the analyses of philosopher Gilles Deleuze, particularly his work, *The Logic of Sense* (2004), through which he argued that such a representational tool as language contributes to the dogma of thought, building categories of right and wrong (or good sense and common sense), stemming from an elusive and illusive rational and autonomous individual. In order to address these concerns, we offer a post-humanist addendum to the PDA tradition. We begin by emplacing education policy within the Anthropocene—a geologic period marked by humankind with significant social implications for all of its institutions. We then pivot to incorporate the recent theorizations on the materiality of language from Maggie MacLure (2013) in order to put forth a tentative (and nervous) operationalization of our post-human/post-qualitative addendum to PDA.

THE ANTHROPOCENE

We live, work, and know the world as complicit producers of the Anthropocene. In a scientific sense, the Anthropocene is our current geologic period—one in which humans are the primary agents of affect and effect on the planet—we have as much power over geologic change as anything else, if not more so, and our imprint on the Earth can be recognized in the Earth's very constitution (Zalasiewics et al. 2011). Such science forces us to grapple with the social consequences of human agency not as separate from nature, but constituent *and simultaneously* constituting of nature. Put more simply, we invent nature, with every decision we make socially and politically regarding how we choose to understand it. In social science, the Anthropocene provides "an ethical injunction to think critically about human and nonhuman agency in the universe" (Zylinksa 2014, p. 62). Applied to PDA in education, the Anthropocene begs attention paid to the non-human agents/actants produced through policy as discourse and the consequences thereof. For example, in examining a policy on school choice, the material conditions of schools matter, particularly as the buildings, artifacts, and supplies afforded across the choices produced through such policy might act upon different children radically differently.

The Anthropocene, as geologic time, marks an epoch in which humans are the dominant form of life on the planet, but also the dominant *force affecting life* of the planet. Humans are no longer subordinate to our environment. Rather, we are able to manipulate, mitigate, and create our environment in ways to serve various needs, desires, or interests. Humans shape and re-create the Earth. We do this metaphorically, through signs and symbols that help make sense of large-scale phenomena like migration and small-scale challenges like settlement development. Through science, technology, and work, humans have learned, over time, that we can also shape and re-create the Earth *literally*. We can change the direction of river-flows. We create dams, and we dry up estuaries. We build skyscrapers on what once was marshland. We experiment with new forms of Earth in controlled laboratory "biospheres." We create earthquakes as we withdraw vital fluids from below the Earth's surface (e.g., hydraulic fracturing). Humans generate hurricane force winds as we raise the temperature of the planet through carbon-based consumption and production.

With dominance comes responsibility. Humans, by taking charge of nature—from indexing of the planet's species to changing its tectonic patterns—also have taken responsibility for the environment. If the environment needs manipulating for our desires or for other species' needs, we seek to understand its relation to self, surroundings, and other beings. We cause and protect other species from extinction.

Not only do we effect change of the environment, we are affected by the environment. Humans, as the dominant form and force of life, are uniquely situated as relationally conscious to what happens around us. As philosopher, Sverre Raffnsoe (2016) shares, "This requisite responsibility has become encompassing to the extent that even singular, hard-to-predict events far beyond human control, such as earthquakes or hurricanes, have entered into the equation" (p. xii). Humans have assumed responsibility for knowing nature, totally, in order to continue our course of manipulating, generating, mitigating, and, ultimately, controlling nature.

Such environmental-social positioning on the planet necessarily raises ontological questions as humans, while not subservient, remain dependent and, in our role as responsible actant, are positioned precariously, in relation to nature—nature that we create. Human actions affect life—not just human life but planetary life. Humans are dependent on how others can respond to the nature we invent—both the nature that is and the nature that may become. Again, Raffnsoe (2016) is instructive:

> They [humans] must be able to answer to, and also to answer for, how they relate to the surroundings in which they find themselves, and which are not merely a result of human creation, while at the same time they must address the reality that they themselves have a decisive effect on the places they inhabit and on how these places effect themselves and others. (p. xiii)

Through our politics of work, our development of science, and our inno-vations of technology, humans have positioned ourselves, ontologically, into a new way of being on the planet. Unanticipated, yet not wholly unexpected, humans—and the social institutions we have created—must wrestle with the new challenges that such positioning demands of us. We must wrestle, through our institutions and the knowledge systems (or discourses) we use and invent to produce them, with what it means to be human in the age of the Anthropocene.

Another defining characteristic of the Anthropocene's social conse-quences is the saturation of knowledge through *mutual mediation*. While humans co-create and re-create our surroundings so extensively that we emerge in geologic history as a life condition for the planet (Raffnsoe 2016), our surroundings boomerang around and back onto our existence, "setting out incontestable conditions for human beings that they have neither explicitly caused nor can easily comprehend" (p. 14). As much as we, as a species, become a condition for planetary life, nature continues to lay down conditions for the human species. This can be seen in climate studies, wherein climate has become understood as interaction between human and nature to such permeating thresholds that it is problematic to regard them separately for analysis. Such mutually defining status of *becoming* illustrate the great paradox of the Anthropocene concept and its conse-quences for the ontological foundations of social research. Drawing again from Raffnsoe (2016):

> While humanity on its part encompasses and embraces the planet and its life forms, the planet with its life forms and its destiny also encompasses and embraces humanity. And if humanity on its part has swelled to colossal size in relation to its surroundings, its surroundings likewise appear colossal on their part in relation to human affairs. (p. 15)

As giant as *the human* might seem, it is not the center of the universe. The human condition is mediated mutually, despite, and in some ways consti-tuting of, its efforts to control, manipulate, and build its landscape to meet its interests. Such subordination in the philosophical foundations of policy discourse and the political discourse that enables policy is a radical shift from the humanist tradition in which an explicit and overwhelming Anthropo-centrism emerges. As such, the Anthropocene concept, and the science of the Anthropocene epoch, each obliterates the long-standing assumptions of objectivist, truth-discovering, politics-making efforts of traditional policy analysis. Rather, to make sense of the political acts that social policy engenders, and/or to build meaning from the uses and generation of policy as a tool for politics and educational practice, third-generation policy research must confront an ontological turn in the foundations of social inquiry and attend to its consequences for method. Such consequences are detailed in the next section.

A Post-humanist and Post-qualitative Addendum

As a strange, yet imminent twist of planes, taking the Anthropocene seriously points toward a need for a non-anthropocentric onto-epistemological orientation. Centering a humanness (i.e., a known/knowable human subject) in analysis, critique, and action does not make sense in a context wherein science itself forces us to reconcile the agency of machines and other things. PDA requires that we uncover and take seriously the discourses in and through which policy is created as well as its own discursive effects. In a world in which humankind operates not solely as a resident species, but as a geologic force, an inventor of nature and of self, rejecting anthropocentrism or decentering humanness opens opportunities to think creatively/freshly about what dominant discourses hold up as real as well as what they obstruct, leave out, or obscure. Hence, post-humanists theorize new ontologies of "becoming-animal," "becoming-earth," and "becoming-machine" (Bennett 2010; Braidotti 2013; Esposito 2015). The move toward *becoming*, rather than *being*, is significant. In the post-human condition, things (including people) protrude into reality as partial and dynamic, never quite what we (or they) aspire to be, yet always en route toward a becoming. Further, the clear categories or delineations of things (e.g., humans, animals, earth, machines) become obfuscated, as hybridity takes center stage in the constantly shifting ecosystems of realities. We address these concepts in more detail toward the end of this section.

This is an optimistic synthesis of the Anthropocene. For here lies great promise: post-humanist and non-anthropocentric ontological productions might indeed afford new tools for excavating the discursive configurations made available from our new material actants, reflected and produced via policy discourses and the discourse *of* policy, where the former are produced through policy texts (in context), and the latter is the knowledge regime that makes policy possible—policy as *dispositif* in Foucauldian terms, perhaps (Foucault 2008).

Pertinent to our contribution to PDA (for the Anthropocene) and the third generation of policy research, it is important to note that the questions around the human raised by post-humanists also raise questions about the relationship between/betwixt the discursive and the material. The term *mangle* has been used by theorists to describe the mutual implication of the discursive and the material in how we can come to know the world (Heckman 2010; Pickering 1995). It is similar to Deleuze and Guattari's (1994) notion of *assemblage*, which emphasizes the unfolding emergence of what humanists termed *reality*. But it is not as simple as an intertwining of language and matter; language-as-discourse and matter-as-actants intra-sect and become entangled (Barad 2007) in non-hierarchical organization. Below, we review ways that three of these mangled ontological becomings have been theorized in the post-humanist literature, emplaced within the Anthropocene.

Becoming-Animal

The traditional humanist subject—white, Eurocentric, healthy, heterosexual, and male—is predicated on the othering and domination of all else. Animals occupy multiple complex positions in relation to the humanist subject—even as they are employed to signify humanist values and cultural norms, their bodies quite literally sustain us as food, as labor, and through companionship. Braidotti (2013) suggests that this interrelation, traditionally grounds for exploitation and othering, breaks down within a post-human paradigm.

Becoming-animal, as an ontology, situates subjectivity in the context of the human as and in relation to animal and vice versa. In the context of the Anthropocene, the humanist understanding of the bond between humans and animals is necessarily negative as it rests in what Braidotti (2013) characterizes as "shared ties of vulnerability" (p. 69) rooted in the destructive impacts of human life on Earth. Post-humanism focuses instead on the human-animal continuum, calling into question our experience of the animal as separate, both subjugated and exploited in the interest of human advancement. At the same time, it rejects the anthropomorphization of the animal as a holdover of humanism that both discounts the animal and reinforces the human/animal distinction. Becoming-animal opens a space in which we can move beyond the binaries to instead investigate the ways in which we—human and animal—intersect, inform, and co-create identities. Within this space, the humanist subject topples from a position of domination. In its place, *Zoe*, life-force that transcends and imbues human/animal, emerges as post-human subject, opening new opportunities to interrogate constructs of otherness.

Becoming-Machine

The post-human subject cannot be understood or conceptualized outside of our technologically mediated reality. Humanist binaries simply do not work in regard to the human/machine relationship. *Zoe*, that vital, interrelational life-force animates, too, our myriad technological connections, reimagining human bodies as part of a complex, interdependent living fabric. Braidotti (2013) posits becoming-machine as an integrated web of new social ecologies that encompass the organic and inorganic. Perhaps in becoming-machine, more than other iterations of post-human subjectivity, it is easiest to recognize the primacy of transversality, the intersectional and interrelational overlaps that weave together the human and non-human, as a dynamic animating force or *Zoe*.

Becoming-Earth

The Anthropocene, so-called given the rise of humanity as a geologic force, has witnessed (and continues to witness) human-caused environmental crisis and destruction, most obviously embodied as climate change. Within this context, the human imagination has grown to encompass both our own macro-agency as a species and the possibility of our self-generated mass extinction. The Anthropocene also creates the conditions for new forms of subjectivity that are geo-centered. Braidotti (2013) writes, "We [critical theorists] need to visualize the subject as a transversal entity encompassing the human, our genetic neighbours the animals and the earth as a whole, and to do so within an understandable language" (p. 82). This is no small task. In our present condition, we might simultaneously experience humanity as both a geologic force and endangered species. At the same time, this collapsing of experience threatens to assign equal culpability across humanity, an unwarranted conclusion. Becoming-earth requires that we intentionally disidentify from humanist values, constructs of hierarchy, and dualism (e.g. male/female), to instead reposition and instead adopt monism as our frame for inquiry. Braidotti (2013) defines monism as "the open-ended, interrelational, multi-sexed, an trans-species flows of becoming through interaction with multiple others" (p. 89). Within this frame, Braidotti suggests that if we position Zoe as subject, we have an opportunity to move beyond compensatory humanism, a space in which we attend to planetary concerns by anthropomorphizing both the Earth and all its inhabitants, living or no, to create new ways of being, imagine new futures, and co-conceptualize our agency within them.

In each of these ontological becomings, we see clear implications for a post-human and materialist approach to PDA. In positing humanness in the frames of becoming-animal, becoming-earth, and becoming-machine, Braidotti (2013) challenges us to re-think the limitations around how PDA conceives of identity and discourse. PDA, and discourse theory more broadly, is rooted in a fundamental binary configuration, what Braidotti calls the *given* (nature) and the *constructed* (culture) (p. 2). PDA focuses specifically on how policy as discourse constructs identities/subject positions. To accomplish this, PDA approaches identity as contextual and relational and decidedly anthropocentric. PDA asserts that identity is historically bound, tied to specific social norms, and so on, but it is limited, in that it interprets subject positions in relation to a human "other" (mother, daughter, sister, etc.) that speaks to individuation. In other words, though we seek to uncover the processes through which identities are created, we experience/represent identity as a product that is singular, bounded, human, and, as a result, incomplete. In theorizing ontologies of *becoming* and situating Zoe as subject, Braidotti (2013) offers new perspectives and, thus, new tools for PDA to employ in its approach to policy as discourse. Should we adopt ontologies of becoming in PDA, we no longer seek to understand how policy constructs the human being, but rather its generative underpinnings. In other words, a post-human PDA for the Anthropocene refocuses on policy's life-force, the intersections of power that produce not only what is, but what could be. Our point here is not that PDA must adopt ontologies of becoming-animal, becoming-earth, or becoming-machine specifically. We offer these examples to illustrate the possibilities that emerge within post-human subjectivity. We suggest that post-human PDA interrogate *becoming* itself—not how policy constructs present knowledges, but how it *generates* new ways of being now and in the future. Within the frame of becoming-animal, to use one of our exemplars, in examining policy on service and emotional support animals, the researcher might explore the generation of new identities that emerge from the space in which the othering of disability status, animal as pet, and animal as technology intersect. To accomplish this, we must look beyond humanist agency to a post-human approach to PDA, employing *becomings* both as ontological frames and as units for analysis.

TOWARD *SENSE* AND EMPLACEMENT

In working toward a post-qualitative inquiry informed by the ontological turn of new materialism and post-humanism, Maggie MacLure (2013) suggests that researchers might consider drawing from *sense* in order to engage with the materiality of language. MacLure reminds that "language is in and of the body; always issuing from the body; being impeded by the body; affecting other bodies" (p. 663). As such, language intra-sects with matter as it becomes representational. Yet, *sense,* a "non-representing, unrepresentable, 'wild element' in language" (p. 658), might provide an opening for PDA to engage with the mangle of language and matter. Sense is a thinking-feeling of a becoming. It cannot be spoken, nor interpreted, and therefore cannot be represented nor representative. However, sense is made known to us in our engagement with data, with social practice, with texts, and within contexts. Sense might be understood as an event (Deleuze 2004). But—an event that takes flight from any number of lines and might never unfold into a becoming . . . anything.

Recalling our discussion of PDA, in which we assert that it requires a recognition of text within context. Gildersleeve et al. (2015) *emplaced* otherwise seemingly disparate political speeches and other texts into a built and subjective context in order to map plausible subjectivation techniques emergent from the immigration policy regime. During analysis, while scouring texts related to immigration and education, politics and political economy, education and opportunity, immigration and democracy, the team, at one point, shared a sense-event when it recognized there was a context that *could be* built if we recognized the materiality of the policy texts they encumbered. From the existing border fencing to the imaginary border wall to Sather Gate at the UC at Berkeley to the immigration forms that migrants must fill out, a zillion kinds of matter mattered and entangled any potential discursive production that the language of policy alone could muster. Such sense-events kept the discursive productions operating on the surface of experience—right at the thresholds of the manglings of education policy. As such, we were able to imagine and map the plausibility of the Latino caste in education policy and college choice. We followed and led the sense-event by entering the mangle or assemblage that continues unfolding as the immigration policy regime from a moment, a line of flight that we could empirically demonstrate as constitutive of a becoming-subject.

POLICY DISCOURSE ANALYSIS IN THE ANTHROPOCENE AND THIRD-GENERATION POLICY RESEARCH

Expecting or working toward sense in PDA might afford the opportunity to consider how the language of texts within context intra-act with matter, both the materiality of language (the building blocks of text) and the matter that becomes represented through language. Of course, *sense* is but one option for reconfiguring how discourse and policy might become engaged in recognition of the Anthropocene and our post-human lines of flight. Our overarching goal in staging this chapter through the tradition of PDA and into the Anthropocene and mangling education policy within the post-human/post-qualitative critique and production of new ways of knowing is not necessarily to say that *sense* needs to be incorporated into PDA, although we think it probably could be beneficial. Rather, we hope to demonstrate that third-generation policy research has an opportunity, and perhaps an obligation, to playfully experiment with how we bring the ontological imperatives of the Anthropocene to bear on education.

We are not alone, nor the first to make such a suggestion. Jasmine Ulmer (2015) drew from post-humanist philosopher Catherine Malabou's concept of *plasticity* (2007, 2010, 2012) and presented it as an approach to policy analysis that could incorporate the becoming nature of the human/non-human entanglement. Ulmer used plastic as an organizing metaphor, analytic, and method for examining technology-centered models of education reforms. She theorized the policy process as plastic—simultaneously shapeable, yet structured, and all the while destructible. Her use of plasticity afforded her the ability to render policy beyond its textual representation, vacillate from outside to inside (and vice versa) of its material manifestation (e.g., outcomes), and provide new directions for policy to consider. According to Ulmer, "plasticity provides a means for understanding how structural elements intra-act within dynamic processes of shaping, reshaping, and unshaping policy" (p. 1101). Her plastic reading of education policy challenges the Anthropocentrism of traditional policy analysis, including the post-structural tradition of PDA described earlier.

Ulmer provides examples of how technology-centered reforms in education materialize from received shape/form—they are presented as (discursive) givens necessary for the digital age of education and workforce development. She then describes how such reforms provide shape/form by materially changing the make-up of instruction (e.g., using tablet technologies in elementary classrooms). Ulmer ultimately draws her plastic reading to demonstrate how technology-centered education reforms might cause disruption (i.e., destruction) by radically re-organizing the teaching and learning exercises of education (e.g., teacher as technologist rather than pedagogue). Ulmer concludes, "this shaping, reshaping, unshaping, and even resistance to shape continuously defines and challenges processes of policy formation" (p. 1103). Her plastic reading, as a (post-humanist and) post-qualitative method for policy analysis, necessarily mangled the discursive and material consequences of education policy.

SUMMARY

Recognizing the entanglement of "the human" with the things that accompany us in our sense of becoming requires that education policy researchers think differently and experiment playfully—yet seriously—with new theoretical and conceptual tools for explaining and designing educational conditions and futures.

Raffnsoe (2016) notes:

> Within new post-disciplinary contexts, academic borders, including borders between the human and the non-human, become more like thresholds that dare us to overstep them, and bridges and passageways that dare us to build them, in order to establish a new independent relationship between that which previously seemed divided. Similarly, the differences become more like accounts that dare us to settle them and balance them appropriately, in order to enable new types of knowledge to come to light. (p. 57)

As education increasingly is emplaced within and expected to act upon dynamic social imperatives, researchers need to develop newly powerful tools that recognize the non-hierarchical organization of our onto-epistemological conditions. Emplacing PDA within the Anthropocene, and providing a post-human and post-qualitative addendum to its representational (i.e., textual and interpretive) tradition, is but one attempt at operating at the thresholds of method and methodology. PDA for the Anthropocene must wrestle with the ontological shifts that "the human" can no longer ignore in our own becoming-history as a geologic force.

Thus, we hope to have offered one plausible passageway to entangling the discursive and material that previously were divided.

Policy researchers interested in taking seriously the Anthropocene and its consequences for human subjectivity via education policy might begin by identifying the material actants that emerge from or produce the policy contexts and regimes under scrutiny. First-steps methodologically might mean shifting focus from the rhetorical development of policy to the materialization of policy regimes. Research questions might become less deterministic and more fluid, affording a dynamism of difference (ala Derrida), to emerge in the empirical readings of education policy. As we have suggested in this chapter, a shift from meaning to sense and from discretion to entanglement is needed in third-generation policy research. These movements suggest that researchers expand the scope of their inquiry. Researchers could stop trying to establish any semblance of boundary for policy and its consequences. Rather, recognizing that any given policy regime acts upon a territory of activities and therefore can be de-territorialized and re-territorialized as the materialization of policy extends into social life.

We reiterate that our goal is to encourage a playfulness with third-generation policy research. One of the greatest strengths of the Anthropocene as a context for inquiry is its indeterminacy. There are fewer and fewer rules for establishing how something can come to be known. As such, the development of new concepts for new explanations—new sense moments, or plastic readings—might serve as new goals or strategies for third-generation policy researchers.

> **Key Connections to Policy Research**
> 1. Identify material actants within policy regime.
> 2. Focus on the materialization of policy regimes, rather than rhetorical development of particular policies.
> 3. Recognize how policy regimes are emplaced within broader material conditions.

REFERENCES

Allan, E. J. (2010). Feminist poststructuralism meets policy analysis: An overview. In E. J. Allan, S. V. D. Iverson, & R. Ropers-Huilman (Eds.), *Reconstructing policy in higher education: Feminist poststructural perspectives* (pp. 11–36). New York: Routledge.

Allan, E. J., Iverson, S. V., & Ropers-Huilman, R. (2010). Introduction. In E. J. Allan, S. V. D. Iverson, & R. Ropers-Huilman (Eds.), *Reconstructing policy in higher education: Feminist postructural perspectives* (pp. 1–10). New York: Routledge.

Ball, S. J. (1994). *Education reform: A critical and post-structural approach.* Buckingham: Open University Press.

Ball, S. J. (2015). What is policy? 21 years later: Reflections on the possibilities of policy research. *Discourse: Studies in the Cultural Politics of Education, 36*(3), 306–313.

Barad, K. (2007). *Meeting the universe halfway.* Durham: Duke University Press.

Bennett, J. (2009). *Vibrant matter.* Durham: Duke University Press.

Bennett, J. (2010). *Vibrant matter: A political ecology of things.* Durham: Duke University Press.

Braidotti, R. (2013). *The posthuman.* Cambridge: Polity Press.

Deleuze, G. (2004). *The logic of sense* (C. Boundas, Ed., M. Lester, Trans.). London: Continuum.

Deleuze, G., & Guattari, F. (1994). *What is philosophy?* (trans: Tomlinson, H., & Burchell, G.). New York: Columbia University Press.

Esposito, R. (2015). *Persons and things.* Cambridge: Polity Press.

Fairclough, N. (1992). *Discourse and social change.* Cambridge: Polity Press.

Fairclough, N. (2006). *Discourse and social change.* Cambridge: Polity Press.

Fairclough, N. (2013). Critical discourse analysis and critical policy studies. *Critical Policy Studies, 7*(2), 177–197. doi:10.1080/19460171.2013.798239

Foucault, M. (1978). *The history of sexuality: Volume I: An introduction* (R. Hurley, Trans.). New York: Vintage Books.

Foucault, M. (2003) *Society must be defended: Lectures at the Collège de France, 1978–1979* (D. Macey, Trans.). New York: Picador.

Foucault, M. (2008). *The birth of biopolitics: Lectures at the Collège de France, 1978–1979* (M. Senellart, Trans.). New York: Picador.

Gildersleeve, R. E. (2013, October). *Discourse and opportunity: Undocumented students and higher education policy.* Invited Paper for the annual meeting of the National Academy of Education, Washington, DC.

Gildersleeve, R. E. (2017). Making and becoming in the undocumented student policy regime: A post-qualitative [discourse] analysis of US immigration and higher education policy. *Educational Policy Analysis Archives, 25*(31).

Gildersleeve, R. E., & Hernández, S. (2012). Producing (im)possible peoples: A critical discourse analysis of in-state resident tuition policy. *International Journal of Multicultural Education, 14*(2).

Gildersleeve, R. E., Cruz, C., Madriz, D., & Melendrez-Flores, C. (2015). Neoliberal futures and postsecondary opportunity: Janet Napolitano and the politics of Latina/o college choice. In P. Perez & M. Ceja (Eds.), *Higher education access and choice for Latino students*. New York: Routledge.

Heckman, S. (2010). *The material of knowledge: Feminist disclosures*. Bloomington: Indiana University Press.

Kuntz, A. M., Gildersleeve, R. E., & Pasque, P. A. (2011). Obama's American graduation initiative: Race, conservative modernization, and a logic of abstraction. *Peabody Journal of Education, 86*, 488–505. doi:10.1080/0161956X.2011.616130

Lather, P., & St. Pierre, E. (2013). Post-qualitative research. *International Journal of Qualitative Studies in Education, 26*, 629–633.

Lemke, T. (2011). *Biopolitics: An advanced introduction*. New York: New York University Press.

Lester, J. N., Lochmiller, C., & Gabriel, R. (2015). Call for papers: Discursive perspectives on education policy, implementation, adaptation, and learning.

Lester, J. N., Lochmiller, C., & Gabriel, R. (2016). Locating and applying critical discourse analysis with education policy: An introduction. *Education Policy Analysis Archives, 24*(102). doi:10.14507/epaa.24.2768

Malabou, C. (2007). An eye at the edge of discourse. *Communication Theory, 17*, 16–25.

Malabou, C. (2010). *Plasticity at the dusk of writing: Dialectic, destruction, deconstruction*. New York: Columbia University Press.

Malabou, C. (2012). *Ontology of the accident: An essay on destructive plasticity*. Cambridge: Polity Press.

MacLure, M. (2013). Researching without representation? Language and materiality in post-qualitative methodology. *International Journal of Qualitative Studies in Education, 26*(6), 658–667.

Massumi, B. (2002). *Parables for the virtual. Movement, affect, sensation*. Durham: Duke University Press.

Pickering, A. (1995). *The mangle of practice: Time, agency, and science*. Chicago: University of Chicago Press.

Raffnsoe, S. (2016). *Philosophy of the anthropocene: The human turn*. New York: Palgrave Macmillan.

Suspitsyna, T. (2012). Higher education for economic advancement and engaged citizenship: An analysis of the U.S. Department of Education discourse. *Journal of Higher Education, 83*(1), 49–72.

Ulmer, J. B. (2015). Plasticity: A new materialist approach to policy and methodology. *Educational Philosophy and Theory, 47*(10), 1096–1109.

Zalasiewics, J., Williams, M., Haywood, A., & Ellis, M. (2011). Introduction: The anthropocene: A new epoch of geological time? *Philosophical Transactions of the Royal Society of London, Series A, Mathematical and Physical Sciences, 369*(1938), 835–841.

Zylinksa, J. (2014). *Minimal ethics for the anthropocene*. Ann Arbor: Open University Press.

Ryan Evely Gildersleeve is Associate Professor and Chair of the Higher Education Department at the University of Denver. His research agenda investigates the social and political contexts of educational opportunity for historically marginalized communities, with a focus on college access and success for Latino (im)migrant families. A critical qualitative methodologist, he is interested in theorizing a post-humanist inquiry that informs social policy for more democratic educational institutions. These lines of research connect in their contributions to understanding how social opportunities become democratic participants in an increasingly global society. He is the author of *Fracturing Opportunity: Mexican Migrant Students and College-Going Literacy* (2010), as well as the recipient of the 2011 Early Career Award from the American Educational Research Association's Division D—Research Methodology. He was a 2012–2013 National Academy of Education/Spencer Foundation fellow, supporting his project *Discourses of Opportunity: Undocumented Students and Higher Education Policy*. Gildersleeve holds a PhD in Education and MA in Higher Education and Organizational Change from UCLA. He is a graduate of Occidental College.

Katie Kleinhesselink is Director of Member Services for Campus Compact of the Mountain West, an organization dedicated to community engagement and the public good through higher education. She is a PhD candidate in the Higher Education Department at the University of Denver. Her research interests include education policy, neoliberalism, and philosophies of the "posts," as well as the GI Bill and the success of veterans on US colleges and university campuses.

Plays Well with Others: The Discourse and Enactment of Partnerships in Public Pre-K

Bethany Wilinski

Introduction

The recent expansion of public pre-kindergarten (pre-K) has been accompanied by calls for its provision through partnerships between school districts and private early childhood education (ECE) providers (U.S. Department of Education 2014; Wat and Gayl 2009). School district-ECE provider partnerships in pre-K have been promoted as a mechanism to "share resources and expertise...to expand access to and increase the quality of all programs, no matter where they are housed" (Wat and Gayl 2009, p. 1). As such, pre-K partnerships have the potential to benefit families, school districts, and ECE providers. This chapter examines pre-K partnerships in the context of Wisconsin's public pre-K program, known as four-year-old kindergarten (4K). School-community partnerships are considered a cornerstone of 4K in Wisconsin. In this discursive analysis of data from an ethnographic study of pre-K policy implementation, I demonstrate the ways a local pre-K partnership reflected but also diverged from state-level partnership discourse.

B. Wilinski (✉)
Michigan State University, East Lansing, MI, USA

© The Author(s) 2017
J.N. Lester et al. (eds.), *Discursive Perspectives on Education Policy and Implementation*, DOI 10.1007/978-3-319-58984-8_7

Wisconsin's pre-K partnership model, the 4K Community Approach (4K-CA), emerged in the early 2000s in response to concerns from local ECE communities that new public pre-K programs would negatively affect the childcare industry by channeling four-year-olds out of private childcare sites and preschools and into public schools (Bulebosh 2000). From its beginnings in La Crosse, Wisconsin, the 4K-CA model took root and spread across the state. In the 2014–15 school year, nearly all Wisconsin school districts provided 4K, and about 25% of those districts implemented 4K through the community approach (Wisconsin Department of Public Instruction 2015). The state has prioritized 4K-CA through 4K start-up grants, which provide districts with funding to explore the implementation of 4K; priority consideration for these grants is given to districts that propose providing 4K through a community approach (Wisconsin Department of Public Instruction 2016). Reflecting its support for 4K-CA, the state Department of Public Instruction (DPI) recently hired a storyteller to travel around the state collecting stories about the "unique benefits" of 4K-CA (Kann 2013). Most recently, the State Superintendent's Advisory Committee released a proposal to create additional incentives for adopting 4K-CA, with a goal "to support traditional school-based models moving to community approaches and to support existing community approach districts to maintain the model" (Forces for Four Year Olds 2016, p. 1).

In Wisconsin 4K, an emphasis on providing pre-K through partnerships is clear: There is an established state vision for pre-K partnerships through 4K-CA, financial support for the development of partnerships, and a local literature that supports partnerships, including case studies of districts that have successfully implemented 4K-CA (Anderson 2015; Bulebosh 2000; Rhyme and Eilers 2005). While pre-K partnerships hold much potential for all stakeholders involved, they can also be fraught with tension, because they bring together the previously separate and distinct ECE and K-12 systems (McCabe and Sipple 2011). Partnerships require institutions with historically different approaches to teaching and learning, that are subject to different pressures, and which have access to different types of resources, to establish new mechanisms for working together to implement public pre-K.

This chapter presents an analysis of the discourse and enactment of pre-K partnerships in Wisconsin in order to highlight the complexity of partnership. In this investigation, I examine the discourse of partnership at the state level, through an analysis of documents and stakeholder perspectives. This discursive analysis reveals how the state positions partnerships within the 4K landscape, producing a "discourse of partnership." I then set this discourse against evidence from one Wisconsin school district—Lakeville—where 4K was enacted through a partnership between the school district and local ECE providers, demonstrating the limits of a partnership in which a clear differentiation between ECE providers and the school district is articulated.[1]

KEY LITERATURE

Access to public pre-K has expanded rapidly in recent years, with the percentage of four-year-olds enrolled in state-funded programs growing from 14% to 29% between 2002 and 2015 (Barnett et al. 2016). State pre-K programs are diverse and take different approaches to implementation (Barnett et al. 2009). While some states provide pre-K exclusively in public elementary schools, many states utilize a partnership model, in which local school districts collaborate with community-based partners such as ECE centers and Head Start (Wat and Gayl 2009).

There are many benefits to providing pre-K through partnerships. Partnerships can enable school districts to bring pre-K programs to scale more quickly by utilizing a community's existing ECE infrastructure (Government Accountability Office 2004; Schulman and Blank 2007). A steady stream of public funds can benefit ECE providers, who often operate close to the margin financially (Schilder et al. 2003; Wat and Gayl 2009). In addition, public funding can lead to improved program quality in ECE sites by supporting infrastructure improvements or increased teacher compensation. Such changes are thought to have a "spillover effect," resulting in benefits to all children at a given site (Schulman and Blank 2007). Pre-K partnerships may also be instrumental in helping school districts create greater alignment between ECE and K-12, leading to greater continuity across the two systems (Kagan and Kauerz 2012; Wat and Gayl 2009). Finally, pre-K partnerships support working families by addressing the need for full-day childcare. Implementing pre-K in sites that also provide care outside pre-K hours bridges an important gap for families who want to participate in pre-K but would be unable to manage the logistics of a part-day pre-K program (Schumacher et al. 2005).

There are also challenges to implementing pre-K through partnerships. Successful partnerships require a shift in the views of both ECE and K-12 professionals and a negotiation of markedly different approaches to teaching and learning in K-12 and ECE (McCabe and Sipple 2011; Takanishi 2010;

Wat and Gayl 2009). Pre-K partnerships can also lead to challenges in pre-K teacher recruitment and retention as a result of significant compensation differences for pre-K teachers in public versus private sites (McCabe and Sipple 2011). Decisions about which private sites are included in partnerships and the level of funding they receive to implement pre-K also affects communities and local ECE systems (Morrissey et al. 2007; Wilinski 2017). Finally, pre-K partnerships require a negotiation of divergent governance norms in the ECE and K-12 systems. Accountability and reporting mechanisms in ECE are typically related to health and safety, whereas accountability in K-12 is framed in terms of student achievement (McCabe and Sipple 2011; Takanishi 2010).

A discursive analysis of how partnership was envisioned at the state level in Wisconsin, examined in light of how one partnership was enacted locally, is an important step toward a deeper understanding of the complexity of bringing the K-12 and ECE systems together for pre-K provision. Takanishi (2010) noted that "Early education and K-12 education are now largely separate cultures with their own values and ways of operating" (p. 30). Thus, bringing ECE and K-12 together is as much a cultural project as it is one centered on funding and logistics. While state-level partnership discourse reveals one vision for how these cultures might be brought together, an investigation of local implementation tells a different story.

METHODOLOGICAL AND THEORETICAL PERSPECTIVE

I use Bakhtin's (1981) notion of dialogism as a framework for understanding how pre-K partnership took on different meanings in state discourse and local implementation. Bakhtin understood the world as heteroglossic, or multi-voiced, where multiple and contradictory perspectives necessarily co-exist. In a heteroglossic world, meaning is created in context:

> At any given time, in any given place, there will be a set of conditions—social, historical, meteorological, physiological—that will insure that a word uttered in that place and at that time will have a meaning different than it would have under any other conditions. (Bakhtin 1981, p. 428)

For Bakhtin, utterances are given meaning through dialogue, a notion he termed "dialogism." Because of the range of possible meanings and as a result of multiple languages and voices that contribute to dialogue, dialogue is necessarily "messy" and "unfinalizable" or open, with multiple different meanings possible. Holquist (2002) explained the Bakhtinian notion of dialogism this way:

> Dialogism argues that all meaning is relative in the sense that it comes about only as a result of the relation between two bodies occupying simultaneous but different space, where bodies may be thought of as ranging from the immediacy of our physical bodies, to political bodies and to bodies of ideas in general (ideologies). (p. 21)

This analysis explores the multiple interpretations of partnership that existed at the state and local level in Wisconsin. Here, dialogism provides a framework for understanding why the discourse of partnership that existed at the state level was not reflected in how Lakeville ECE providers experienced their relationship with the school district. The state-level meaning of partnership took a very different shape at the local level, where a new vision of partnership developed as ECE providers interacted with the school district around 4K. Through the interaction of these two "bodies," partnership was given new meaning.

This analysis is framed by an understanding of discourse as "type of social practice" (Fairclough 1992, p. 28). In the tradition of critical discourse analysis, discourse is assumed to be a productive practice that "both reflects and constructs the social world" (Rogers 2004, p. 5). I draw on policy documents, reports, and the perspectives of state DPI officials to construct the state's vision of 4K partnership. This vision conveys the "values, beliefs...and attitudes" of the state related to 4K partnerships, creating a normative discourse of partnership (Souto-Manning 2014, p. 159). By setting this discourse of partnership against the experiences and perspectives of ECE stakeholders in Lakeville, we can begin to understand how a divide between the school district and the ECE community was perpetuated despite the two systems coming together to provide 4K in this community.

Method/Analytic Approach

This chapter is drawn from a larger ethnographic study of 4K policy enactment in Lakeville, which focused on understanding how teachers in different institutional contexts made sense of and implemented 4K policy (Wilinski 2017). I conducted fieldwork in three 4K teachers' classrooms from October 2012 to July 2013. Fieldwork included 300 hours of classroom observation, 3 semi-structured interviews with each focal teacher

Table 7.1   Data sources

Data type	Description
Interview	Marty Jameson, former State Department of Public Instruction (DPI) official
	Helen Moyers, City of Lakeville Child Care official
	Annette Simons, ECE partner site administrator
	Melanie Gustafson, ECE partner site director
	Denise Sanderson, ECE partner site director
	Maura Evans, ECE partner site director
Document	*Stories Highlighting the Unique Benefits of the 4K Community Approach*, Report commissioned by DPI
	Vision for Continuous Promotion of High Quality 4K and 4KCA in Wisconsin, Report by the State Superintendent's Advisory Committee on 4K and Community Approaches
	Sandbox Synergy: La Crosse Launches Innovative Preschool Partnership, Article in Wisconsin School News sponsored by DPI
	The Wisconsin Forces for Four-Year-Olds Community Initiative, Report prepared for DPI and funded by the PEW Charitable Trust

(nine interviews total), interviews with administrators at each site (six interviews total), interviews with other ECE stakeholders in Lakeville (nine interviews total), and one interview with a state education official. In addition, I observed staff meetings (four) and planning meetings (four) at each focal site, district-wide 4K steering-committee meetings (three), and one school board meeting. I also collected documents from the state and school district websites pertaining to 4K and 4K partnerships.[2]

In this chapter, I use a subset of this data to examine the state-level discourse of 4K partnership, and how the state's vision for partnership related to the way stakeholders in the Lakeville ECE community experienced their district's 4K partnership. Table 7.1 provides an overview of the data analyzed for this chapter.[3]

I included these four reports in my analysis because they were all requested or sponsored by the state DPI. Although the DPI may not have influenced how partnerships were represented in these publications, the presence of reports that focus specifically on 4K partnerships reflects the DPI's commitment, investment, and promotion of these partnerships over the years.[4]

I used the qualitative data analysis software MAXQDA to analyze documents and interview transcripts. Analysis was conducted in two overarching phases: First, I coded state-level documents to construct the state's discourse of partnership. Second, I compared this with how ECE stake-holders described their experiences working with the school district to develop and implement 4K. In the first phase, I used a process of open coding to look for themes in the state's discourse partnership (Saldana 2016). To do this, I read through each of the four documents included in my analysis, looking for elements that described aspects of partnerships, with a particular focus on passages that conveyed a rationale for partnering or a vision of what partnerships entail. After generating a list of 75 codes, I looked for themes across the codes and condensed them into four broad categories: process of creating 4K-CA, benefits of partnership to school district, benefits of partnership to ECE providers, and challenges of part-nership. The first set of codes fell into these categories because the docu-ments analyzed were primarily focused on describing how 4K-CA came to be, the types of support and collaboration needed for 4K-CA, and how 4K-CA benefits the institutions involved in its provision. I then organized these coded excerpts into a display (Miles et al. 2014). In the display, I listed the four categories derived from coding in the left-hand column. Then, I read through the data excerpts in each of these categories and copied and pasted the excerpts that best illustrated each category in the right-hand column. Once complete, I used this display to write the narrative of state-level partnership discourse.

In the second round of coding, I attempted to analyze interview tran-scripts using the codes created in the first cycle of coding. As I did this, however, I realized that most of the ways ECE stakeholders in Lakeville described the partnership contradicted the state's conceptualization of partnership. As a result, I used versus coding (Saldana 2016) to capture these competing visions of partnership. In versus coding, the researcher employs binary terms to identify salient divisions among individuals, groups, organizations, or processes. In this analysis, I applied versus codes to illus-trate where local stakeholders' experiences stood in contradiction to the state-level discourse of partnership. Thus, in this cycle of coding, I read through interviews with ECE stakeholders and developed and applied versus codes that captured this contradiction. Codes included: top-down versus bottom-up, enhance versus detract from ECE ecology, economic benefit versus economic burden, us versus them, trust versus mistrust, and collaboration versus control. After creating versus codes, I went back to the excerpts created in the first coding cycle and collapsed them into the newly created codes. Then, I read through all coded excerpts and wrote an analytic memo for each versus code, in which I described how local experience converged or diverged from state-level discourse. Through analytic memos, I sought to tease out "the reasons why the opposition exists. . .and to try to explain how the two oppositional characteristics may exist in the same empirical space" (Gibson and Brown 2009, p. 141, as cited in Saldana 2016, p. 117). In the process of re-reading excerpts and developing memos, I realized that the tension between state-level discourse and the experiences of local stakeholders was best captured in a phrase used by the former superintendent of La Crosse, where he described working in partnership as moving from a "we/they" to a "we/us" mentality (Bulebosh 2000). This became the central organizing feature of my analysis, and it is the theme that I use to demonstrate that Lakeville's 4K partnership, from the perspective of ECE providers, remained grounded in a "we/they" mentality instead of moving to the "we/us" mentality envisioned by state-level partnership discourse.

FINDINGS

While the state-level discourse of partnership described an idealized vision of partnership, in which the school district and local ECE providers worked collaboratively to provide 4K, ECE stakeholders in Lakeville experienced an ongoing division between the school district and ECE providers as 4K policy was implemented. In this section, I describe how the partnership was envisioned at the state level, and then how it was experienced by ECE stakeholders in Lakeville.

State-Level Discourse of Partnership

State-level documents and reports about 4K create a vision of the form and function of 4K partnerships in Wisconsin. Within the DPI, and even among state legislators, 4K-CA is a point of pride; it is promoted as something uniquely beneficial to children, families, ECE providers, and school districts (Graue et al. 2016; Kann 2013). In this section, I demonstrate how state-level discourse about 4K-CA constituted an idealized vision of 4K partnership. The discourse of partnership focused on the policies and processes that facilitated partnership and on the relationships that characterized partnerships.

Policies and Processes that Facilitate Partnership
The state policy framework for public pre-K was positioned as critical to the establishment of local pre-K partnerships, called 4K-CA. Reporting on 4K included an emphasis on how the flexibility of state 4K funds enabled the development of unique partnerships. For example:

> One of the benefits of the 4K-CA approach is that each participating community can design the program to fits [sic] the needs of their specific community. There is no expectation nor mandate that one model will fit all communities. (Kann 2013, p. 22)

One report includes a quote from a DPI official, who similarly described the benefit of this flexibility:

> The [state] funding streams do have some specific requirements, but they actually give you enough wiggle room to put together a model that works for everyone, without getting hung up over things like titles and role responsibilities. (Bulebosh 2000, p. 10)

Former DPI official Marty Jameson similarly noted that the reason 4K-CA worked so well in Wisconsin was because of the state's emphasis on local control in education. He asserted:

> This thing works because, community by community, they discovered it themselves. Most states are much more top down in their approach to education. They have blue ribbon committees and when they come up with the latest new idea it's implemented and mandated. (July 2013 interview)

These excerpts express a sentiment that partnership was possible in Wisconsin because of the flexibility written into state 4K policy, which allowed local communities to develop a model of 4K that worked best for them. In the discourse of partnership, a state policy with minimal requirements was not enough to ensure that school districts and local ECE providers would collaborate to develop pre-K partnerships. A key ingredient to the type of partnering envisioned by the state was a bottom-up process that brought all stakeholders to the table and allowed them to play equal roles in developing 4K. The challenge with a truly bottom-up approach was that it required that stakeholders give up some control and be open to new perspectives. A 2005 report on 4K-CA underscored this idea:

Communities that include all stakeholders in the planning process early on, and view them as equal partners are most successful in breaking down many of the traditional barriers that that impede start-up efforts. Missing from these communities is divisiveness that can be characteristic among collaborating agencies competing for scarce resources. (Rhyme and Eilers 2005, p. 20)

A quote from the former superintendent in La Crosse, the first district in Wisconsin to develop a 4K partnership, provides a concrete example of what this might look like in practice:

We had monthly public information meetings for anyone who wanted to come....It was a good opportunity for those with the deepest concerns to step forward. . . . And by going out and working with our child care providers, we really knew what the issues were. Nothing jumped out from behind the bushes at us. (Bulebosh 2000, p. 12)

In La Crosse, the pioneer and gold standard in Wisconsin 4K partnerships, the development of 4K-CA took six years, precisely because the district encouraged so much community participation and gave up some of its control over the process. The superintendent who led the development of 4K-CA in that district explained:

We all had to give up something....This is why we call collaboration the highest order. All organizations truly have to shift from a "we/they" mentality to "we/us." Over time it's been proven that we needed to have that understanding. (Bulebosh 2000, p. 8)

This shifting of perspective was critical, particularly because the school district had to be the one to initiate the development of 4K. Marty Jameson explained that, because of this, it was especially important for the school district to give up some of its power:

[The school district] has to lead in all these communities. We've had no example of childcare ever leading. The superintendent has to be in the position of saying, "We understand what our role is, but I'm gonna organize the meetings, I'm gonna be the lubricant to pull it together." Childcare has no central organization, no central authority. ...[Then], "Whatever the answer is – if it winds up in the public school, fine, but it will be created from the bottom-up by everyone in the room. And I won't heavy handedly dictate anything. You come up with the answer." (July 2013 interview)

Partnership thus required not only bringing all stakeholders together, but ensuring that the stakeholders with the most power (e.g. school district superintendents) were willing to give up some control of the negotiations and to accept the outcome that was determined by stakeholders to be most beneficial to children and families. In spite of the fact that the vision for stakeholders coming together with "no one in charge" was somewhat mythologized in Wisconsin 4K history, the discourse of partnership did include recognition that not all attempts to develop partnerships were successful. Marty Jameson described how "powerful people" such as school district officials and teachers' union leaders, if they were inflexible and unwilling to compromise, could "hijack" the process of developing a partnership. He explained:

> You just have to get enough people in the conversation so it doesn't get hijacked. . . .It's all been hijacked when it becomes top-down. . .(Pointing to a map of Wisconsin that indicates where large school districts are implementing school-based 4K)Yeah, this has all been hijacked by powerful people. It becomes all distorted and you can't get the power back. You gotta believe in distribution of power. (July 2013 interview)

The issue of power and control, and the perception among community ECE providers that they were not equal partners with the school district, informed Lakeville ECE stakeholders' perpetuation of a "we/they" mentality in describing their relationship with the school district. A recent report on 4K-CA addresses the challenges of collaboration, suggesting the development of "community collaboration councils," envisioned to "help to equalize the power among the districts and the community partners and ensure collaborative decision-making and policy development" (Forces for Four Year Olds 2016, p. 1). In the discourse of partnership, distribution of power among 4K stakeholders was envisioned as essential to partnership, even as it acknowledged the difficulty of accomplishing this goal.

Characteristics of Relationships Between Partners
Collaborative relationships formed during the development of 4K were envisioned to extend into its implementation. In state-level discourse, partnering entailed: re-defining the relationship between the school district and ECE providers, positioning the school district as a learner, and resource sharing. A report on the benefits of 4K-CA asserted that as a result of partnering, "School districts now see the community centers as an extension

of the school program and they act accordingly in terms of making their resources available to the centers" (Kann 2013, p. 26). This idea that a school district would come to see ECE providers as an extension of itself reflected the notion that partnership helped school districts and ECE providers overcome the historical separation of their two systems. Bridging the divide between ECE and K-12, according to the discourse of partnership, would also involve school districts learning from ECE providers:

> The 4K Community Approach program helps school districts gain a better understanding of the needs and challenges of the early childhood programs in their community. . . .With this knowledge, school districts are more committed and better able to work cooperatively with their community partners to provide quality early learning for children. (Kann 2013, pp. 38–39)

This characterization of the school district as a learner disrupts how school districts are typically positioned vis-à-vis ECE providers, where school districts are the education experts and ECE providers provide care (Takanishi 2010). Partnership in Wisconsin 4K was instead conceptualized as a mechanism to foreground the expertise of community providers, who would be able to share their years of experience with the school district, a relative newcomer to ECE.

Finally, the discourse envisioned that school-community partnerships would enhance ECE providers' access to resources. The logic was that if the school district viewed ECE partners as an extension of itself, they would make school district resources readily available to ECE providers. Examples provided in the *Unique Benefits of 4K-CA* report underscore this:

> The 4K Community Approach program has nurtured collaborative partnerships between school districts and the community child care and early childhood education programs. As a result, school districts commonly offer professional development training sessions which include 4K staff from the community sites. They also often invite the child care teachers from the community sites who work with children younger than four-year-olds to attend the training sessions. They sometimes even schedule the trainings during the evening or on Saturdays to better accommodate the scheduling needs of the childcare teachers. Both the 4K teachers and the teachers of younger children have improved their practices as a result of the training they've received. (Kann 2013, p. 28)

The 4K Community Approach program has brought the curriculums and resources from the school district to the child centers in an unprecedented fashion. (Kann 2013, p. 26)

The expected infusion of school district resources, which ECE providers would most likely be unable to afford on their own, are positioned as both evidence of the strong functioning of the partnership and as a benefit to ECE centers for participating in 4K.

In state-level discourse, partnerships were developed through collaboration between the school district and community ECE providers, characterized by shared decision-making and a distribution of power. Such collaboration in the development of 4K would feed into a partnership that situated expertise within the ECE community, and in which school district resources could be leveraged to improve the quality of ECE centers. The reality of Lakeville's partnership, as I describe in the next section, did not fully align with the state's conceptualization of partnership.

Enactment of Partnership in Lakeville

In this section, I describe how the partnership imagined in state-level discourse looked very different in local implementation. Achieving the state's vision for a pre-K partnership would have required moving from a "we/they mentality to a we/us [mentality]," as described by the former La Crosse superintendent (Bulebosh 2000, p. 8). Evidence from interviews with Lakeville ECE stakeholders suggests that while a partnership technically existed in Lakeville, members of the ECE community continued to perceive significant differences between themselves and the school district, grounding the partnership in a "we/they" mentality. This mentality was characterized by the perception that the school district had more power in the setting up of 4K policy than ECE sites did, that K-12 and ECE were fundamentally separate systems, with different ways of operating, and that the school district did not have the expertise nor the appropriate structures to provide 4K at the same level of quality as ECE providers.

Power and Control
ECE providers' perception that, in spite of the pre-K partnership, their work was still very separate from that of the school district was informed an awareness that the school district was ultimately in control of 4K. Maura

Evans, an ECE partner site director, asserted that the Lakeville school district, because of its size, was not very good at shared decision-making:

> And I know some districts they really pair with the community, but they're smaller. I think that's part of the issue with Lakeville. They're big, they're used to being, and I hate to say dictate, but they are. And I think as time goes on they'll be more willing to give us the credit we deserve and maybe let some of the expectations fall on us, so to speak. (February 2013 interview)

From Evans' point of view, the school district dictated the terms of the relationship and of 4K, rather than drawing on the expertise of ECE sites in the way state-level partnership discourse imagined. One challenge that resulted from the school district making some unilateral decisions about 4K was initial uncertainty over how many 4K slots would be allocated to each ECE partner. Administrators described their worry that they would not be able to provide 4K to all of their existing families; this fear was compounded by the fact that they had no control over the allocation of 4K slots. Denise Sanderson explained:

> I think for year one [of 4K] the registration process and the number of slots and the number of families, lining all that up was a big fear. Initially, we weren't going to have enough spots to serve our current families. And we weren't getting direct answers at the time. (January 2013 interview)

Although the process of allocating slots eventually became more transparent and caused far less anxiety in the second year of 4K, the process remained out of ECE partners' control because the school district was obligated, per an agreement with the local teachers' union, to carefully control how many 4K slots were offered in ECE sites. As Sanderson described, "That takes the control of who is in our center out of our hands" (January 2012 interview).

Maura Evans experienced a different challenge in relation to the allocation of 4K slots. In the first year of 4K, although she was struggling to fill all of the 4K classes at her center, the school district opened a new 4K classroom at a nearby elementary school. This development meant there was no way Evans would fill all of her 4K seats. She explained:

> I had difficulty because they opened up Fieldstone Elementary 4K after...they hadn't even filled my center. So I'll be honest—I was kind of vocal, asking "Wait a minute, why are you opening up another school when you haven't even filled our slots?" (February 2013 interview)

The school district did not address this issue, and Evans' 4K slots went unused, yet there was nothing she could do about the situation; the nature of the 4K partnership in Lakeville meant that if ECE providers wanted to be part of 4K, they had to accept that there were some aspects of the program over which they had no control.

Another exemplar of power imbalance in the Lakeville partnership was how the nature of community-wide 4K meetings changed over time. Prior to the implementation of 4K, these regular meetings had been venues for stakeholder input and defining a shared vision for 4K. Once 4K was underway, however, the meetings became a venue for the school district to pass on information to ECE partners. City of Lakeville childcare official Helen Moyers explained:

> [Before 4K started], there was a 4K advisory committee. And that was really kind of cool, because it was the school district, and community representatives, and center directors. But [now]...it's just a meeting with directors. It's a way for the school district to pass on information. Which is very nice, but it does not at all play the role that the advisory committee did, in trying to figure out whether this is working well or not. (January 2012 interview)

After 4K began, the structure intended to facilitate critical discussion of community priorities for four-year-olds changed. The perception that 4K meetings were now perfunctory, a way to pass on information, reinforced a "we/they" mentality by underscoring that decision-making related to 4K was not shared equally among the school district and ECE partners. All the same, these meetings were viewed as essential by ECE stakeholders, who worried that in the absence of regular meetings, ECE partners would be "Out of sight, out of mind" (Denise Sanderson, January 2013 interview). Sanderson elaborated on this and explained that she felt the need to regularly remind the school district that ECE providers were also part of 4K:

> We sometimes have to wave our arms and say, "Hello! We're over here!" [The school district is] so used to not having to think about community sites...As we were winding down year one [the district said], "Well, now that year one is done, maybe we don't need a steering committee." And I said, "No nonononononono!" We still need to be coming together and talking, because this is a collaborative effort. The players all need to be there and we need to see each other and communicate with each other. (January 2013 interview)

ECE stakeholders like Sanderson did not perceive their relationship with the school district as one in which ECE becomes an extension of K-12, as the discourse of partnership envisioned. Instead, they recognized that the power dynamic of the 4K partnership was skewed in favor of the school district, and they worried that they might be left out of decision-making altogether if they did not continually assert their presence.

Separate Systems and Expectations
Even as they hoped for a more collaborative relationship with the school district, there was recognition among ECE stakeholders that the school district was a very different and incompatible system. Annette Simons, an ECE partner site administrator, described it as a challenge of not speaking the same language:

> My vantage is that the district, like [our center] or any other institution, has its own language and its own...system. It's large, and we are small. And I don't know if the school district was ready or, it was ready and knew how to communicate and deal with...the small little off-sites and how to speak our language. And we didn't know how to listen to their language. (January 2012)

In this view, working in partnership would require each side to learn to speak the other's language. Yet, some differences between the two systems would be impossible to overcome. For example, administrators spoke of the process of creating 4K, which required a lot of people's time and effort to come up with a plan. Everything had to be cleared through the school district's legal department, however, which almost always resulted in changes to the agreed-upon plan. Because of the way it worked and the systems to which it was accountable, the school district would always have the final say in some matters. According to Denise Sanderson, coming to understand this reality was part of the process of working with the school district:

> I've come to appreciate the district for what it is. You know, early childhood centers tend to [think of it as] "the big bad school district." But, I've come to appreciate what [the school district's] process is. I understand how they operate. Sometimes I don't understand *why* they operate that way, but I understand their process, which makes it easier for me to figure things out. (January 2012 interview)

Sanderson acknowledged that the school district likely had reasons for doing what it did, even if she did not always understand. This view helped her make sense of decisions about 4K that puzzled her.

Beyond the fact that the K-12 and ECE systems had very different ways of operating, a significant challenge to the partnership was that the school district, because it was not a state-licensed ECE provider, was exempt from complying with regulations associated with the provision of high-quality ECE. The result was that public school 4K classrooms and ECE center 4K classrooms were held to a different standard. There was some contradiction in the structure of Lakeville's 4K policy: In order to qualify to partner with the school district, ECE centers had to be accredited by the National Association for the Education of Young Children (NAEYC) or the city of Lakeville, which had standards and regulations designed to ensure the provision of high-quality programming. For example, accreditation standards limited teacher–student ratios to 1:8 and maximum group size to 16. In addition, accredited centers were required to employ certain practices aimed at promoting children's development and socialization, such as the requirement that meals and snacks be served "family style."

As 4K was developed, it became clear that, although the teachers' union had stipulated that ECE partner sites be accredited in order to ensure quality in 4K, public school 4K sites would not be held to the same standards. Helen Moyers explained:

> [You need to understand] that [public school 4K classrooms] don't have to follow state licensing [regulations]. Especially they don't have to follow ratios. And we know that student-teacher ratios is one of the primary indicators of quality. So, [ECE centers would need] an assistant to have 15 children, and the school district said, "Oh well, we always have an aide assigned." And you're going, "Really?"[5] Or when [the district] wants to have 18 or 20 kids [in one 4K class]. And you're going, "We can't have that. Licensing forbids it." And city standards and NAEYC standards are even stricter. And for [the district] to say, "Yes you have to do that, but we don't have to follow those ideas of quality", that was difficult during those planning meetings. (January 2012 interview)

Moyers described being surprised by the school district's unwillingness to comply with state licensing regulations and accreditation standards. This reinforced a separation between the school district and the ECE community, at least in the eyes of ECE providers, because the district was able to make claims about quality and enforce quality standards for ECE providers while simultaneously not holding itself to those standards. Adhering to maximum group size and teacher-student ratios would have made 4K more costly for the district to provide, because it would require hiring additional teachers.

That the school district distinguished itself from the ECE providers when it came to complying with rules related to quality fueled a more general suspicion of whether the school district and public school 4K teachers were qualified to provide 4K. Moyers, for example, was concerned that an unwillingness on the part of school district 4K teachers to adhere to relatively simple regulations related to quality might manifest itself in other aspects of 4K teaching. She explained:

> So, I'm meeting with a [school district] 4K teacher yesterday and she's telling me how when she does lunch they just serve all the kids. And I work with an early childhood program in the same space that I have a required change saying, you need to set up your meals so that self-serve, so the children are learning how to use utensils. And the [school district] 4K teacher said, "Oh it takes too much time." And I said, "Absolutely. It takes more time—you are right!" And she said, "Well we can't do that." I let it go, but at the end I said, "I'd ask you to rethink that. In terms of your goals for these children, we want them to be able to do that." I can find 10 things that they're learning during a snack or during a lunch. But I was caught because [she just said] "We're not doing that. It takes too much time." And if that's true about snack, can we talk about what that must be like with language or literacy? Math? Open-ended art activities? (January 2012 interview)

If this interaction had taken place in an accredited center, Moyers would have been able to enforce her request. However, because she was speaking with a school district-employed 4K teacher, she could only suggest the change, but had no power to enforce it. That this teacher appeared unwilling to harness important opportunities for learning by allowing children to serve themselves at lunch and snack led Moyers to question the teacher's practice more generally. As I describe in the next section, this suspicion— that public school 4K teachers and the school district were not well-positioned to provide 4K—was shared by other ECE stakeholders in Lakeville.

Appropriate Environments and Expertise

A final element of the relationship between the school district and ECE providers that defined the partnership was a belief on the part of ECE partners that the school district was not well equipped to serve four-year-olds. Two sub-themes animated this perspective: infrastructure and expertise. First, ECE providers questioned the appropriateness of public school buildings for young children, a perspective that grew out of an understanding that ECE centers were purposefully designed for four-year-olds while public school buildings were not. Denise Sanderson explained:

> I'm not bashing the district, it's just—our center was built for four-year-old children. The school district buildings, some of them were not, and they're having to be retro-fitted. [They have] bathrooms down the hall [and not in classrooms], that kind of thing. The children are probably going to be absolutely just fine. But [our center is] just so purposeful and accommodating to the age that we're serving. (January 2013 interview)

From Sanderson's point of view, school buildings constructed with older children in mind created a structural limitation to the school district's ability to provide high-quality 4K. In a separate interview, Sanderson said that if she could change anything about 4K, "I would have 4K completely in community sites *that were designed for early childhood education*" (January 2012 interview). This perspective, which was echoed by other ECE stakeholders, drew clear distinctions between ECE and K-12 and perpetuated a "we/they" mentality.

Second, beyond structural concerns, ECE providers expressed mistrust in the school district and public school 4K teachers' understanding of young children and ability to teach them effectively. For example, Helen Moyers said, "The truth is, I believe that we are much better positioned, even than the school district is, because they're new at this" (January 2012 interview). The "we" in this assertion was childcare providers. This we/they binary was based in an assumption that ECE providers had greater expertise in teaching young children, given their understanding of developmentally appropriate practice and significant experience. Denise Sanderson's concern that, "Teachers who are teaching [4K in public schools] may not have ever touched a four year old before" (January 2012 interview) grew out of this perspective. The logic was, if 4K teachers had never "touched a four-year-old," it would be hard for them to provide 4K that was as high quality as what was provided by the ECE community. Moyers explained:

Early childhood care and education people are very committed to children and families...They also know what is developmentally appropriate and...they know what a four-year-old can handle...and needs to learn. So they have worked very hard to look at their own curriculums and the [state early learning standards] to make sure that those are connected. Personally, I'm not so sure that it's as connected to those teachers in [public school 4K classrooms]...[4K teachers in ECE sites] are under a great deal of scrutiny, and I don't get the sense that the 4K teachers in the public schools are. (January 2012 interview)

Moyers' articulated her belief that not only did ECE teachers have a better understanding of what and how four-year-olds learned, they were also more motivated to do a good job at 4K, perhaps more so than public school 4K teachers. In addition, the stakes may have been higher for ECE providers, where losing a contract to be a 4K partner could put a site's economic viability in jeopardy.

SUMMARY

As ECE partners in Lakeville interacted with the school district to provide public pre-K, they created a new meaning of partnership that differed significantly from the state's idealized vision of partnership. Bakhtin's notion of dialogism, which asserts that meaning is made through interaction, provides one framework for making sense of local variation in policy implementation. Although Wisconsin's state 4K policy was designed with variation in mind, the state's conceptualization of pre-K partnership was relatively monolithic; it articulated a clear vision of how districts and community ECE providers would work collaboratively to develop a 4K program to meet the needs of children and families. The state envisioned this as a bottom-up process, characterized by a distribution of power. Moreover, 4K partnerships were supposed to create new linkages between ECE and K-12, leading to a shift from a we/they mentality in which the two systems were viewed as separate, to a we/us mentality in which each system was seen as an extension of the other.

In Lakeville, however, even as they partnered with the school district, ECE stakeholders continued to view their work in opposition to the school district. The perspectives of these stakeholders demonstrate that this perspective grew out of a recognition that, despite the partnership, the school district retained more power and control over 4K than ECE providers, that the ECE and K-12 systems were fundamentally different, and a belief that the school district and its teachers were not well equipped to provide high-quality 4K. Whether the differences between ECE providers and the school district were real or perceived, they informed the way ECE providers came to conceptualize partnership.

Although this was a study of one school district, the findings are applicable in contexts beyond Lakeville. While pre-K partnerships are widely promoted, there is a limited body of research that investigates the nature and complexity of such partnerships (Casto et al. 2016; Wilinski 2017). Yet, as the findings from this study underscore, the way different stakeholders conceptualize partnership matters because it has implications for how partners work together to provide pre-K. In the case of Lakeville, even if the school district perceived that they were working collaboratively with ECE providers, the fact that ECE stakeholders saw a divide between the two is significant, and likely had an effect on the way the partnership functioned. Remaining rooted in a we/they mentality likely prevented Lakeville from achieving the type of collaborative partnership envisioned in state discourse.

Key Connections to Policy Research
1. Bringing together ECE and K-12 systems for the provision of pre-K is a complex process. There is a need to better understand the nature of pre-K partnerships in order to reconcile differences between discourse and enactment of partnerships.
2. Stakeholders involved in pre-K partnerships may have diverse interpretations of partnership. These perspectives must be reconciled in order for collaboration to occur.
3. Creating new linkages between ECE and K-12 may require state-level support. In Wisconsin, collaboration councils are being promoted to help facilitate the development of partnerships.

NOTES

1. All names of people and places are pseudonyms.
2. A limitation of this study is that I was unable to interview any school district officials, despite repeated requests to speak with them.

3. I only included data from 4K administrator interviews, as these were the stakeholders who worked most closely with district officials in the development and implementation of 4K.

4. In a different study, we found that state legislators and DPI officials cited 4K partnerships as a key feature of Wisconsin 4K and a point of pride in the state's educational landscape (Graue et al. 2016).

5. Moyers' skepticism of the district's commitment to have a teacher's aide in public school 4K classrooms was not unfounded. For the public school 4K teacher who participated in this study, having a consistent aide was a struggle over the two years she taught 4K. At least for this teacher, being assigned an aide was not a given.

REFERENCES

Anderson, S. (2015, September). Developing young learners: 4K programs are preparing students for kindergarten and beyond. *Wisconsin School News*, 4–8. Retrieved from https://issuu.com/wischoolnews/docs/wsn_sept_2015/6

Bakhtin, M. M. (1981). Discourse in the novel. In M. Holquist (Ed.), *The dialogic imagination: Four essays by M. M. Bakhtin* (pp. 259–422). Austin: University of Texas Press.

Barnett, W. S., Friedman, A. H., Hustedt, J. T., & Stevenson-Boyd, J. (2009). An overview of prekindergarten policy in the United States: Program governance, eligibility, standards, and finance. In R. C. Pianta & C. Howes (Eds.), *The promise of pre-K* (pp. 3–30). Baltimore: Paul H. Brookes Publishing Co.

Barnett, W. S., Friedman-Krauss, A. H., Gomez, R. E., Horowitz, M., Weisenfeld, G. G., Clarke Brown, K., & Squires, J. H. (2016). *The state of preschool 2015*. New Brunswick: National Institute for Early Education Research.

Bulebosh, N. (2000, June). Sandbox synergy: LaCrosse launches innovative preschool partnership. *Wisconsin School News*, 5–12.

Casto, H. G., Sipple, J. W., & McCabe, L. A. (2016). A typology of school-community relationships: Partnering and universal prekindergarten policy. *Educational Policy, 30*(5), 659–687.

Fairclough, N. (1992). *Discourse and social change*. Cambridge, MA: Polity Press.

Forces for Four Year Olds. (2016). *Vision for continuous promotion of high quality 4-year-old kindergarten (4K) and 4-year-old kindergarten and community approaches (4KCA) in Wisconsin*.

Government Accountability Office. (2004). *Prekindergarten: Four selected states expanded access by relying on schools and existing providers of early education and care to provide services*. Retrieved from http://www.gao.gov/products/GAO-04-852

Graue, M. E., Wilinski, B., & Nocera, A. (2016). Local control in the era of accountability: A case study of Wisconsin preK. *Education Policy Analysis Archives, 24*(60), 1–26.

Holquist, M. (2002). *Dialogism: Bakhtin and his world* (2nd ed.). New York: Routledge.

Kagan, S. L., & Kauerz, K. (2012). Early childhood systems: Looking deep, wide, and far. In S. L. Kagan & K. Kauerz (Eds.), *Early childhood systems: Transforming early learning* (pp. 3–17). New York: Teachers College Press.

Kann, B. (2013). *The unique benefits of the 4K community approach or 54 reasons to implement the 4K community approach.* Madison: Department of Public Instruction. Retrieved from http://dpi.wi.gov/sites/default/files/imce/early-child hood/4kca/pdf/54_benefits_4kca_list.pdf

McCabe, L., & Sipple, J. W. (2011). Colliding worlds: Practical and political tensions of prekindergarten implementation in public schools. *Educational Policy, 25*(1), e1–e26.

Miles, M. B., Huberman, A. M., & Saldana, J. (2014). *Qualitative data analysis: A methods sourcebook.* Washington, DC: SAGE.

Morrissey, T. W., Lekies, K. S., & Cochran, M. M. (2007). Implementing New York's universal pre-kindergarten program: An exploratory study of systemic impacts. *Early Education & Development, 18*(4), 573–596.

Rhyme, A. R., & Eilers, A. M. (2005). *A case study on the expansion of four year old kindergarten and the Wisconsin Forces for Four-year-olds community initiative.* Wisconsin Department of Public Instruction. Retrieved from http://www.collaboratingpartners.com/docs/WIk4study5-26-05.pdf

Rogers, R. (2004). An introduction to critical discourse analysis in education. In R. Rogers (Ed.), *An introduction to critical discourse analysis in education* (pp. 1–18). Mahwah: Lawrence Erlbaum Associates, Publishers.

Saldana, J. (2016). *The coding manual for qualitative researchers* (3rd ed.). Thousand Oaks: SAGE.

Schilder, D., Kiron, E., & Elliott, K. (2003). *Early care and education partnerships: State actions and local lessons.* Cambridge, MA: Education Development Center, Inc. Retrieved from http://www.researchconnections.org/childcare/resources/1515

Schulman, K., & Blank, H. (2007). *A center piece of the preK puzzle: Providing state prekindergarten in child care centers.* Washington, DC: National Women's Law Center. Retrieved from http://www.nwlc.org/sites/default/files/pdfs/NWLCPreKReport2007.pdf

Schumacher, R., Ewen, D., Hart, K., & Lombardi, J. (2005). *All together now: State experiences in using community-based child care to provide pre-kindergarten.* Washington, DC: Center for Law and Social Policy. Retrieved from https://www.brookings.edu/wp-content/uploads/2016/06/200502lombardi.pdf

Souto-Manning, M. (2014). Critical narrative analysis: The interplay of critical discourse and narrative analyses. *International Journal of Qualitative Studies in Education, 27*(2), 159–180. http://doi.org/10.1080/09518398.2012.737046

Takanishi, R. (2010). PreK-third grade: A paradigm shift. In V. Washington & J. Andrews (Eds.), *Children of 2020: Creating a better tomorrow* (pp. 28–31). Washington, DC: Council for Professional Recognition; National Association for the Education of Young Children.

U.S. Department of Education. (2014). *What are preschool development grants?* Retrieved from http://www2.ed.gov/programs/preschooldevelopmentgrants/pdgfactsheet81115.pdf

Wat, A., & Gayl, C. (2009). *Beyond the schoolyard: Pre-K collaborations with community-based partners.* Washington, DC: The Pew Center on the States. Retrieved from https://www.nmefoundation.org/getmedia/c9544bc4-2128-4ec5-8446-d7858f12868b/BeyondtheSchoolYard

Wilinski, B. (2017). *When pre-K comes to school: Policy, partnerships, and the early childhood education workforce.* New York: Teachers College Press.

Wisconsin Department of Public Instruction. (2015). *95 percent of public school districts offer 4K.* Retrieved from https://dpi.wi.gov/news/releases/2015/95-percent-public-school-districts-offer-4k

Wisconsin Department of Public Instruction. (2016). *Four year old kindergarten grants.* Retrieved from http://dpi.wi.gov/early-childhood/kind/4k/start-up-grants-schedule

Bethany Wilinski is Assistant Professor at Michigan State University in the Department of Teacher Education. She studies domestic and international early childhood education policy. Her research focuses on how teachers make sense of and implement early childhood policies and how policy shapes families' access to early childhood programs. Her international work is based in Tanzania, where she is involved in research, curriculum development, and teacher training projects for Michigan State University's Tanzania Partnership Program.

Reframing Misbehavior: Positive School Discipline and the New Meaning of "Safety" in Schools

Hilary Lustick

Introduction

Since 2011, the federal government has become increasingly interested in stemming the disproportionate suspension of students of color (as well as the overall spike in suspensions and expulsions nationwide). The Supportive School Discipline Initiative, a joint venture launched in January of 2014 by the Department of Education (ED) and the Department of Justice (DOJ), has released a School Climate Guidance Package meant to support schools in implementing alternatives to *exclusionary discipline* practices like suspension and expulsion. The package is certainly a step in the right direction from zero tolerance policies. However, it neglects to acknowledge that, while racial disproportionality in discipline has been a phenomenon since school desegregation, federally mandated zero tolerance discipline policies exacerbated racial disparities in discipline (Anfinson et al. 2010; Gregory et al. 2010; Hoffman 2012; Pots et al. 2003; Skiba et al. 2002; Stader 2004; Verdugo 2002). Instead, ED holds districts entirely responsible and

H. Lustick (✉)
Texas State University, San Marcos, TX, USA

© The Author(s) 2017
J.N. Lester et al. (eds.), *Discursive Perspectives on Education Policy and Implementation*, DOI 10.1007/978-3-319-58984-8_8

employs discursive strategies that make such accountability seem coherent, natural, and logical.[1]

Just as form follows function in architecture, the wording of a policy determines not only its implementation but also how the public will understand the problem at hand. In this chapter, I argue that Critical Discourse Analysis (CDA; Fairclough 1992) is a useful methodological approach for analyzing the Supportive School Discipline Initiative, allowing us to separate how ED is framing the problem of school discipline; the political reasons for ED's chosen frame; and additional problems their solution may present. Thus, in this empirical chapter, I begin by offering a brief overview of the key literature related to zero tolerance policies. Then, I discuss my analytical and methodological approach, providing a brief overview of CDA. After this, I describe my data sources and methods of analysis. The remaining sections of the chapter describe my key findings and highlight some critical implications of policy researchers.

KEY LITERATURE

Zero tolerance policies are a set of harsh, uniform school discipline policies that date back to the early 1990s but whose logic are rooted in the "get-tough" anti-drug laws of the 1980s (Alexander 2010; Kafka 2011). Under the zero tolerance regime, schools were warned to coordinate effectively with law enforcement officials and procure proper surveillance equipment, with the emphasis being on excluding threatening students. The implications for students of color were dramatic. The Kirwan Institute (2015) found that Black students comprised 18% of the total US K-12 public school population, but comprised 35% of the total number of students suspended.

Researchers and advocates have long challenged zero tolerance policies on the grounds that (a) they have been correlated with increased exclusionary discipline, disengagement, and dropout for students of color (American Psychological Association 2008), and (b) there is mixed evidence as to whether exclusionary discipline improves schools for those who do not get excluded (Gregory et al. 2010; Essex 2000; Mongan and Walker 2012). There is, however, research suggesting that these policies have an adverse impact on students of color. There is also evidence that methods of *positive discipline*, such as restorative justice practices or Positive Behavioral Interventions and Supports (PBIS), reduce the need for suspension (Allman and

Slate 2011; Chin et al. 2012; Hachiya 2010; Osher et al. 2010; Timothy and Russo 2001).

In a testimony to the U.S. Commission on Civil Rights, Keleher (2000) provided suspension and expulsion data in 12 cities across the USA and found that in each case, suspensions and expulsions for students of color were at least twice that of White students. On the one hand, he, like others, argued that these disparate impacts are largely because of how the policies are implemented. On the other hand, he also noted that the policies themselves "can curtail the expression of reasonable professional judgment by school educators and administrators and limit students' and parents' right to due process" (Keleher 2000, p. 4). His recommendations included federal support (e.g., resources and funding) to districts for developing alternatives to suspensions that reduce racial disproportionality in disciplinary practices.

ED's Guidance Package is technically a matter of taking Keleher's advice. The DOJ is launching investigations into cities with racially disparate discipline records and providing suggestions for alternatives to suspensions. Politically, however, it is not so simple for the federal government to declare a moratorium on zero tolerance policies. Recent incidents in Chicago, Illinois, and Newtown, Connecticut, for example, make it difficult—rhetorically and pragmatically—to ignore the need for strong security measures in schools. ED, therefore, must find a way to mitigate the effects of zero tolerance policies without drawing attention to the fact that these problems find their origin in how public policy itself has contributed to schools' current predicament. As I will demonstrate, discursive strategies or discursive techniques are a means by which to smooth over this contradiction and focus all of the attention on the responsibilities of school staff. The language of the new Guidance Package transforms the preoccupation with "safety" from safety against violence to safety for students who are perceived to misbehave.

METHODOLOGICAL PERSPECTIVE

Fairclough's (1992) theory and method of CDA pays particular attention to the ways in which language both represents and reinforces ideology. Discourse is understood, then, as a site of ideological power and, thus, a potential site of resistance and transformation (Fairclough 1992, p. 87). Through discourse, power is articulated and, moreover, asserted. Analyzing discourse was, for Fairclough, an analysis not only of power but of how power is wielded. In Gramscian terms, he argued that power is most effective when "the ideologies embedded in discursive practices...become naturalized, and achieve the status of 'common sense'" (Fairclough 1992, p. 87). To understand the power of a text, therefore, we must examine not merely content but the way in which content is delivered and the subjects are implicated. These choices are the unspoken, invisible, powerful components by which hegemony is fueled.

The CDA of Government Texts

Fairclough (1992) argued that sophisticated producers, such as government departments, will construct documents for multiple consumers. One strategy of such "speech accommodation" (p. 24) is to *intertextualize* the discourse of multiple audiences in a method that signifies alliance with those audiences' ideologies (p. 101). Discursive techniques make this reasoning appear natural and righteous, as if all responsibility lies not in policy but in school-level practices. This entails a careful and consistent choice of *grammatical structure, word choice,* and *phrases* that signal more inclusive ideology about schooling and discipline. A CDA approach, detailed in the following Methods and Analytic Approach section, explicates the hegemonic, "common sense" notion of protecting misbehaved students—one that, in the case of my study, draws attention away from the policies that have exacerbated racial disproportionality in discipline.

METHODS AND ANALYTIC APPROACH

Five documents were included in this analysis. I selected the four major items that were part of the Guidance Package, omitting only a compendium of state discipline policies and a book of resources for building positive discipline in schools. I omitted these documents because their contents were largely derived from sources other than the Supportive School Discipline Initiative and were thus not necessarily composed by ED staff (although a separate discursive analysis could perhaps be applied to the compendium's sorting process). Two of the documents I analyzed were speeches given by Secretary of State Arne Duncan that related directly to the Supportive School Discipline Initiative but were intended for different audiences than the documents themselves. While some of the content of these documents overlap, they were strikingly different in what elements of the issue they chose to focus on and what language they used. The language they had in common, therefore, was significant; it helps us to understand what ideologies were central to the ED's message. Different wordings, in conjunction with different intended audiences and genres, suggested to which stakeholder interests ED staff were beholden.

The descriptions of the documents are as follows, and copies of each can be found on the ED website, www2.ed.gov. I transcribed the videotaped speech by Arne Duncan found on this website and analyzed this transcription along with the other documents. Like the documents on the Guidance Package, no author was listed for these speeches. I therefore consistently cited the US ED as the author.

Duncan Video

On the ED website, where all Guidance Package materials can be found, a video recording of Secretary of Education Arne Duncan giving a brief framing of the guidance package can be found. He described the need to both protect schools against violence and disruption, and avoid removing students from instructional time on the other. The speech's intended audience was practitioners, though it is also open to the public.

Duncan Speech at Frederick Douglass High School, January 8, 2014

The Secretary of Education chose Frederick Douglass High School in Baltimore, MD, which had in recent years increased its performance on state exams while decreasing its suspension and expulsion rates, as a press site for officially announcing the guidance package. Its intended audience was the media and public, practitioners, students, and parents affiliated with the high school.

Dear Colleague Letter (Letter to School Officials)

This extensive letter was addressed to school officials and teachers. Its main sections are an overview of racial disparities in the administration of school discipline; the legal framework under which the federal government has investigated school districts for discriminatory suspension practices; and a detailed description of what discriminatory discipline can look like. The document also discusses how the federal government conducts its investigations into possible discrimination cases and makes suggestions for remedying and record-keeping so that schools can track their own progress in administering just discipline. The appendix also provides extensive supplementary information, such as recommendations for training school security and pedagogical staff.

Guiding Principles

A section of the Dear Colleague Letter includes Guiding Principles; these principles distinguish between discipline practices that intentionally discriminate against students of particular groups ("different treatment") versus inadvertently disadvantage students of certain racial groups ("disparate impact"). Because the Guiding Principles were so extensive and detailed, and were clearly intended for legal interpretation in federal investigations, I thought it worthwhile to analyze them as a document separate from the Dear Colleague Letter.

Overview of Supportive School Discipline Initiative

I included also an overview, which provides a more succinct version of some of the background information detailed in the Dear Colleague Letter. It opens with statistics on the schools-to-prison pipeline, specifically its disparate impact on students of color and African American students in particular. It then describes how the initiative was funded and managed, including its budget and how various monies are allocated to "reinvigorate" Civil Rights Data Collection (CRDC) and conduct research on school discipline practice. The intended audience of this document is not explicitly stated, but its specific information about budgets and the origins for the initiative suggests it might be of interest to advocates or politicians. As it includes proposals for future work, it may also serve as a planning document or a groundwork for funding proposal.

Method of Analysis

To analyze the Guidance Package and accompanying speeches, I first coded each document for words or phrases that related to school safety or discipline. I divided these words into adjectives, nouns, and phrases. My criteria for culling a noun or adjective for analysis was that it: (a) appear in relation to school discipline in at least two of the documents and (b) appear more than once in at least one of the documents. These frequencies may seem low, but documents varied in length from a single-page speech to a 20-page letter. I next looked at exactly *how* these terms were used in the documents.

For example, when "safe school climate" was used, was it described as protecting non-disruptive students from threats at school, disruptive students who need positive rather than exclusionary discipline, or an ideal overall school environment? In expanding my units of analysis from individual words and phrases to how these words and phrases were discussed in context, I was able to apply the constructs Fairclough (1992) recommended for analyzing phrasing, grammar structure, and word choice.

FINDINGS

Across all documents, the adjectives employed most often in reference to discipline were *positive* and *support(ive)*. The most common nouns were *school climate, safety, prevention, zero tolerance policies, and rigor*. Additionally, I noted two key phrases lifted directly from the advocacy discourse around reducing disproportionality; these included *rethinking schools* and *schools to prison pipeline*. These words and their tallies across the five documents are listed in Fig. 8.1.

Documents varied in how often they used the listed terms. For example, "positive" and "support(ive)" appeared in Secretary Duncan's video speech and guiding principles, but not in the other documents. School climate, zero tolerance, and school safety also appeared in Duncan's speech at Frederick Douglass High School, but not in the other documents. The phrase "schools to prison pipeline" appeared in the overview but nowhere else, and "rethinking schools" appeared both in the title of the Frederick Douglass speech and several times in its body. I interpreted these variations to be based on what Fairclough called *consumption*—which highlights the various audiences and contexts in which these speeches occurred (Fairclough 1992, p. 71). In addition, the documents varied in how often they used the listed terms. The following section provides an in-depth analysis of these terms, their contexts, and their intertextualities.

Misbehaved Students as Subjects, Not Objects, in the Discipline Process

Previous rhetoric around zero tolerance policies referenced school discipline for violence, labeling such behavior (and, by extension, such students) as a "threat" to be removed from the school site. In its Guidance Package, ED chose to focus on a different subset of hypothetical students: those students marginalized by race who misbehave mildly, or perhaps do not misbehave at all. In this new frame, such students were positioned as potential targets for

Document Name	Duncan Video (380 Words)	Duncan Speech at Frederick Douglass High School	Dear Colleague Letter	Initiative Overview	Guiding Principals
Intended Audience	Practitioners/Advocates	Students, Practitioners Parents, Media, Press	Practitioners	Unspecified	Practitioners
Adjectives: Positive	5				
Support(ive)	1				2
Disciplined	1		2		
Nouns: School Climate	2	1			
Prevention	1	2			
Zero Tolerance Policy		2			
Phrasing: Rethinking Schools		3			
Schools to Prison Pipeline				2	

Fig. 8.1 Common words and phrases related to safety and/or discipline

unjust discipline, and schools were cast as needing to work harder to protect and engage them as a matter of civil rights and educational equity.

The concepts of CDA surface the grammatical elements of this new frame. One "typical example" of racial discrimination listed in the Dear Colleague Letter depicted "similarly situated students of different races [that] are disciplined differently for the same offense" (ED 2013, p. 7). Here, students who misbehaved were subjects of a story—victims of unjust suspension and expulsion policies whose enactors were left unidentified, and therefore remained arbitrary and void of logic, intelligence, and feeling. By framing misbehaving students as victims, the Guidance Package emphasized students' humanity and focused discipline reform on protecting their well-being. Simultaneously, this ignores the fact that educators do more than dole out suspensions and expulsions to unsuspecting students. Significant qualitative research suggests this dynamic is typically more nuanced (Devine 1996; Nolan 2006) and that it is often the result of educators trying to cooperate with school-level police officers—a direct result, therefore, of zero tolerance policies. To ignore this component is to deny the policy's, and, therefore, government's role in discipline, laying responsibility entirely on the school.

The passive voice was a grammatical construction that the ED used to render students as subjects in school discipline. For example, the Dear Colleague Letter stated that "African-American students *were disciplined* more harshly and more frequently because of their race than similarly situated white students" (ED 2013, p. 4); in Duncan's video speech, he noted that "African American students are three times more likely than their white peers *to be suspended or expelled*" (ED 2013) (emphasis mine).

Fairclough (1992) explained that grammar is a "system of options...from which we make selections...depending on social circumstances" (p. 26). "'Passivization,' the conversion of an active clause into a passive clause...may be associated with ideologically significant features of texts" and "allow the agent of a clause to be deleted" (p. 27). In the absence of a subjectified actor with his or her own (perhaps racist, perhaps nuanced) reasons for suspending a student, this construction focuses our attention on the student victimized by these practices. Similarly, this grammatical choice "nominalizes" (p. 27) students of color, positioning them as sympathetic antagonists in frequent references to the discriminatory discipline narrative (i.e., some paraphrasing of "students of color are disproportionately expelled and suspended"). Considering that the intended audience is largely made of practitioners, we also have to consider that such passivization aligns with notions of "support," "guidance," and "positive" discipline by addressing the needs of students rather than the faults of educators.

Overall, ED's grammatical constructs and word choices framed students who misbehave as in need of support. In addition, ED framed the adults who educate them as responsible for protecting them from unjust exclusion, as well as providing a physically and academically positive space for all students. I argue that such grammatical constructions, therefore, served a hegemonic purpose: they centered a drama of unjust discipline on marginalized students and placed complete responsibility on educators to resolve that drama. Larger discussions of policy and society were left unspoken and, therefore, ED absolved itself of responsibility beyond the guidance it provided.

"Positive" and "Supportive" School Discipline

The language of the Supportive School Discipline Initiative—from its title, to its "Guiding Principles," to the speeches used to promote it online and around the country—is decidedly different from that of zero tolerance policies. Rather than emphasize what will *not* be tolerated, as "zero tolerance" implies, the new terminology seems to signal a focus on what *should* happen in schools—in fact, "should" is a word Secretary Duncan used twice in his 380-word video speech to prescribe educator behavior. The terms "positive" and "supportive" are key components of "Positive Behavioral Interventions and Supports," a popular alternative approach to school discipline demonstrated to reduce the need for suspension and expulsion (TA Center on Positive Behavioral Interventions and Supports, November 20, Adkins 2012; Blank 2013; Cavanaugh 2013; Coyle 2013; Deutsch 2013; Dirsmith 2013; Eacho 2013; Gilmour 2005; Guardino 2013; Hendrix 2004; Kok 2015).

Even the titles of the Initiative's various documents—"Guiding Principles," "Guidance Package," and "Dear Colleague Letter"—sound less like federal mandates and more like collegiate suggestions. These titles reinforce the notion that such guidance is all the government is required to provide in order to stem racial disproportionality in school discipline. In the 380-word videotaped speech posted to the Guidance Package website, Secretary of State Arne Duncan used the word "positive" five times. He distanced himself (and, thus, the DOE) from the logic of zero tolerance policies by intertextualizing language from alternative models that practitioners are likely to recognize. Even for those not familiar with PBIS, "supportive" and "positive", are intuitive. They signal a radically different, even opposing, purpose for discipline than school safety or punishment. Discussing these terms under the guise of "guidance" allowed ED to ignore the zero tolerance discipline policies it enacted and still, in some cases, supports.

ED also studiously avoided terms that do relate to zero tolerance policies, including the term "safety" that was invoked so often to justify harsh discipline in the past. In contrast to these explicit references to positive school discipline, the word "safe" only appeared once in Duncan's video speech, and not to discuss violence or even the safety of those people violence might threaten. Instead, it was used to discuss the "safe and supportive" school environment that educators must create in order to reduce the need for exclusionary discipline. Similarly, the Dear Colleague

Letter declared that "schools are safer when all students feel comfortable and are engaged in the school community" (ED 2013, p. 5). One might expect it to be invoked in the speech at Frederick Douglass, with parents and students present, but instead this was used as an opportunity to outright denounce the way school-level staff enact zero tolerance policies and the exacerbation of the schools to prison pipeline. While "safe" has been used to describe the school environment zero tolerance policies were meant to protect, it is now being used to describe the climate educators must provide to "protect" students from the inequities associated with repeated and disproportionate suspension. As hegemonic tools, the terms peppering these documents frame discipline as a school-level issue, absolving entities beyond school staff of any responsibility.

Key Phrases and Metaphors

In addition to reframing the discourse around discipline for educators, the government also signaled its alliance with education advocates who have protested zero tolerance policies and disproportionate discipline since the 1990s. The documents associated with the initiative, particularly the speeches delivered in public contexts, incorporated phrases associated with such advocacy statements. A prime example of strategic phrase placement was the use of the phrase "school-to-prison pipeline" in the Overview. The Overview stated that, in 2012, the DOJ awarded $840,000 to the School Discipline Consensus Project for dismantling "what is commonly named the schools-to-prison pipeline" (www.csgjusticecenter.org). The project engaged "practitioners from the fields of education, juvenile justice, behavioral health, and law enforcement, as well as state and local policymakers, researchers, advocates, students, and parents to collaboratively develop a comprehensive set of recommendations for change agents working to address this issue" (www.csgjusticecenter.org).

This description evidences a new ED focus in the discourse on discipline: dismantling the schools-to-prison pipeline. Use of this phrase, which initiated from education advocacy discourse in the 1990s (American Civil Liberties Union 2014; Losen et al. 2013; Knight and Wadhwa 2014), signaled two things. First, it evidenced a commitment to protecting equal access to education for students who misbehave in school or who are disproportionately represented in school discipline. Second, since racial disproportionality is strongly linked to zero tolerance policies, the discursive act of articulating this focus was a signal of alliance with anti-racist criminal justice reform. Similarly, ED was trying to reframe how various actors are implicated in designing justice in school discipline practice. Fairclough (1992) explained that discourse both describes practice and is, itself, practice.

Another discursive mechanism used here was the grammatical listing of various stakeholders (including educators, lawyers, and advocates) who are, under this initiative, working together and in opposition to the schools-to-prison pipeline. Zero tolerance policies frame discipline as a matter of exclusion, drawing a line between behaving and misbehaving students. The use of "schools-to-prison pipeline," together with a laundry list of stakeholders, drew a different division. ED allied itself with an advocacy movement focused on education as a civil right and, thus, distanced itself from the same federal policies as the former Democratic administration (the Clinton Administration) put in place. In essence, ED intertextualized its protestors so that their language looked like its own.

Lastly, it is critical to note the absence of presence. What was not listed is as important as what was listed. One of the chief populations blamed for the schools-to-prison pipeline was not school officials but the police who were assigned to schools as part of zero tolerance funding (Nolan 2006). Police officers contribute to a prison-like atmosphere in schools and often escalate what would in the past have been a minor disciplinary issue into a legal issue complete with ordinance-issuing. However, ED effectively bypassed this dynamic—and the government's responsibility for it—by placing all focus and responsibility on teachers and administrators to keep schools safe. Fairclough called this *modality*—the strategy by which an authorial body organizes information to create an objective "truth" where there is, in fact, a collection of complicated and intersecting phenomena. The audience and purpose of the ED documents declared, without ever having to say as much, that teachers and principals were the target of discipline reform and must be, by extension, the problem.

Limitations of Critical Discourse Analysis

CDA risks being too critical. The author's bias is also inextricable from the analysis process, and, I, as the author of this piece, am certainly biased toward supporting non-punitive methods of discipline, as well as to suspecting any government initiative that holds schools and districts accountable for specified outcomes without providing accompanying support in the form of training and capacity-building. In this case, I became interested in this topic upon noting the lack of acknowledgment that the

Supportive School Discipline Initiative paid to the role federal education policy played in implementing zero tolerance policies, even when disconcerting evidence about their impact had begun to accumulate. It is, therefore, more than conceivable that the findings identified for this chapter are different than they may have been for someone with different attitudes toward school discipline; indeed, someone with a different attitude toward the subject of positive school discipline would likely not have conducted a critical policy analysis at all.

Also, while in this chapter I assumed that the Supportive School Discipline Initiative signified ED's wielding of hegemonic power, it could also signify that ideas like the "schools to prison pipeline" have gathered legitimacy on their own and are thus transferrable from one sphere to another. Mautner (2010) demonstrated how the "market society" (Mautner 2010, p. 1) colonizes education through discourse, particularly evident in the terminology educators begin to borrow from the business world. While CDA leads us to suspect ED's motives, we must also be aware of the real possibilities for social change signified by its new discursive practice.

SUMMARY

This chapter elucidates an intentional reframing of school discipline that could have powerful implications for civil rights both in and beyond the school. The language of supportive discipline practices has the potential to reframe how practitioners, advocates, criminologists,[2] and policymakers discuss young people: perhaps these fields will start using clinical or guidance-related terms rather than criminalizing, behavior-oriented terms. On the other hand, this discourse also places all the responsibility on teachers and schools to both educate students who are disruptive and protect all students from harm. The use of "guidance" language furthermore takes responsibility out of the hands of the federal and local governments that both created zero tolerance policies and provided the law enforcement to uphold them—factors that, in many cases, exacerbated a prison-like atmosphere in schools. In framing the "Guidance Package" as such, the government frees itself of the responsibility to support schools in developing the professional capacity to address racist pedagogical and disciplinary practices. Through discursive techniques, it is possible to talk about socially just discipline without ever addressing the policies and circumstances that lead to unjust discipline outcomes.

ED's reframe affords opportunities for the researchers and advocates whose language it intertextualizes. The Dignity in Schools Campaign, for example, has already pasted photographs of Duncan to the page on its website describing recent work, with the organization claiming that the Guidance Package is a result of its constituents' organizing (Dignity in Schools Campaign 2014). It could take further advantage of this moment by harnessing chunks of Duncan's speech (specifically quotes involving the "schools to prison pipeline" or "rethinking schools" that spoke specifically to advocates) to demand from policymakers the resources and funding to schools that enact positive discipline approaches. The benefits of intertextuality can go both ways—and should, lest the government co-opt advocacy terminology so completely that it is used to punish schools rather than empower communities.

Key Connections to Policy Research
1. How a policy is written has the potential to frame the political context in which it will be implemented.
2. In light of the first point above, it is crucial for the wording of a policy to be analyzed in its political context, not taken at face value.
3. Equity-based initiatives, like the Supportive School Discipline Initiative, must support local change, not just command the same.
4. The "support" described in point three starts with how a problem and the policy addressing it are worded. Critical Discourse Analysis (CDA) allows us to see how this works, and make more effective recommendations as a result.

NOTES

1. I use the acronym "ED" to signify Guidance Package authors, as specific name(s) are not listed.
2. Concurrently with the Supportive School Discipline Initiative, the DOJ and ED are also launching an initiative to reform the juvenile justice system (Shaw 2014).

REFERENCES

Adkins, K. E. (2012). *Exploring the effectiveness of a school wide positive behavior support program*. Ed.D., Wilmington University, Delaware. ProQuest Dissertations and Theses (1284866978).

Alexander, M. (2010). *The new Jim Crow: Mass incarceration in the age of colorblindness.* New York: The New Press.

Allman, K. L., & Slate, J. R. (2011). School discipline in public education: A brief review of current practices. *International Journal of Educational Leadership Preparation, 6*(2), 1–7.

American Civil Liberties Union. (2014). *School-to-prison pipeline.* Retrieved from https://www.aclu.org/school-prison-pipeline

American Psychological Association Zero Tolerance Task Force. (2008, December). *Are zero tolerance policies effective in the schools?* American Psychological Association. Retrieved from http://www.apa.org/pubs/info/reports/zero-tolerance.pdf

Anfinson, A., Autumn, S., Lehr, C., Riestenberg, N., & Scullin, S. (2010). Disproportionate minority representation in suspension and expulsion in Minnesota public schools: A report from the Minnesota department of education. *International Journal on School Disaffection, 7*(2), 5–20.

Blank, J. E. (2013). *Use of behavioral disciplinary techniques with the implementation of SWPBIS and its impact on students' prosocial motivation.* Ph.D., University of Delaware. ProQuest Dissertations and Theses (1319306997).

Cavanaugh, B. J. (2013). *Implementation science and preventative behavioral supports in schools.* Ed.D., The University of Maine. ProQuest Dissertations and Themes (1461392001).

Chin, J. K., Dowdy, E., Jimerson, S. R., & Rime, J. (2012). Alternatives to suspensions: Rationale and recommendations. *Journal of School Violence, 11*, 156–173.

Coyle, L. A. (2013). *Students' lived experiences with the positive behavioral interventions and supports (PBIS) program in middle school.* Ph.D., Capella University. ProQuest Dissertations and Theses (1447009344).

Deutsch, A. J. (2013). *A case study of first year implementation of positive behavioral Interventions and supports in a high school.* S.S.P., Western Carolina University. ProQuest Dissertations and Theses (1355174693).

Devine, J. (1996). *Maximum security: The culture of violence in inner city schools.* Chicago: Chicago University Press.

Dirsmith, J. K. (2013). *The impact of school-wide positive behavioral interventions and supports on academic achievement.* D.Ed., Indiana University of Pennsylvania. ProQuest Dissertations and Theses (1346190745).

Dignity in Schools Campaign. (2014). *Updates.* Retrieved from www.dignityinschools.org

Eacho, T. C. (2013). *Violence and disorder, school climate, and PBIS: The relationship among school climate, student outcomes, and the use of positive behavioral interventions and supports.* Ph.D., University of Maryland, College Park. ProQuest Dissertations and Theses (1432193995).

Essex, N. L. (2000). Zero tolerance approach to school discipline: Is it going too far? *American Secondary Education, 29*(2), 37.

Fairclough, N. (1992). *Discourse and social change.* Cambridge: Polity Press.

Gilmour, S. L. J. (2005). *What factors contribute to a commitment and implementation of a more restorative approach to discipline in schools?* M.A., Royal Roads University, Canada. ProQuest Dissertations and Theses (305348276).

Gregory, A., Skiba, R. J., & Noguera, P. A. (2010). The achievement gap and the discipline gap. Two sides of the same coin? *Educational Researcher, 39*(1), 59–68.

Guardino, D. M. (2013). *The disproportionate use of discipline: An investigation of the potential impact of school-wide positive behavioral interventions and supports.* Ph.D., University of Oregon. ProQuest Dissertations and Theses (1399994802).

Hachiya, R. (2010). *Balancing student rights and the need for safe schools.* ProQuest Dissertations, LLC.

Hendrix, G. M. (2004). *A test of reintegrative shaming theory's concepts of interdependence and expressed shame in restorative justice conferencing.* M.S., Michigan State University. ProQuest Dissertations and Theses (305156510).

Hoffman, S. (2012). Zero benefit: Estimating the effect of zero tolerance discipline policies on racial disparities in school discipline. *Education Policy, 28*(1), 69–65.

Kafka, J. (2011). *The history of "zero tolerance" in American public schooling.* New York: Macmillan.

Keleher, T. (2000). *Racial disparities related to school zero tolerance policies: Testimony to the US commission on civil rights.* Oakland: Applied Research Center. http://www.arc.org

Knight, D., & Wadhwa, A. (2014). Expanding opportunity through restorative justice: Portraits of resilience at the individual and school level. *Schools: Studies in Education, 11*(1), 11–33.

Kok, S. (2015). *An in-depth analysis of high school student and teacher perceptions of PBIS.* Ed.S., University of Nebraska at Omaha. ProQuest Dissertations and Theses (1504640206).

Losen, D., Kim, C., & Hewitt, D. (2013). *The school to prison pipeline.* New York: NYU Press.

Mautner, G. (2010). *Language and the market society: Critical reflections on discourse and dominance.* London: Routledge. (Chapters 2, 3).

Mongan, P., & Walker, R. (2012). "The road to hell is paved with good intentions": Ahistorical, theoretical, and legal analysis of zero tolerance weapons policies in American schools. *Preventing School Failure, 56*(4), 232–240.

Nolan, K. (2006). *Police in the hallways: Discipline in an urban high school.* Minneapolis: University of Minnesota Press.

Osher, D., Bear, G. G., Sprague, J., & Doyle, W. (2010). How can we improve school discipline? *Educational Researcher, 39*, 48–58.

Pots, K., Njie, B., Detch, E. R., & Walton, J. (2003). *Zero tolerance in Tennessee schools: An update.* http://www.comptroller.state.tn.us/orea/reports/zerotoler2003.pdf

Shaw, L. (2014, April 21). *Suspensions hit minorities, special-ed students the hardest, data show.* http://seattletimes.com/html/education/2023423257_schooldisciplinexml.html

Skiba, R. J., Michael, R. S., Nardo, A. C., & Peterson, R. L. (2002). The color of discipline: Sources of racial and gender disproportionality in school punishment. *The Urban Review, 34*(4), 314–342.

Stader, D. (2004). Zero tolerance policy: The good, the bad, and the ugly. *The Clearing House, 78*(2), 62–66.

The Kirwan Institute. (2015). *Racial disproportionality in school discipline: Impact bias is heavily implicated.* Retrieved from http://kirwaninstitute.osu.edu/racialdisproportionality-in-school-discipline-implicit-bias-is-heavily-implicated/

Timothy, J., & Russo, C. J. (2001). An alternative approach to zero tolerance policies. *School Business Affairs, 67*(7), 43.

United States Department of Education. (2013). *School climate and discipline guidance package.* Retrieved from http://www2.ed.gov/policy/gen/guid/school-discipline/index.html?utm_source=E-News%3A+School+Discipline%2C+Hillary+Clinton%2C+and+Early+Ed&utm_campaign=enews+1%2F15%2F14&utm_medium=email

Verdugo, R. R. (2002). Race-ethnicity, social class, and zero-tolerance policies: The cultural and structural wars. *Education and Urban Society, 35*(1), 50–75.

Hilary Lustick is Assistant Professor of Educational and Community Leadership at Texas State University. She specializes in community leadership, action research methods, and culturally responsive discipline. Her empirical and theoretical research on restorative justice in urban public schools has appeared in *Race, Ethnicity, and Education, International Journal for Leadership and Education,* and the *Youth and Society Series* from Emerald.

CHAPTER 9

Critical Discourse and Twenty-First-Century Education Reform Policy

Jasmine Ulmer and Sarah Lenhoff

INTRODUCTION

In this chapter, we examine how the discourses of education reform intersect with twenty-first-century policies that purport to prepare students to be productive members of a global economy. Through the example of a national reform organization that promises to deliver twenty-first-century skills and competencies for career and college readiness, we demonstrate how discourse shaped and revealed the aims of the program as it was implemented in three high schools. In the process, we approach policy language as a form of discourse. We suggest that education discourse shapes policy initiatives at the same time that it influences the everyday practices of schooling and society. In other words, discourse does more than passively exist in policy documents, speeches, and mission statements. Rather, discourse is active language that—once absorbed into how educational stakeholders think, speak, and act—has the capacity to filter down and influence interactions with individual students. From there, we argue, discourse has the potential to position students (or future workers) within a global

J. Ulmer (✉) • S. Lenhoff
Wayne State University, Detroit, MI, USA

© The Author(s) 2017   175
J.N. Lester et al. (eds.), *Discursive Perspectives on Education Policy and Implementation*, DOI 10.1007/978-3-319-58984-8_9

economy. Put simply, discourse can become policy, which, in turn, can become public pedagogy (Giroux 2004). To demonstrate, we share examples of discourse that reside at the intersection of policy, power, critical theory, and education to illustrate how critical discourse methodologies might inform educational policy research.

This chapter builds upon a larger ethnographic comparative case study that analyzed how the language used to describe a twenty-first-century skills-focused reform organization influenced implementation of the program (Lenhoff and Ulmer 2016). We used a critical approach to discourse (Wodak 2004) to examine the stated and implicit audience for the school reform program, which we called "Transforming Schooling." We found a problematic misalignment regarding the discourses through which the program was described: although the reform organization advertised the program as being "for all" students, local implementers described the program as only being appropriate "for some" students. This misalignment led to deficit discourses that blame low-performing students for not achieving academic success in the program. Findings suggested that local actors would benefit from examining the discursive claims of outside vendors and considering what external reform programs are able to achieve across varied school settings. Furthermore, the study also raised significant questions regarding not only "for whom" the program was intended, but "for what" purpose the program prepared students. In the process of critically examining data, we identified a second potential misalignment between the stated aims of the program and the goals of the leaders charged with implementing it. Because a critical analysis of the purposes of the program was beyond the scope of the previous study, we take up the question of program aims here within this chapter.

We begin by analyzing how the discourse of twenty-first-century education reform has informed three decades of federal policy initiatives. We next discuss a neoliberal policy agenda through the theoretical lens of critical pedagogy before discussing critical discourse from Foucauldian and Freirean methodological perspectives. We then analyze ethnographic data to identify the following discourses that illustrate "for what" students in the reform program were being prepared: "the real world," "corporate culture," and "revenue and growth." We conclude by discussing implications for educational policymakers, educational reform organizations, and local stakeholders. We suggest that an examination of how discourses intersect with policy is important in understanding the objectives and impact of contemporary reform agendas, particularly given the financial incentives associated with the expansion of some reforms.

KEY LITERATURE

Discourses related to twenty-first-century education have permeated educational policymaking in recent decades. The turn of the last century was a rhetorical opportunity for state and federal policymakers alike as the promise of the new millennium emerged alongside the opportunities of an interconnected global economy. According to a vision expressed by politicians, policymakers, and business leaders, the year 2000 had the potential to usher in a bright future. Yet, in order to realize the economic success and prosperity that this future might hold, those in power identified a need for new models of workforce preparation. The educational systems of the past would no longer be adequate for educating students to become workers in this future world. Entrants into the modern workforce would need different skills to navigate what business theorists described as the "New Economy" and the "Next Society" (Drucker 2002). As twenty-first-century discourse shaped twenty-first-century policy frames, public education was charged with providing students with workforce skills for the next century.

Several policy initiatives and events responded to calls for twenty-first-century education. For example, the National Governors Association convened an influential education summit in 1989. The summit led to the unsuccessful federal proposal of *America 2000: An Education Strategy* in 1991 and the subsequent passage of the *Goals 2000: Educate America Act* in 1994. In introducing *America 2000*, President George H.W. Bush outlined the potential for what laid ahead through the discourse of twenty-first-century education. He remarked,

> the 21st century has always been a kind of shorthand of the distant future–the place we put our most far-off hopes and dreams. And today, the 21st century is racing toward us–and anyone who wonders what the century will look like can find the answer in America's classrooms. (U.S. Department of Education 1991, p. 1)

This was a plan, as Bush explained, to "reinvent American education–to design New American Schools for the year 2000 and beyond" (p. 6). After *America 2000* failed to achieve momentum, *Goals 2000* took its place. President William Jefferson Clinton introduced *Goals 2000* by noting that the act would put the country into a strong global position for the twenty-first century. This would be achieved, in part, by "abolish[ing] the outdated distinction between academic learning and skill learning" (Clinton 1994, p. 929). The years that followed saw US education policy discourse move toward an educational system designed to generate skilled workers who would be technology savvy, productive, collaborative, and competitive in a global workforce (Riley 2004; Sahlberg 2006).

The Partnership for 21st Century Skills, known as P21, was instrumental in creating a framework to guide these efforts. The group emerged from a coalition of educational stakeholders, policymakers, and business leaders in 2002.[1] Prominent founders included the U.S. Department of Education, the National Education Association (NEA), and one-half-dozen well-known technology corporations (Partnership for 21st Century Skills [P21] 2016). One of P21's main contributions involved the 2002 release of the Framework for 21st Century Skills, which became the primary reference point for what a twenty-first-century education should entail. The most recent version of the framework (in 2011) contained 5 themes, 5 support systems, and 12 skills. Support systems included standards, assessments, and effective instruction, and skills were categorized into three domains: learning and innovation; information, media, and technology; and life and career. To further streamline the framework, the NEA (2012) later repackaged key skills in the framework into the four Cs: critical thinking, communication, collaboration, and creativity. Each iteration of the framework further refined the language used to describe and implement twenty-first-century education policy.

As schools and other organizations responded to policy language offered by different versions of the Framework for 21st Century Skills, education policy discourse remained attuned to the workforce needs of the business community. The framework already acknowledged some of these needs by including themes related to "financial, economic, business and entrepreneurial literacy." Moreover, P21 had collaborated with business groups to produce reports such as, "Are They Really Ready to Work? Employers' Perspectives on the Basic Knowledge and Applied Skills of New Entrants to the 21st Century U.S. Workplace" (The Conference Board, Corporate Voices for Working Families, the Partnership for 21st Century Skills, & the Society for Human Resource Management 2006). According to this report, US employers remained concerned that incoming workers needed skills related to professionalism/work ethic, oral and written communications, teamwork/collaboration, critical thinking/problem solving, and technology. Consequently, employer needs have encouraged education policies that promote project-based learning, one-to-one computing, and other skills that educational technology can support.

The influence of twenty-first-century discourse upon education policy contributed to the creation of a large (and expanding) school improvement industry. As Rowan (2002) observed,

> more than 80% of all local education agencies in the United States contract with outside sources for professional and technical services in a given year, services that are provided by over 3,700 business establishments earning over $3.7 billion per year. (p. 289)

At that time, the overall educational reform industry was valued at $17 billion with an anticipated annual growth rate of 10 percent (Rowan 2002). In 2009, Burch estimated that the federal and state expenditures on education totaled more than $750 billion annually, of which $80 billion went to external vendors. Accordingly, the availability of public education funds as an untapped market remain of great interest to venture capitalists and private entities (English 2016). From a neoliberal perspective, it could be argued that the discourse of twenty-first-century education not only is concerned with providing economic opportunity for students, but that it has increased economic opportunity for external providers, as well.

Given the commodification of education and the proliferation of reform organizations promising to deliver future workforce competencies and skills, it is important to examine the ways in which reforms are positioned as being available for purchase. This is particularly the case in a climate of privatization, deregulation, decentralization, and globalization (Singh et al. 2005). Although researchers have investigated the conditions under which educational reforms are likely to be effective (e.g., Barron et al. 1998; Penuel 2006), few studies have examined the implications of the policy language used to sell, buy, and implement those same policies—including policies related to twenty-first-century education reform. Such an examination is significant in a time when educational services function as economic commodities and public education operates in a market economy.

METHODOLOGICAL AND THEORETICAL PERSPECTIVE

Because the organization we refer to as Transforming Schooling is a curriculum reform program, we turn to critical pedagogy scholars and philosophers who have theorized about discourse. In so doing, we draw from Henry Giroux, Peter McLaren, Michel Foucault, Paulo Freire, and others to situate this chapter within critical methodological and theoretical perspectives. Each of these scholars emphasize pedagogy throughout their respective works as a contested site of cultural politics (e.g., Foucault 1977; Freire 2000; Giroux 1992, 2003; McLaren 1999, 2015).

Critical pedagogy scholars often use discourse to theorize how curriculum is shaped by economic trends. They approach discourse as a "form of cultural production, linking agency and structure through the ways in which public and private representations are concretely organized and structured within schools" (Giroux 1988, p. 199). Discourse, in this regard, becomes a means of transmitting, producing, and reproducing power. In the process, the ways in which power and discourse interact provide an important theoretical account of how language, history, politics, and experience join forces to "produce, define, and constrain" elements of educational practice (p. 196). It is within these contexts that Giroux (2003) suggests that educational leaders have prioritized opportunities for commercial investment at the expense of social improvement. This is why he describes the need for "new understanding[s] of how culture works as a form of public pedagogy; how pedagogy works as a moral and political practice; how agency is organized through pedagogical relations; [and] how politics can make the workings of power visible and accountable" (Giroux 2004, p. 502). Critical discourse offers a means to generate the new understandings of pedagogy and politics for which he calls.

Critical discourse emphasizes how and why particular knowledges are generated within particular times, places, systems, and institutions, including—and especially—through the use of pedagogy (McLaren 2003b).[2] To illustrate, critical pedagogy scholars view curriculum as "much more than a program of study, a classroom text, or a course syllabus. Rather, it represents the *introduction to a particular form of life; it serves in part to prepare students for dominant or subordinate positions in the existing society*" (McLaren 2003a, p. 86, emphasis in original). This is part of a hidden curriculum that, according to McLaren (1999, 2015), reproduces hegemonic interests and works to maintain a compliant working class. Notably, Giroux and McLaren theorize pedagogy and critical discourse alongside other scholars (e.g., Carlson and Apple 1998; Hall 2001; hooks 1994) whose works are informed by Michel Foucault and Paulo Freire.

Foucault's macro-analytical stance provides insight into how discursive language influences society. He often writes of the ways in which institutions produce discourse, including educational systems. For Foucault (2002), discourses are constituted by a series of related statements. Discourses are a form of power/knowledge that reveal and reference the invisible structures of society that govern how we talk, write, think, and act (Foucault 1980). Yet, as Foucault (1977) explains, discursive practices do more than produce discourse: "They are embodied in technical processes, in institutions, in patterns for general behavior, in forms for transmission and diffusion, and in pedagogical forms which, at once, impose and maintain them" (p. 200). In other words, pedagogies create and receive discourse. This is significant within the context of a twenty-first-century education discourse because pedagogies transmit a policy emphasis upon skills and global economic competitiveness; at the same time, pedagogies also work to "impose and maintain" messaging around twenty-first-century learning. Discourse constitutes pedagogy as pedagogy constitutes discourse.

Alongside Foucault, we also take up Freire. Although offering a useful approach to discourse taken in and of itself, each theorist emphasizes pedagogy and discourse differently. For Foucault, pedagogy is a secondary apparatus that shapes and takes its shape from discourse. For Freire, in contrast, pedagogy *is* discourse. Whether developing a pedagogy of the oppressed (2000), freedom (2001), or hope (2014), Freire situates different pedagogies within different macro discourses of society. In this sense, Freirean discourses produce social practices as social practices simultaneously produce discourses (Freire 2001). This is not incommensurate with Foucauldian approaches to discourse. Rather, we draw distinctions between the two theorists because Foucault's interests lie in discourse, whereas Freire's interests lie in pedagogy. It is the intersection thereof that generates productive understandings of the interrelationships between discourse and pedagogy in twenty-first-century education reform policy. The confluence of discourse, pedagogy, and politics is important to examine because, as Freire (2000) writes, "The language of the educator or politician... like the language of the people, cannot exist without thought; and neither language nor thought can exist without a structure to which they refer" (p. 96). Through Freire and Foucault, then, we examine the discursive structures of twenty-first-century education policy reforms as they emerged over the course of this study.

METHOD/ANALYTIC APPROACH

As we have described in the previous section, our analytic approach resides at the nexus of Foucauldian and Freirean discourse. Because we examine discourses that have the potential to illustrate the hidden aims and unintentional effects of twenty-first-century policy reforms, these discourses reveal power differentials and the implications thereof in selected schools. In this section, therefore, we begin by providing brief descriptions of the study site and data collection procedures. We then return to Freire and Foucault to explain our analytic approach.

Research Setting and Context

We build upon previous research that examines how three high schools implemented a twenty-first-century skills reform program (Lenhoff and Ulmer 2016). Over the last two decades, the organization Transforming Schooling has grown from a small, project-based reform initiative in one US high school into a full-scale reform model that now operates in more than 150 elementary and secondary schools in the US (as well as several schools outside the country). This growth, in part, can be attributed to its acquisition by, and subsequent spin-off from, a reform network with a broad portfolio of reform projects. Some of the Transforming Schooling implementation sites have been recognized by P21 as "exemplars of 21st century learning," and the organization has successfully acquired external funding from federal and philanthropic sources. Day-to-day operations are managed by a small number of staff at headquarters; most employees work from remote sites to support implementation in schools.

Three Transforming Schooling sites were examined in this study. All were high schools in a Midwestern state that began implementing the reform program in 2010. Sites differed by school characteristics, student demographics, and previous academic success. School 1, located in a small city, performed in the top quartile statewide. School 2, a suburban school within a school, performed around the state average. School 3, located outside a large metropolitan area, contracted with Transforming Schooling after failing to meet adequate yearly progress; joining the lowest 5 percent of schools in the state; and becoming a School Improvement Grant program site. Student populations also varied across school sites. School 1 primarily served white, middle-income students, whereas Schools 2 and 3 served more students of color and from low-income households.

Data Collection

As described previously in more detail (Lenhoff and Ulmer 2016), we collected data in two phases. Lenhoff collected data from 2010 to 2012 as part of a larger ethnographic comparative case study. The initial dataset included semi-structured interviews ($n = 20$), participant observations ($n = 37$), organization documents ($n = 44$), and publicly available online materials ($n = 6$). Lenhoff also conducted interviews with Transforming Schooling staff and personnel in local school sites (such as classroom teachers, instructional coaches, school principals, and district administrators). Interview questions investigated participants' perspectives on pedagogical and curriculum reforms and were supplemented by more than 120 hours of participant observations across sites. Both authors then collected follow-up materials created between 2010 and 2015 to examine changes in the organization's external discourse over time; these data were sourced from websites, videos, press releases, and other promotional materials.

Analytic Approach

When conducting our previous discursive examination of the intended audience of the reform program, we noticed discrepancies between the stated and the actual aims of the program. In developing this chapter, we re-read the datasets to look for discursive statements that revealed the objectives of the reform program. We drew from Foucault to identify these statements and to consider the ways in which they contributed to broader discourses. This was an iterative process in which we repeatedly compared analyses with data to identify potential discourses. This also offered a means of producing validity through repeated readings and saturated analysis of data (per Jäger 2001). In addition, we found that a move toward Freire necessitated an additional, yet important, analytical strategy. Given that Foucault primarily seeks to identify discursive formations, whereas Freire seeks to liberate people from them, the combination of Foucault and Freire involved (1) critically questioning the statements that create discursive formations (Jessup and Rogerson 2004) and (2) considering how they might translate into transformative aims. Put simply, analysis is insufficient in and of itself for Freire. Rather, analysis should also lead to the potential for action. As such, we report our analysis of data in the findings section before discussing how Freirean approaches to pedagogy might provide a grassroots counterbalance to the top-down discourses of twenty-first-century education reform.

FINDINGS

We found that the aims of twenty-first-century learning could be distilled into three discourses across study sites: "for the real world," "for corporate culture," and "for revenue and growth." Notably, these discourses differ from the stated aims of Transforming Schooling. In online and informational materials, the school reform organization instead advertised itself as being "for" college readiness, career readiness, and civic life. Such promotional discourses were present in the organization's outward-facing website (which included optimistic reports, infographics, videos, and text). To a lesser extent, the discourses of college readiness, career readiness, and civic life were espoused by reform organization leadership as well. On-site observations and in-depth interviews, however, presented significant differences between the ideals of what the reform program claimed to be "for" and the realities that drove day-to-day priorities in reform schools and classrooms. As we shall explain, this contributed to discursive misalignment and disappointment on the part of some implementers. Even though teachers expressed support for the organization's stated goals of preparing students for college, career, and civic life, they also expressed discomfort with being asked to fulfill goals that were thought to be unfeasible or did not align with their expectations of appropriate college preparatory pedagogy.

For the "Real World"

When asked what the Transforming Schooling program was preparing students "for," reformers and implementers used the term "real world." Yet, rather than preparing students to succeed in a "real world" of college, career, and civic life through rigorous collegiate pedagogy, the program often seemed to prepare students for low-skill jobs in the global marketplace. For example, when a school reform coach and classroom teacher discussed a female student with challenging behaviors, they discussed this student's future in terms of whether or not she would be able to work in a fast-food drive-through window without swearing at customers.

It was not, however, that teachers were not interested in exposing students to high-level collegiate thinking and college-preparatory content. They were. This is part of why teachers expressed frustration that they could not "do everything." To illustrate, multiple teachers in Schools 1 and 2 were observed as saying that they felt an uncomfortable tension with having to choose between what they considered necessary college-prep content and the "real world" skills that were part of the program, such as collaboration. As one teacher leader at School 3 explained, preparing students for the "real world" meant preparing students to work as a member of a team to be successful in collegiate settings. This same teacher leader, however, was unsure whether or not college was a realistic goal for many students:

> *These kids seriously will get D's and E's back on their projects and still think 'I'm going to be a veterinarian.' So the mindset is completely off. And that is something that is a district cultural issue. It is not just a [reform program] cultural issue. Because these kids have always been told, 'oh, you can do this.' And that is fine to have hopes for kids, but at the same time ...*

This teacher ultimately believed that students are responsible for themselves and shared that the school reform program "cannot change students' mentalities. I think it can only give them a new direction." Notably, she was not the only teacher to question whether or not students had the capacity to succeed within the program. Other teachers also expressed frustration at what they perceived to be a misalignment between what the Transforming Schooling program purported to be for and what they believed was possible in practice. This frustration manifested in deficit views of students, in which teachers blamed students and their circumstances for not being able to prepare them for college, career, and civic life. Importantly, however, the Transforming Schooling staff was unresponsive to teachers' concerns that students were not meeting expectations, leading coaching staff to in turn view teachers through deficit lenses.

For Corporate Culture

The Transforming Schooling model was transmitted to teachers, in part, through training visitations to model schools throughout the organization, known as demonstration sites. For some teachers, these demonstration sites perpetuated corporate culture and pedagogy. More specifically, visiting a demonstration site allowed teachers to experience firsthand what implementation of the curriculum should look like; the practices on display in demonstration schools then were to be emulated when teachers returned home to their own schools. Teachers were able to travel to demonstration sites located in other states. In recalling a demonstration site visit, one science teacher at School 1 expressed being overwhelmed by the nature of both the students and facilities:

> *You walk in and it is like every student center or commons is like a fine university. It is open spaces and kids sitting at a little café table working and I had never seen this in a high school and I am like, 'this is like a college campus.' You know huge... little work areas and lounges and you know big lighting and very high ceilings and glass block and very, very professional looking—more like a corporate office than a traditional school.*

Though the teacher began to describe aesthetics of the school as something that might belong on an elite college campus, the discussion quickly shifted into the professional, and hence corporate, appearance of the reform school. This underlying emphasis on corporate culture was present throughout multiple data sources, including interviews, observations, and organizational rubrics.

As previously mentioned, educators repeatedly expressed concerns about spending too much time teaching twenty-first-century skills and not enough time teaching content. A humanities teacher at School 2 reported that because the reform organization "is mainly concerned with preparing students for the business workplace," the program did not serve students who did not want to go into business well. The second author observed classroom activities in which students pretended to work for a major corporate entity and constructed business pamphlets, guides, infomercials, and digital portfolios. Across the reform organization and school sites, teachers and instructional leaders used terms that invoked corporate imagery when describing curriculum and pedagogy, such as "project briefcase" (a lesson plan bank) and "systematize the school structure." Teachers then reflected business language back to instructional coaches. Instead of asking how students might work together more effectively in groups, they asked questions such as, "How do we get teams to be synergistic?" In the same professional development session in which teachers were being trained to fit their classrooms into a corporate-style culture, teachers indicated that there were not enough opportunities provided to reflect upon their own instructional practice.

Corporate language also was embedded throughout a 2010 version of a rubric that describes expectations for successful school sites; little has changed in the four years following initial data collection, according to recent information on the organization's website. To illustrate, a criterion for advanced-level proficiency in the rubric involved aligning school culture with the "professional environment of the workplace." The involvement and support of business partners were key throughout the rubric. Indicators of advanced-level proficiency included program alumni who garner reputations as entrepreneurs, external partnerships in which businesses function in an advisory capacity and provide fiscal resources and support to schools, and climates in which businesses and other community groups perceive schools as valuable assets (and again provide resources and financial support). Each of these indicators was predicated upon Transforming Schooling sites fostering active participation from business partners in their local communities.

For Revenue and Growth

In following the overall strategy of hosting site visits, one district hosted a partners breakfast to advertise the school reform program to the local business community, targeted industries (e.g., manufacturing, health care, and a nearby major research university), as well as politicians and media outlets. Per organizational rubrics, the goals were not only to find local business partners who might be able to support students at a later date, but also generate goodwill and a positive reputation for the reform organization. At the breakfast, a principal began by discussing economic prosperity and the need to increase students' ability to generate income, especially in a difficult economy.

Even though reform organization personnel stated that community tours generally are discouraged in the first year of operations, a district leader seemed particularly fixated on tours, including whether or not outside visitors could be charged admission fees for tours. This leader told school principals that they should always be "on" so that tours can be scheduled "whenever"; school leaders indicated that they would be able to host as many as two visits each month, with somewhere between 20 and 25 guests per visit. Reform staff did not discourage this and indicated that tours provide students with opportunities to be guides while allowing teachers to reinforce skills that they are trying to teach, "like money."

As the organization continued to expand in scale, funding continued to be a major focus. In part, funding concerns were tied to larger economic challenges and changes in federal spending. As one school leader explained in an interview, principals across the organization share fundraising ideas:

Where are you going to find pockets of money, unless you go to industry themselves? So I think that there's a benefit to being a school that is focused on providing the needs that industry is asking for and that businesses are asking for, so in return for producing these students... we're looking for help in placing kids in internships. We're also looking for help in finding financial resources as well. Once you privatize everything, who do you go to for funding if you can't go to tax dollars?

The funding alluded to here was not simply the estimated $150,000 annual fee for reform organization support, or maintaining staffing in the face of salary reductions and teacher layoffs, but also funding to support the expansion of new reform school sites. With regard to scaling up, one instructional coach explained that organizational leaders had begun to tie bonuses and raises to the creation of new school reform sites. In fact, there were several strategies employed by Transforming Schooling in order to scale up the program throughout the country: (1) become certified as a preferred service provider to failing schools that were required to partner with an outside entity to support turnaround efforts, (2) expand the program into elementary and middle schools, and (3) offer a special "certification" for teachers who completed the appropriate Transforming Schooling training. These certified Transforming Schooling teachers could then serve as surrogates for the organization itself. By way of illustration, School 3 was a new effort by Transforming Schooling to expand into low-performing "turnaround" schools. These efforts have continued to occur since the initial data collection in 2010.

The growth of external funding seemed equally important. One reform district liaison anticipated that millions of dollars in federal funding might be allocated to the state for college access. This leader viewed this as a "legitimate partnership opportunity" for Transforming Schooling reform sites, especially given that—according to this liaison—major philanthropic foundations indicated that they would rather sub-grant to reform organizations than allocate money directly to schools. Transforming Schooling later was awarded a substantial grant from a national philanthropic foundation to pilot math and literacy modules aligned with the Common Core State Standards Initiative (2016).

Summary

Twenty-first-century education policy reforms have led scholars to debate the influence of corporations and private entities in public education (Labaree 1997; Reckhow and Snyder 2014). Increasingly, these debates are predominately international in scope (Ball 2007, 2012; Davies and Bansel 2007). Because a globalized economy relies upon a workforce with a particular set of skills—such as those promoted by twenty-first-century reform organizations—the spheres of economics and education have converged. This convergence creates questions regarding the intended purposes of education reform policy, including whether reforms are designed to produce "real world" competencies, reproduce corporate culture, or stimulate revenue and growth for outside entities. This convergence also serves to explain, as Giroux (2003) writes, how "[c]orporate culture does not reside only in the placement of public schools control of corporate contractors. It is also visible in the growing commercialization of school space and curriculums" (p. 121). As economic considerations inform education, the ways in which schools reflect public and private agendas cannot be separated from discourse (Giroux 1988).

Critical policy scholars in education, therefore, might turn to critical discourse studies as a means of studying the effects of globalization on pedagogy, politics, and policy.[3] As we have shown here, Foucault potentially helps scholars to identify discursive statements and formations. Similarly, Freire potentially helps scholars to consider the effects of pedagogical discourse, particularly as it intersects with language, power, politics, history, ideology, and society.

Therefore, in considering how this study extends the use of critical theory, we conclude by discussing the transformative aims of critical research. Both Foucault and Freire inspire different critical moves. Foucault encourages scholars to critically question discursive policy formations, whereas Freire encourages scholars to move toward collective and collaborative action. When Foucault's conceptualizations of power as a productive force are considered alongside Freire's critical social consciousness, their writings highlight possibilities that are already present within education. It is within this vein that critical research might engage

schools as sites of possibility, that is, as places where particular forms of knowledge, social relations, and values can be taught in order to educate students to take a place in society from a position of empowerment rather than from a position of ideological and economic subordination. (Giroux 1988, p. 192)

These engagements might take the form of a local, "situated pedagogy" (Shor and Freire 1987). Such a pedagogy might take shape as "a collaborative discourse... in which thought, action, and reflection combine in informed, enlightened, and committed action" (McLaren and da Silva 1993, p. 56). In the process, discourse might shift from a past-tense analysis to a present-day tool for supporting public educational systems that serve students within a democratic society.

This raises the question of how such a local and situated pedagogy might be constructed. In turning to Freire and scholars who have drawn from his work, we briefly describe one promising avenue through which this might occur: a critical pedagogy of place. For Gruenewald (2003), place-based pedagogies are designed to positively shape both the social and ecological places in which people live. This involves "read[ing] the texts of our own lives and... making a place for the cultural, political, economic, and ecological dynamics of places whenever we talk about the purpose and practice of learning" (p. 10–11). In these ways, a critical pedagogy of place decenters educational aims that support corporate culture, revenue, and growth. Instead, it offers a move toward social, ethical, and environmental responsibility, as well as a future in which students are critical thinkers and community members rather than corporate commodities. Rather than scale purportedly one-size-fits-all twenty-first-century education reform models, then, curriculum reform organizations might be repurposed to scale difference through critical place-based education. This might involve variations on social justice curriculum, ecopedagogy, Indigenous education, and other approaches to teaching and learning that recognize "expanded notion[s] of justice demanded by the recognition of the interrelationship among culture, economics, and environment" (Gruenewald 2005, p. 206). In so doing, place-based discourses might re-imagine education as a series of local systems that are designed to serve students and the unique, diverse, and vibrant places in which they live. Given that the twenty-first century has only just begun, there is time yet for such alternative visions to emerge.

In sum, rethinking the productive power of discourse is important in educational policy. Freire (2000) repeatedly emphasizes how pedagogy can create social change *with* people rather than create social change *for* people. Analyses of who and what policy is for, then, might consider the ways in which Freire discourages top-down policy solutions in favor of grassroots, participatory, and dialogical change. Creating change on behalf of people, as Freire suggests, creates a power imbalance that privileges elite and powerful members of society, often at the expense of those whom they are claiming to serve and protect. Freire's writings thus offer a productive lens through which others might pair critical theory with critical discourse. Such a pairing might further examinations of who creates twenty-first-century education policies, how they are implemented within a particular reform program, and who and what potentially benefit.

Key Connections to Policy Research
1. Education leaders may want to consider the ways in which the goals for their schools align with the stated goals of potential education reform partners, as misalignment could disrupt implementation.
2. Before selecting an education reform program, education leaders may benefit from evaluating whether the program's stated goals are supported through implementation mechanisms and messages to teachers and students.
3. Language can shape implementation of reform; therefore, education reformers may consider how the messages they convey through promotional materials, training, and discussions about implementation are aligned with reform goals.
4. Critical theories can inform discursive studies in educational policy.

NOTES

1. P21, or the Partnership for 21st Century Skills, since has changed the longer version of its name to the Partnership for 21st Century Learning.
2. In this chapter, we take up critical discourse studies through the writings of Foucault and Freire. This approach slightly differs from that of Critical Discourse Analysis (CDA). We make this choice because CDA emphasizes sociolinguistic traditions, whereas critical discourse studies tend to be more closely aligned with theoretical readings of data. Because we draw from critical pedagogy scholars who work within the field of critical discourse studies, we make similar moves for the purposes of methodological and theoretical consistency.
3. It is important to note that Foucault and Freire are but two potential critical theorists who might inform discursive policy studies. For example, critical

scholars might also consider the writings of Mikhail Bakhtin or Hannah Arendt. Each of these scholars offers a number of concepts that could inform, enhance, and expand discursive policy studies in education.

REFERENCES

Ball, S. J. (2007). *Education plc: Understanding private sector participation in public sector education.* Oxon: Routledge.

Ball, S. J. (2012). *Global Education Inc.: New policy networks and the neo-liberal imaginary.* Oxon: Routledge.

Barron, B. J., Schwartz, D. L., Vye, N. J., Moore, A., Petrosino, A., Zech, L., & Bransford, J. D. (1998). Doing with understanding: Lessons from research on problem-and project-based learning. *Journal of the Learning Sciences, 7*(3–4), 271–311.

Burch, P. (2009). *Hidden markets: The new education privatization.* New York: Routledge.

Carlson, D., & Apple, M. (1998). Introduction: Critical educational theory in unsettling times. In D. Carlson & M. Apple (Eds.), *Power/knowledge/pedagogy: The meaning of democratic education in unsettling times* (pp. 1–40). Boulder: Westview Press.

Clinton, W. J. (1994). *Public papers of the presidents of the United States: 1994.* Washington, DC: United States Government Printing Office.

Common Core State Standards Initiative. (2016). About the standards. Retrieved January 12, 2016 from http://www.corestandards.org/about-the-standards/

Davies, B., & Bansel, P. (2007). Neoliberalism and education. *International Journal of Qualitative Studies in Education, 20*(3), 247–259.

Drucker, P. (2002). *Managing in the next society.* Oxford: Butterworth-Heinemann.

English, F. (2016). Toward a metanoia of global educational leadership. In R. Papa & F. English (Eds.), *Educational leaders without borders: Rising to global challenges to educate all* (pp. 63–82). Cham: Springer.

Foucault, M. (1977). History of systems of thought. In D. F. Bouchard (Ed.), *Language, counter-memory, practice: Selected essays and interviews* (D. F. Bouchard & S. Simon, Trans.) (pp. 199–204). Ithaca: Cornell University Press.

Foucault, M. (1980). *Power/knowledge: Selected interviews and other writings, 1972–1977.* New York: Pantheon.

Foucault, M. (2002). *The archaeology of knowledge* (A. M. Sheridan Smith, Trans.). New York: Vintage (Original work published 1969).

Freire, P. (2000). *Pedagogy of the oppressed* (M. B. Ramos, Trans.). New York: Bloomsbury Publishing (Original work published 1970).

Freire, P. (2001). *Pedagogy of freedom: Ethics, democracy, and civic courage* (P. Clarke, Trans.). Lanham: Rowman & Littlefield (Original work published 1998).

Freire, P. (2014). *Pedagogy of hope: Reliving pedagogy of the oppressed* (R. R. Barr, Trans.). London: Bloomsbury Publishing (Original work published 1992).

Giroux, H. A. (1988). Critical theory and the politics of culture and voice: Rethinking the discourse of educational research. In R. R. Sherman & R. B. Webb (Eds.), *Qualitative research in education: Focus and methods* (pp. 189–209). New York: Routledge Falmer.

Giroux, H. A. (1992). *Border crossings: Cultural workers and the politics of education.* New York: Routledge.

Giroux, H. A. (2003). Education incorporated? In A. Darder, M. Baltodano, & R. D. Torres (Eds.), *The critical pedagogy reader* (pp. 119–125). New York: Routledge Falmer.

Giroux, H. A. (2004). Public pedagogy and the politics of neo-liberalism: Making the political more pedagogical. *Policy Futures in Education, 2*(3–4), 494–503.

Goals 2000: Educate America Act of 1994, 20 U.S.C. § 5801 (1994).

Gruenewald, D. A. (2003). The best of both worlds: A critical pedagogy of place. *Educational Researcher, 32*(4), 3–12.

Gruenewald, D. A. (2005). More than one profound truth: Making sense of divergent criticalities. *Educational Studies, 37*(2), 206–215.

Hall, S. (2001). Foucault: Power, knowledge and discourse. In M. Wetherell, S. Taylor, & S. J. Yates (Eds.), *Discourse theory and practice: A reader* (pp. 72–81). London: Sage.

hooks, b. (1994). *Teaching to transgress.* New York: Routledge.

Jäger, S. (2001). Discourse and knowledge: Theoretical and methodological aspects of a critical discourse and dispositive analysis. In R. Wodak & M. Meyer (Eds.), *Methods of critical discourse analysis* (pp. 32–62). Thousand Oaks: Sage.

Jessup, H., & Rogerson, S. (2004). Postmodernism and the teaching and practice of interpersonal skills. In S. Barrett, C. Komaromy, M. Robb, & A. Rogers (Eds.), *Communication, care and relationships: A reader* (pp. 74–83). New York: Routledge.

Labaree, D. F. (1997). Public goods, private goods: The American struggle over educational goals. *American Educational Research Journal, 34*(1), 39–81.

Lenhoff, S. W., & Ulmer, J. B. (2016). Reforming for "all" or for "some": Misalignment in the discourses of education reformers and implementers. *Education Policy Analysis Archives, 24*(108), 1–29.

McLaren, P. (1999). *Schooling as a ritual performance: Toward a political economy of educational symbols and gestures* (3rd ed.). Lanham: Rowman & Littlefield.

McLaren, P. (2003a). Critical pedagogy: A look at the major concepts. In A. Darder, M. Baltodano, & R. D. Torres (Eds.), *The critical pedagogy reader* (pp. 69–96). New York: Routledge Falmer.

McLaren, P. (2003b). Revolutionary pedagogy in post-revolutionary times: Rethinking the political economy of critical education. In A. Darder, M. Baltodano, & R. D. Torres (Eds.), *The critical pedagogy reader* (pp. 151–184). New York: Routledge Falmer.

McLaren, P. (2015). *Life in schools: An introduction to critical pedagogy in the foundations of education.* New York: Routledge.

McLaren, P., & da Silva, T. T. (1993). Decentering pedagogy: Critical literacy, resistance and the politics of memory. In P. McLaren & P. Leonard (Eds.), *Paulo Freire: A critical encounter* (pp. 47–89). London: Routledge.

National Education Association. (2012). *An educator's guide to the "four c's": Preparing 21st century students for a global society.* Washington, DC: National Education Association.

Partnership for 21st Century Learning. (2016). Our history. Washington, DC. Retrieved July 12, 2016 from http://www.p21.org/about-us/our-history

Partnership for 21st Century Skills. (2011). Framework for 21st century learning. Washington, DC. Retrieved July 13, 2016 from http://www.p21.org/storage/documents/docs/P21_framework_0116.pdf

Penuel, W. R. (2006). Implementation and effects of one-to-one computing initiatives: A research synthesis. *Journal of Research on Technology in Education, 38*(3), 329–348.

Reckhow, S., & Snyder, J. W. (2014). The expanding role of philanthropy in education politics. *Educational Researcher, 43*(4), 186–195.

Riley, K. A. (2004). Schooling the citizens of tomorrow: The challenges for teaching and learning across the global north/south divide. *Journal of Educational Change, 5*(4), 389–415.

Rowan, B. (2002). The ecology of school improvement: Notes on the school improvement industry in the United States. *Journal of Educational Change, 3* (3–4), 283–314.

Sahlberg, P. (2006). Education reform for raising economic competitiveness. *Journal of Educational Change, 7*(4), 259–287.

Shor, I., & Freire, P. (1987). *A pedagogy for liberation: Dialogues on transforming education.* Westport: Bergin & Garvey.

Singh, M., Kenway, J., & Apple, M. W. (2005). Globalizing education: Perspectives from above and below. In M. W. Apple, J. Kenway, & M. Singh (Eds.), *Globalizing education: Policies, pedagogies, and politics* (pp. 1–29). New York: Peter Lang.

The Conference Board, Corporate Voices for Working Families, the Partnership for 21st Century Skills, & The Society for Human Resource Management. (2006). Are they really ready to work? Employers' perspectives on the basic knowledge and applied skills of new entrants to the 21st century U.S. workplace. Authors. Retrieved July 15, 2016 from http://files.eric.ed.gov/fulltext/ED519465.pdf

U.S. Department of Education. (1991). *America 2000: An education strategy. Sourcebook.* Washington, DC: Author. Retrieved July 12, 2016 from http:// files.eric.ed.gov/fulltext/ED327985.pdf

Wodak, R. (2004). Critical discourse analysis. In C. Seale, G. Gobo, J. F. Gubrium, & D. Silverman (Eds.), *Qualitative research practice* (pp. 185–202). Thousand Oaks: Sage.

Jasmine Ulmer is Assistant Professor of Educational Evaluation and Research at Wayne State University. Her research agenda develops critical qualitative methodologies, including discursive approaches to educational policy studies. Her work has appeared in *Discourse: Studies in the Cultural Politics of Education,* among others.

Sarah Lenhoff is Assistant Professor of Educational Leadership and Policy Studies at Wayne State University. Her research focuses on education policy development and implementation, organizational improvement, school choice and externally sponsored school reform. Her articles have appeared in *American Educational Research Journal, Educational Policy,* and others.

Reading and Dyslexia Legislation: Analytic Techniques and Findings on the Framing of Dyslexia

Rachael E. Gabriel and Sarah Woulfin

Introduction

Reading achievement is frequently used as a barometer for the success of schools and the efficacy of reform efforts. As such, it is often the target of education policy mandates at the state and federal level. In this study, we draw upon framing theory to analyze how education policy problems and solutions related to reading are formulated during the policymaking process (Benford and Snow 2000; Goffman 1974). We are also interested in how language is used to construct particular versions of problems, solutions, and social phenomena, such as reading achievement and reading difficulty. In order to investigate how language is used within written testimony provided to policymakers as education bills were being considered, we conducted a discourse analysis from a social constructionist perspective. In the sections that follow, we describe the context of the legislation of interest, and then discuss our theoretical and methodological approach. We conclude the chapter by describing findings produced from our analysis as they related to understandings of the state's role in education policymaking,

R.E. Gabriel (✉) • S. Woulfin
University of Connecticut, Storrs, CT, USA

© The Author(s) 2017   197
J.N. Lester et al. (eds.), *Discursive Perspectives on Education Policy and Implementation*, DOI 10.1007/978-3-319-58984-8_10

constructions of reading difficulty, and uses of discourse analysis and framing theory for understanding the social construction of education-related phenomena (e.g., achievement, disability) and the subject positions of stakeholders in the education policymaking enterprise.

KEY LITERATURE

Reading Instruction in State and Federal Policy

Literacy instruction (specifically reading assessment, remediation, and instruction) is perhaps the most heavily legislated aspect of public schooling in the USA. As represented in Table 10.1, over the past three decades, policymakers have devoted significant attention to issues of reading. While Title I provided funding for the preparation and support of Reading Specialists and reading materials in schools serving low-income students, the National Reading Panel set forth particular sets of ideas about what counts as appropriate and effective reading instruction. Reading First, a branch of the 2001 No Child Left Behind Act, allocated resources to states implementing systematic, explicit reading programs that specified lessons on the Big 5: phonemic awareness, phonics, fluency, vocabulary, and comprehension. Currently, many states and districts are refocusing efforts around enacting Common Core-aligned literacy instruction and assessments, and/or adjusting to the latest iteration of each state's high-stakes testing program.

As the timeline (Table 10.1) demonstrates, reading instruction, assessment, and/or achievement have often been at the center of education-related policies at the federal level, with reading cast as both a problem (low scores indicating lack of competitiveness or equity) and solution (reading professionals, materials, and accountability solve problems of competitiveness or equity) to broader social phenomena, including poverty, equity, equality, and social economic opportunity.

The timeline (Table 10.1) indicates a pattern of federal involvement in reading instruction that, with one notable, failed exception, is limited to either (a) investigating the state and impact of reading achievement or (b) funding positions, programs, and people aimed at increasing equal opportunities to develop literacy. The exception to this pattern was the prescriptive package of coaching, instruction, assessment, and remediation activities included in the NCLB's (2001) Reading First program, which was discontinued when it failed to achieve desired results. The nature and

Table 10.1 Timeline of federal reading policies

1964—Economic Opportunity Act funded headstart programs to provide educational materials and opportunities to low-income children

1965—Elementary and Secondary Education Act (ESEA)—Title I funded Reading Specialists and reading materials for schools serving low-income schools

1969—National Assessment of Educational Progress (NAEP, the "Nation's Report Card") is administered for the first time, and resulted in the collection of nationwide statistics on reading and mathematics achievement

1983—President Reagan commissioned a report on the state of education in the United States, *A Nation at Risk*, used NAEP data to sound the alarm on American competitiveness and spark the interest/involvement of the business community in education and the standards movement for teachers and students

1997—Congress funded an interdisciplinary National Reading Panel that would evaluate existing research and evidence to find the best ways of teaching children to read. Their report and summary document was finished in 2000 and widely circulated in 2001

2001—No Child Left Behind Act (NCLB) included the Reading First program, which required low-performing schools to adopt a particular model for reading coaching, assessment, and instruction in grades K-3 based, in part, on the findings of the National Reading Panel

2004—Reauthorization of the Individuals with Disabilities Education Act (IDEA) required providing adequate instruction and intervention for students to help keep them out of special education. Response to Intervention programs in reading and math were created in response

2007—A federally funded Reading First Impact Study concluded that the $1 billion/year program increased time for reading instruction and the use of particular instructional practices, but had no impact on students' comprehension and only a small impact on decoding achievement. The program was subsequently defunded

2016—Every Student Succeeds Act (ESSA) includes the "Literacy Education for All, Results for the Nation" ("LEARN") grants for new school libraries, and grants to states to create comprehensive K-12 literacy programs

substance of reading assessment, instruction, and remediation has been left to the states and/or to individual districts.

State Policies Related to Reading

Reading assessment, instruction, and remediation are referenced in the text of more state legislation than any other academic subject because of the fundamental and far-reaching implications of basic and critical literacies. Literacy rates are mentioned in legislation related to housing, incarceration, health, and civic responsibility, and the development of literacy is a major focus of legislation related to educational experiences for general and specific populations from early childhood through adult life. Unlike federal legislation, state legislation is often much more specific and can be more prescriptive about *how* reading is assessed, taught, and remediated. However, state legislators must contend with the wide range of approaches, ideologies, and politics associated with reading instruction. Though the National Reading Panel's report and summary tried to cut through the many controversies about the research base for effective beginning reading instruction, the primacy and diversity of understandings of reading, explanations for reading difficulty, and efforts to support meaningful growth continue to proliferate. Efforts to dramatically improve trends in beginning reading or adolescent and adult literacy rates seem to be a permanent fixture on the policymaking agendas of states and municipalities. Yet, adolescent literacy rates have remained stagnant over the past 30 years, and researchers consistently identify differences in the measured achievement of students based on gender, class, race, disability label, and language learner status. This has led to a combination of legislation that addresses literacy as part of broader social policies, tax and funding policies, and more specific policies related to subgroups of students, including those who have difficulty learning to read.

State Policies Related to Dyslexia

Over the past 5 years, more than 24 states have considered and/or passed revisions to laws concerning the reading instruction, specifically legislation related to the instruction of children with dyslexia (Youman and Mather 2013). The term "dyslexia" refers to a specific kind of learning disability that manifests in the area of reading. It is itself a contested category within and outside of educational policy settings (Elliott and Grigorenko 2014). Neuroscientists and developmental psychologists have disagreed about its etiology, diagnostic criteria, and the nature of its relationship to reading disability or reading difficulties in general. Within education, researchers have similarly disagreed about the operational definition, assessment criteria, and instructional implications of dyslexia. More recently, advances in neuroimaging have allowed scientists to develop consensus understandings of several aspects of dyslexia, including its genetic origin, pattern of neural activation, and responsiveness to intervention.

As Elliott and Grigorenko (2014) noted, "questions about the existence or otherwise of dyslexia have raged periodically for many years" (p. 1), but legislation directing educators to screen, identify, assess, and intervene in cases of dyslexia is relatively new. Over the last decade, advocacy groups, most often those mobilized by parents of children with dyslexia, have gained power both in number, influence, and legislative reach. The group "Decoding Dyslexia, a parent-led grassroots movement" (Decoding Dyslexia 2015) has planted chapters organizing for advocacy in 48 states and British Columbia over the last 5 years. Their advocacy mission includes five policy goals:

1. A universal definition and understanding of "dyslexia" in the state education code.
2. Mandatory teacher training on dyslexia, its warning signs, and appropriate intervention strategies.
3. Mandatory early screening tests for dyslexia.
4. Mandatory dyslexia remediation programs, which can be accessed by both general and special education populations.
5. Access to appropriate "assistive technologies" in the public school setting for students with dyslexia.

Items 2–5 are dyslexia-specific versions of mandates that already exist in most states' statutes for reading difficulties in general (e.g., early identification through universal screening, appropriate assessment and intervention, teacher preparation and support). Since reading achievement is a key measure of the success of a school system and/or the impact of reform, there may indeed be multiple pieces of legislation that mandate the same thing for a different purpose (see Table 10.2). Table 10.2 illustrates four current state laws that concurrently require a similar set of reading-related activities (e.g., universal screening). In each case, however, a legislative mandate such as "universal screening" is aimed at different populations of students with potential difficulties (e.g., low-income students, students with dyslexia) with a different intention (e.g., equity in opportunities to achieve based on socioeconomic status vs. access to specific assessments, diagnoses, and remediation programs for students with dyslexia).

Whereas 7 states had laws that specifically mentioned dyslexia prior to 2008, 24 have considered and/or passed related legislation (Davis Dyslexia Association International 2015). Some states have multiple laws addressing dyslexia (e.g., Louisiana with nearly five), while others have only one (e.g., New Hampshire). In other words, activity related to education legislation that specifically targets dyslexia has nearly quadrupled over the last 3 years. This increase can likely be explained by a similar increase in the number and size of advocacy groups focused on dyslexia (Decoding Dyslexia 2015), but

Table 10.2   Matrix of mandates from reading-related legislation in Connecticut

	Act Concerning Early Reading Success Grants, 1999	Act Concerning Closing the Achievement Gap, 2011	Education Reform Act, 2012	Act Concerning Students with Dyslexia, 2015
Universal screening for reading difficulties	X	X	X	X
Progress-monitoring for reading	X	X	X	X
Provision of research-based interventions	X	X	X	X
Preparation of teachers to identify and address reading difficulties	X	X	X	X
Assessment of teachers' knowledge about reading	X	X	X	X
Professional development for teachers focused on reading	X	X	X	X

neither the recent rise in policy activity nor the rise in advocacy efforts has an apparent catalyst. Thus, questions remain about policymaking and implementation of legislation related to dyslexia. Questions related to implementation are especially important in states where new legislative mandates are not explicitly connected to a funding stream. In the instance described within this chapter, legislation related to the achievement gap is part of a package of legislation that includes dedicated funding, but legislation related to dyslexia was proposed and approved in isolation, without a dedicated funding mechanism. In such cases, unfunded mandates related to dyslexia present different levels of burden to districts with varying funding/financial need, which may lead to an unequal distribution of implementation efforts across the state.

Theoretical Framework

Framing theory helps researchers understand the relationship between macro-level ideas, individuals, and organizational change. With the goal of persuading individuals or organizations to mobilize for change, frames promote and justify particular ideas (Benford and Snow 2000). Frames "cast issues in a particular light" (Campbell 2005, pp. 48–49). Accordingly, a frame can emphasize certain ideas, while downplaying others (Coburn 2006; Fiss and Zajac 2006). As Coburn (2006) noted, "policy problems do not exist as social facts awaiting discovery. Rather they are constructed as policymakers and constituents construct the social world as problematic" (p. 343). Framing theory enables an interrogation of the construction of policy problems and remedies. Framing theory has been used in the fields of sociology, political science, and education. Scholars have used framing theory to examine federal welfare and social program legislation, and local policies regarding homelessness (Cress and Snow 2000; Schneider and Ingram 1993). Educational researchers have drawn on framing theory to grapple with the ways in which reading policies and district reforms are defined and communicated (Coburn 2006; Park et al. 2012).

Framing plays a role in defining issues and potential solutions or motivating action at the macro- and meso-levels (Benford and Snow 2000). Diagnostic frames construct the underlying problem, while prognostic frames delineate a solution for an issue. Additionally, motivational frames can inspire other organizational actors to change. Implementation researchers have used frame analysis to attend to the content and objectives of frames (Coburn 2006; Park et al. 2012). Specifically, these researchers have analyzed how principals engage in framing with teachers, as well as district leaders' prognostic framing associated with state education policy in order to understand both the process and pattern of implementation. By attending to the nature and influence of framing within and across organizations, these researchers have applied framing theory at the meso-level.

Similar to the notion that frames construct policy problems, solutions, and motivations, we also draw upon discursive psychology, in that we assume "people use discourse rhetorically in order to accomplish forms of social action," (Jorgensen and Phillips 2002, p. 118); that is, the language of talk and text in particular settings constructs and is constructed by the social realities worked up in that setting. In this way, this chapter reports on micro- and macro-features of dyslexia policy framing. We draw on naturally occurring material, in this case, written testimony submitted to the state legislature, in order to engage with discourse and rhetoric "occasioned" by the policymaking process. In doing so, we engage with what Wetherell (1998) referred to as a synthetic approach to discourse analysis inspired by traditions of discourse analysis that combine fine-grained analysis of the action orientation of talk and text with traditions that engage a broader focus on power and positioning (see Wetherell 1998). Given that written testimony does not include many of the micro features of transcribed talk often analyzed by conversation analysts (Schegloff 1997), including turn-taking sequences, pacing, pauses, and intonation, our analysis attends to the production of text, the sequence of ideas, and word choice. Using extracts that include frames identified within policy-related documents, we engage in a discourse analysis (Potter and Hepburn 2008; Potter and Wetherell 1987) of the construction of reading difficulty as a public policy problem in a northeastern US state. This synthetic approach enables us to highlight the multiple ways in which different stakeholders present the problems of and solutions to reading difficulty, and the subject positions rhetorically identified for various stakeholders.

Methodological Approaches

In order to identify trends in recent dyslexia legislation, we performed a hand search of state legislative databases for each of the 50 states and Washington, DC. Copies of the most recent version of bills ($n = 24$) related to dyslexia in each state were downloaded and compiled for further analysis, which was guided by the following question: What change does this legislation require? Using this question as a focus for reading, we read each bill and created a matrix that described the state, title of the bill, and new requirements.

Our initial analysis proceeded in a four-step process. First, we identified relevant policy documents, as described above. Second, we coded for concepts from framing theory: frame alignment, which includes "the actions taken by those who produce and invoke frames in an attempt to connect these frames with the interests, values, and beliefs of those they seek to mobilize" (Coburn 2006, p. 347); and frame resonance, "the degree to which a frame is able to create such a connection...with individuals and motivate them to act" (Coburn 2006, p. 347). Third, we conducted recoding to identify information related to the following set of linked analytic questions:

1. Who are the actors named in documents related to each bill?
2. What is the problem this bill attempts to address?
3. What is the mechanism by which this bill intends to address the problem?
4. What values and beliefs are made relevant within the description of the problems and policy solutions for each bill?

As a final step, we created a matrix with information related to each of these questions to facilitate comparison and additional interpretation within and across pieces of legislation. Notably, we coded and analyzed data individually, periodically consulting and meeting to co-analyze data and discuss analytic techniques. The collaborative analyses clarified findings and enabled us to martial additional evidence, when necessary, in support (or rejection) of particular claims.

Data for this study also included written testimony received by the education committee as they were considering four recent instances of reading-related legislation. Testimony provided to the committee is scanned and stored in online archives and subject to the state's open meetings law. We also reviewed the latest iteration of each bill and the related law (if applicable). This included the testimony of 148 individuals and organizations and the text of three recent pieces of reading-related legislation: House Bill 6432 (now Public Law 11–85); House Bill 5350; and House Bill 5562. Table 10.3 indicates the number and percentage of written testimonies submitted by stakeholder group. We defined stakeholder groups using labels included in the letterhead or introductory sentences of each submission.

It is interesting to note that there was significant overlap in some cases. Some state organizations submitted testimony for all three bills. For example, the teachers union organizations, and organizations like the state association of boards of education submitted testimony in all three. However, it is important to note that the submissions of organizations and commissions often addressed multiple bills in one letter. That is, organizations regularly commented on several bills at a time as part of regular

Table 10.3 Stakeholder representation

Bill	Non-profit literacy organizations	Teachers/ professors	Parents	People with dyslexia	For-profit companies	Non-profit organizations and school administration
HB5562 (105 total)	6 (5%)	21 (19%)	35 (32%)	15 (14%)	8 (7%)	20 (18%)
HB5350 (20 total)	1 (5%)	2 (10%)	–	–	3 (15%)	14 (70%)
HB6432 (22 total)	–	–	–	–	1 (5%)	21 (95%)

correspondence with the legislature. For this reason, their submission may not indicate a bill of particular interest or priority. In addition to overlap in some of the non-profit organizations across bills, one representative from a for-profit organization which provides professional development to teachers about reading instruction testified for all three bills, even when no other for-profit organizations were present (e.g., HB6432).

There was less overlap with teachers, parents, literacy volunteers, or individuals who self-identified as people with dyslexia. However, there were several instances where a husband and wife would each submit testimony and/or a parent and child from a single family would each submit individual testimony.

We engaged in further analysis of extracts from testimony identified as relating to the problem and solution frames. This stage of analysis took up a discursive framework guided by a social constructionist perspective (Jorgensen and Phillips 2002) within which we assumed that language—in this case the text of written testimony—is constitutive rather than representative or reflective of a social or cognitive reality (Edwards 1997). Specifically, we analyzed the subject positions (Davies and Harre 1990) made available within problem and solution frames by considering both how the speaker identified themselves, and how they used language to position themselves and others within descriptions of problems and solutions related to each policy. We did this by first attending to introductions and then noting what other individuals and entities (e.g., school systems, children, companies, researchers) were made relevant and in what ways.

By engaging in frame analysis to identify extracts, we were able to focus on a subset of more than 300 pages of testimony. We treated each frame as a case. This created a manageable dataset for intensive, line-by-line analysis and allowed us to focus our analysis on segments of text within which we believed participants were engaging in the construction of policy problems and solutions. As described in the previous sections, we coded each frame along multiple dimensions, and we created memos to draft findings and identify supporting evidence. Though it could be argued that all testimony is broadly aimed at constructing problems and solutions, our use of extracts coded as "problem" or "solution" frames enabled us to parse out cases from the testimony. In effect, frame analysis was a mode to funnel and focus data for this particular investigation. However, these analyses are not generalizable across state or policy contexts. Instead, we aim to apply framing theory as a lens to view and comprehend the dynamics of policymaking and implementation. We encourage other scholars to use this theory for studying other policies and contexts.

FINDINGS

Results of the frame analysis included two major themes that reveal important differences in how reading was constructed as a policy problem. In short, within legislation related to the achievement gap, *the ability to read* was framed as a collective challenge exacerbated by socioeconomic problems and ameliorated by policies that simultaneously increase funding and accountability for public schools. On the other hand, *reading difficulty* was framed as an individual problem exacerbated by the public school system and ameliorated only by private providers and particularly for-profit programs (e.g., educational psychologists, consultants, and tutors).

The Ability to Read

Within testimony, frames served to construct a policy problem that reflected poorly on the state as a whole or as a collective of individuals. This statewide problem is illustrated in the example below:

> If you cannot read by third grade, you are not going to make it in school. Our prisons are full of men and women who cannot read and whose reading level is between third and fifth grade. It is the most critical finding in our achievement gap.

The testimony included motivational frames meant to spur action to solve the problem of ability to read. Specifically, in testimony related to the passage of HB5350, a representative of a local non-profit organization stated: "we argue that a child reading at grade level by 3rd grade is a critical public policy issue," noting that literacy rates are tied to prison population sizes and recidivism rates. Motivational frames frequently included references to the prison population and to the reputation of the state by referencing statistics related to the achievement gap. For example, several people reiterated that: "Connecticut has the largest academic achievement gap in the country," and that, "the achievement gap is a broken bridge in our state." Furthermore, they declared that, "these reforms can help put Connecticut in the lead nationally for education innovation."

Diagnostic frames within testimony related to achievement gap legislation were often related to the timing of effective intervention, with an emphasis on addressing low achievement in the early grades, when it can be more readily and economically addressed. For example, a local education lawyer explained:

> I am acutely aware that by the time a student with such difficulties enters middle school or high school a great deal of time and effort must be expended by the district to try and ameliorate the difficulties. Addressing a child's reading needs early on through methods that have been thoroughly researched will reduce the need to expend resources later on.

The connection to research-based methods and references to the cost to districts appeared frequently across frames related to achievement gap legislation.

It follows, then, that many of the prognostic, or solution-oriented, frames included reference to increased funding for early intervention, as well as the universal use of screening and assessment tools used to identify difficulty in the early grades. For example, a non-profit executive wrote:

> Effective schools have an integrated mix of instructional leadership, clear and focused missions, safe and orderly environments, a climate of high expectations for everyone, frequent monitoring of student progress, positive home-school relationships and opportunities for students to learn and have time on task.

The financial burden on the districts for additional testing and services was explicitly linked to the eventual financial burden on the state because of incarceration rates. So the decision to legislate universal screening, research-based methods, and a "third grade trigger law," which suggests students be retained if they are not reading on grade level by third grade, were framed as economic imperatives and as the appropriate expression of moral or social values. Across testimony related to this legislation, references to children and teachers were all general or hypothetical (e.g., "a child" or "children"), rather than personal or individual; this indicates that both the problem and solution of ability to read were framed as a collective, societal issue.

Reading Difficulty

In contrast to the motivational frames for achievement gap legislation focusing on the state or society at large, testimony on reading difficulty, whether told by parents or people with dyslexia labels, were intensely personal. These stories consistently used first names, described individuals, and often highlighted an individual's emotions or emotional damage. For example, one parent began his written testimony with the following personal narrative:

> I'm writing to tell you my story, or more accurately my daughter's story...She will tell you that she is dyslexic and that will probably be all she tells you about herself. She won't tell you that she is beautiful, smart and funny. Or, that she is her daddy's little ladybug. Or, that she is happy. There was a time when she would have but those times are gone, or at least they are few and far between. The system has done this to her.

Stories from personal experiences, such as the examples above, were frequently used to bolster motivational and diagnostic frames. These stories often used emotion words when describing the problem, such as: "disturbing," "frustrating," "painful," or "angry," unlike the broader, generalized statements contained in diagnostic frames related to achievement gap legislation.

Diagnostic frames were largely consistent across testimony related to dyslexia legislation, frequently defining the problem as the failure of public schools or individual teachers to identify and provide adequate services, thereby necessitating the use of outside private consultants to diagnose and remediate difficulty. One example of this is from the opening narrative of another parent (emphasis is original):

> NO TEACHER OR SPECIAL EDUCATOR EVER TOLD US OUR SON OR DAUGHTER ARE DYSLEXIC. We had to figure it out for ourselves, with outside testing and refusing to just accept the words "don't worry, we are handling it."

Though some testimony indicated that the schools should have known because such difficulty runs in the family, or because parents explicitly flagged the possibility, inadequate diagnosis and response on the part of a teacher, school, or district was consistently implicated within diagnostic frames. For example,

I have four children – two are dyslexic. My oldest child is now 20 years old and we never knew he was dyslexic until he was 16 years old. He was given the incorrect, very broad label of "central auditory processing disorder" and never received the proper instruction or intervention for his dyslexia. My son had to navigate school on his own, constantly criticized by teachers as "not trying hard enough" …He graduated high school HATING school and is now on his third college, still struggling through, trying to earn his Bachelor's degree.

Both quotes above share the implication that a school's negligence has caused significant, lifelong harm to individuals. Furthermore, where testimony related to achievement gap legislation positioned parents as central, private consultants, tutors, and programs were repeatedly included in prognostic frames on reading difficulty.

Stakeholders

Continuing our frame analysis, we considered who was engaging in this framing. Thus, we turn our attention to the positioning of stakeholders within each frame. In the section that follows, we discuss the role of parent groups and demographic differences involved in the framing of each reading-related policy in order to understand the motivations and scope of various legislative efforts to improve the teaching and learning of reading. We note, however, that the actors involved in framing dyslexia are markedly different from those implicated by laws aimed at raising reading levels, in general, or providing screens for general reading difficulty. In particular, parents, for-profit organizations, and individuals with reading difficulties were heavily involved in this particular state at the historical moment when dyslexia-specific legislation was passed. Although most submissions come from the same set of non-profit organizations and educational administrators (e.g., superintendents, chancellors), the majority of submissions (46%) for the dyslexia bill came from private citizens, particularly the parents of children with dyslexia. Additionally, though approximately 20 submissions are common for most bills before the education committee, this bill received over 100. This provides evidence of the intensity of interest and debate regarding dyslexia.

Prognostic frames related to achievement gap legislation tended to define two stakeholders as key to the solution to problems described above: parents and the state. The analyzed solution frames contained references to parents and the state, in concert, as solving the achievement gap problem.

For example, the quote below comes from the written testimony of Executive Director of the state's commission on children, and it explains that parents have the most knowledge about their children, while it is the state's responsibility to ensure parents have knowledge about schools.

> The parent trigger brings in parents as a key stakeholder. No one knows better than a parent how a child learns and how a child is performing. But just as you train your superintendents on how to link performance evaluation to teachers in section 3 of this bill, you will need to ensure that parents are trained in knowing what an effective school is.

In this case, the speaker used a combination of an extreme formulation (Pomerantz 1986) "no one knows better," which bolstered the claim by both highlighting and naturalizing the assertion that parents carry important knowledge as common knowledge. The second half of the quote above is directed to the informal "you," referring to the education committee, indicating that it is within their power ("just as you train superintendents"), and it is a necessity ("you will need to ensure") that they support parents in developing their knowledge so that they can advocate on behalf of their children. Similarly, another representative of a non-profit organization wrote: "We laud the inclusion of parental engagement provisions in this bill, as parents are children's first and most important teachers." The pattern of positioning of parents as "key" and "most important" can be found across testimony related to this bill. Ironically, no parents testified in hearings related to this bill, yet they provided the majority of testimony related to dyslexia.

It is important to also consider how these solution frames attribute fault. Both use extreme case formulations when blaming teachers and schools, but achievement gap testimony does so indirectly. That is, testimony related to achievement gap bills highlighted the importance of parents, and of parents who are empowered to hold schools accountable which logically diminishes the importance of schools. In testimony related to dyslexia legislation, teachers' knowledge, expertise, and judgment are directly and frequently challenged within diagnostic frames, and the provision of intensive training for teachers is specifically requested within prognostic frames.

By contrast, testimony related to individuals with dyslexia suggested that teachers were part of the problem. More specifically, frames attributed the difficulty of students with dyslexia to teachers' lack of knowledge and awareness to identify or support students with dyslexia. In scenarios outlined by testimony related to individuals with dyslexia, individual teachers were implicated as the actors required changing in order to ensure adequate identification and remediation of difficulties. In particular, testimony concentrated upon teachers' low knowledge/skills related to reading difficulties and their inconsistent application of systematic reading programs or assessments. And a common prognostic framing was to indicate the need for teachers to be adequately trained. Specifically, many parents asserted that the state should require a specific kind of training for a minimum number of hours as described in the quote from a parent reproduced below:

> It is also interesting to note that I currently have 36 hours of training in Orton-Gillingham instruction (one of the best methods to help children with dyslexia to read and learn) – MORE than all the special education teachers in all the public schools my children have attended. These teachers claim to be OG trained, but when I asked, they have only attended a Saturday workshop for 4–5 hours of training. That is not enough instruction to be considered "trained" in the OG Method, or any other.

The capitalization of "more" functions to draw attention to the significance of the amount of training and to minimize the expertise and understanding of the "all the special ed teachers in all the public schools" with which the speaker has had experiences. The generalizations, "all the teachers" and "all the schools," added weight to the assertion, and the note about the speaker's own advanced training in this area worked to construct her as an expert who knows more than teachers, which further bolstered her claims. References to Orton-Gillingham methods as administered by private tutors based on the prescriptions of private evaluators were very common across testimony submitted by parents, as well as representatives of for-profit education companies.

Despite general recognition that the diagnosis and remediation is a subject of debate among researchers and practitioners, and that Orton-Gillingham methods in particular, though popular, have a questionable research base (Ritchey and Goeke 2006), parents consistently presented diagnosis and Orton-Gillingham intervention as the clear and obvious choice for all students with dyslexia. In order to support this claim, they frequently referenced ideas and statistics from the Yale Center on Dyslexia and Creativity, which is positioned as the local authority on the subject. Such references appear multiple times in parent and for-profit testimony, but one example below illustrates the binary positioning of schools versus private providers.

> We have had numerous PPT/IEP team meetings this year and we are still in dispute about this topic. We are still requesting an independent evaluation to be done at the Learning House in Guilford, CT. My husband and I believe that the school district has not identified our son and the Learning House would be able to identify our son' linguistically and reading barriers. We believe the Learning House would identify and create an individualized reading plan for our son to share with our school district to ensure our son's educational IEP for reading, spelling, and writing interventions would be tailored to his specific reading and writing barriers.

In the situation described above, the parents constructed the school as negligent and obstructionist, while constructing the private provider as the only viable option for parents who want individualized, tailored instruction. The theme of schools being obstructionist resonates across submitted testimonies, often in connection with the theme of lost or wasted time. Delays in diagnosis were measured in years of age or years of school, not months or days, and time spent in school pre-diagnosis was described as frustrating and painful. This construction of the problem of reading difficulty, casting schools in a negative light, used emotion words and personal narratives to bolster frames.

IMPLICATIONS FOR POLICY RESEARCH

As states continue to revise and consider new legislation aimed at improving the identification and of reading difficulties, it is important to understand how reading, and dyslexia specifically, is framed as policy problems. Research is needed on multiple steps of policymaking and implementation because problem frames help direct the selection of solutions and the positioning of stakeholders. Furthermore, this study extends our understanding of the active, contextualized, and, at times, conflicting constructions of educational policy issues. Though schools are viewed as a site for solutions to the problem of achievement gaps in reading, they are viewed as the source of the problem of undetected/untreated dyslexia among individuals. Likewise, though private providers are not present in discussions of reading achievement as a social issue, they are positioned as necessary sources of specialized knowledge and services, which school policies and personnel are lacking. Finally, where dyslexia, constructed as an emotional, individual tragedy connected with a sense of frustration and loss for students and families, low reading achievement among students was constructed as an embarrassing failure of public policy that was discussed in terms of its damage to the state's reputation as much as its potential damage to individual lives. These disparate constructions of different cases of reading difficulty (individual and societal) explain the layering of similar policies, but may also suggest a proliferation of efforts and social realities that stymies policy coherence and therefore limits implementation.

In addition, this study has implications that could guide implementation efforts and future policymaking. Finally, we generated important links between the fields of policy, reading instruction, and organizational sociology. In particular, we uncovered the nature of various stakeholders' framing of reading policy issues. We discussed how the ability to read was framed as a collective concern, while reading difficulty was portrayed as an individualized, personal problem. Additionally, we investigated the rhetorical tools of stakeholders' advocacy related to reading policy in a state. This highlights the interplay between the public and legislators, as well as the narratives and perspectives playing a role in shaping policies.

SUMMARY

In testimony related to reading legislation in this northeastern state, schools were positioned as failing in their missions and as the source of the policy problem. Non-profit organizations (in the case of the Achievement Gap legislation) and parents (in the case of dyslexia legislation) consistently asked the state to step in to hold schools accountable for better outcomes by increasing regulation, accountability, training, and sometimes funding. Teachers, schools, and districts, on the other hand, were consistently positioned as failing to ameliorate problems of ability and difficulty.

While testimony related to the achievement gap suggested that equitable funding and more accountability would decrease the number of students who struggled to learn to read, testimony related to dyslexia suggested that teacher knowledge and the use of particular programs and assessments was required if schools were to "do their job" and educate all children. Further, though teachers and schools were blamed for poor student outcomes in testimony related to both the achievement gap and dyslexia, testimony regarding the achievement gap described hypothetical teachers or teachers as a collective group, and often excused their failures because of weak oversight and professional development. On the other hand, testimony regarding dyslexia was often more personal, describing individual teachers, schools and districts, and describing their actions and knowledge levels inexcusable.

One potential reason for the remarkable consistency in parent framing and positioning is related to the reason for the parent involvement—the involvement of an advocacy organization which provided talking points and templates for letter-writing and testimony construction. However, we were not concerned with the specific volume or number of instances as much as the ways in which certain messages are repeated and become sedimented or taken for granted within communities where such discourses are engaged (Laclau and Mouffe 1985).

Testimony related to the achievement gap and those related to dyslexia used contrasting motivational, diagnostic, and prognostic frames that resulted in different conceptualizations of reading as a policy problem and varied positioning of stakeholders. We suggest that these conflicting perspectives on reading as a policy problem created the appearance that new legislation was needed to (re-)create or layer atop policies that already exist concerning the screening, assessment, and remediation of reading difficulties. Another possibility is that failure to fully implement practices related to screening and remediation for all students remains especially problematic for students with dyslexia. Finally, it could be argued that universal screens and interventions put in place to prevent low achievement in reading are not deemed as sufficient or effective solutions to the problems of individual students whose parents have social, geographic, and financial access to private providers.

Key Connections to Policy Research
1. When analyzing the progression of related policies over time, it is important to understand the content, position, and rhetorical tools within the testimony submitted for consideration in policymaking processes.
2. Investigating both the texts of policy and the texts that contributed to their development can allow analysts to identify exactly how language is used to frame and construct policy problems and legislative remedies.

REFERENCES

Benford, R. D., & Snow, D. A. (2000). Framing processes and social movements: An overview and assessment. *Annual Review of Sociology, 26,* 611–639.

Campbell, J. L. (2005). Where do we stand? Common mechanisms in organizations and social movements research. In G. R. Davis, D. McAdam, W. R. Scott, & M. N. Zald (Eds.), *Social movements and organizational theory* (pp. 41–68). Cambridge: Cambridge University Press.

Coburn, C. E. (2006). Framing the problem of reading instruction: Using frame analysis to uncover the microprocesses of policy implementation. *American Educational Research Journal, 43*(3), 343–379.

Cress, D., & Snow, D. (2000). The outcomes of homeless mobilization: The influence of organization, disruption, political mediation, and framing. *American Journal of Sociology, 105*(4), 1063–1104. Retrieved from http://www.jstor.org/stable/3003888

Davies, B., & Harre, R. (1990). Positioning: The discursive production of selves. *Journal for the Theory of Social Behavior, 20*(1), 43–63.

Davis Dyslexia Association International. (2015). *Dyslegia: A legislative information site.* Retrieved from http://www.dyslegia.com/state-dyslexia-laws/

Decoding Dyslexia. (2015). *Information sheet.* Retrieved from http://www.decodingdyslexia.net/info.html

Edwards, D. (1997). *Discourse and cognition.* London: Sage.

Elliott, C., & Grigorenko, E. (2014). *The dyslexia debate.* Cambridge: Cambridge University Press.

Fiss, P. C., & Zajac, E. J. (2006). The symbolic management of strategic change: Sensegiving via framing and decoupling. *Academy of Management Journal, 49*(6), 1173–1193.

Goffman, I. (1974). *Frame analysis: An essay on the organization of experience.* Boston: Northwestern University Press.

Jorgensen, M., & Phillips, L. (2002). *Discourse analysis as theory and method.* London: Sage.

Laclau, E., & Mouffe, C. (1985). *Hegemony and socialist strategy: Towards a radical democratic politics.* London: Verso.

Park, V., Daly, A. J., & Guerra, A. W. (2012). Strategic framing: How leaders craft the meaning of data use for equity and learning. *Educational Policy, 27*(4), 645–675.

Pomerantz, A. (1986). Extreme case formulations: A way of legitimizing claims. *Human Studies, 9,* 219–229.

Potter, J., & Hepburn, A. (2008). Discursive constructionism. In J. A. Holstein & J. F. Gubrium (Eds.), *Handbook of constructionist research* (pp. 275–293). New York: Guildford.

Potter, J., & Wetherell, M. (1987). *Discourse and social psychology: Beyond attitudes and behaviour*. London: Sage.

Ritchey, K., & Goeke, J. L. (2006). Orton-Gillingham and Orton-Gillingham-based reading instruction: A review of the literature. *Journal of Special Education, 40* (3), 171–183.

Schegloff, E. A. (1997). Whose text? Whose context? *Discourse and Society, 8,* 165–187.

Schneider, A., & Ingram, H. (1993). Social construction of target populations: Implications for politics and policy. *The American Political Science Review, 87* (2), 334–347.

Wetherell, M. (1998). Positioning and interpretative repertoires: Conversation analysis and poststructuralism in dialogue. *Discourse and Society, 9,* 387–412.

Youman, M., & Mather, N. (2013). Dyslexia laws in the USA. *Annals of Dyslexia, 63* (2), 133–153. doi:10.1007/s11881-012-0076-2

Rachael E. Gabriel is Assistant Professor of Literacy Education at the University of Connecticut. She is an associate of the Center for Education Policy Analysis and the Center on Post-Secondary Education and Disability at the University of Connecticut. Her research interests include teacher preparation, development and evaluation, as well as literacy instruction, interventions, and related policies. She is the author of *Reading's Non-Negotiables: Elements of Effective Reading Instruction* (2013) and co-editor of *Evaluating Literacy Instruction: Principles and Promising Practices* (2015) and *Performances of Research: Critical Issues in K-12 Education* (2013). In addition to serving as an associate editor of *Educational Administration Quarterly,* Gabriel is also on the editorial boards of the *American Educational Research Journal, Educational Policy Analysis Archives, Journal of Literacy Research,* and *Reading & Writing Quarterly.*

Sarah Woulfin is Assistant Professor in Neag's Department of Educational Leadership at the University of Connecticut. She studies the relationship between education policy, leadership, and instructional reform. Woulfin is an associate editor for *Educational Administration Quarterly.* She is on the Editorial Review Board of *Reading Research Quarterly.*

CHAPTER 11

Constructing Teacher Effectiveness in Policymaking Conversations

Rachael E. Gabriel

Introduction

Since 2009, 46 states and the District of Columbia have revised policies for the evaluation of teachers, thus ushering in a new generation of tools and approaches for teacher evaluation. State teacher evaluation policies codify definitions of what it means to teach (Raudenbush 2009), what teachers are expected to do (Darling-Hammond 1990, 2013), and which ways of teaching and learning are to be encouraged or resisted by articulating a set of values for classroom teaching and student learning (Connors 2013). By identifying tools and approaches for the measurement of teaching quality, such policies inscribe particular definitions of teacher effectiveness—a construct that has often been debated and reconstituted over the history of research and evaluation in US public schools (Marzano et al. 2012). In this study, I analyze transcripts from the Teacher Evaluation Advisory Committee (TEAC) meetings in Tennessee, which was the first state to pilot and implement a new generation of teacher-evaluation policies. As the forerunner of a national trend, Tennessee's example is regularly highlighted by

R.E. Gabriel (✉)
University of Connecticut, Storrs, CT, USA

© The Author(s) 2017
J.N. Lester et al. (eds.), *Discursive Perspectives on Education Policy and Implementation*, DOI 10.1007/978-3-319-58984-8_11

politicians and reformers alike (Duncan 2012; Garrison 2014; Heitin 2012; Horn and Wilburn 2013). In addition, the consultants involved in Tennessee's initial teacher evaluation policymaking process have since contracted with at least ten other states to craft similar forms of legislation (Gabriel and Paulus 2014). Tennessee is therefore taken as an influential case of teacher evaluation policymaking within which the discourses of evaluation and effectiveness policies can be examined.

KEY LITERATURE

In many ways, the story of new-generation teacher evaluation policies has been a story about public displays of teacher effectiveness, with debates about tools for evaluation in the news (e.g. Gabriel and Lester 2013a), in academic settings (see Baker et al. 2010), in policy settings (e.g. Gabriel and Paulus 2014) and in the courts (Amrein-Beardsley and Collins 2012). Though policies differ across states, new-generation teacher evaluation policies have a great deal in common (Doherty and Jacobs 2013). Unlike their weaker predecessors (Weisberg et al. 2009), they are comprehensive packages of policy that link annual evaluation with other systems related to teacher quality including: mentoring and induction, data use protocols, professional development, merit pay, promotion, hiring/firing and tenure. Accountability through teacher evaluation was at the center of the Obama administration's education agenda, playing a central role in Race to the Top (R2T) grant competition criteria, and criteria for No Child Left Behind (NCLB) waiver applications. The high stakes attached to new-generation policies, and their prominence in national conversations, fueled a series of public debates about measures of teacher effectiveness, as well as large-scale investigations of teacher effectiveness (see Kane and Staiger 2012), which contribute to the social and political context of Teacher Evaluation Advisory Committee (TEAC) conversations and similar conversations across the country.

Researchers have outlined at least two pathways by which teacher evaluation systems might increase overall teacher quality (Firestone 2014): (1) by identifying and providing a rationale for the removal of low-performing teachers and (2) by identifying specific areas for professional development that would increase the average quality of the teaching force. So far, studies of the first pathway indicate that relatively few teachers are found significantly below standard even under new-generation evaluation schemes (e.g. Anderson 2013; Barge 2012; Keesler and Howe 2012).

Thus, economists predict that simply removing the lowest performing teachers will only minimally raise the mean average for teacher quality (Hanushek 2012). Instead, the second pathway, differentiated and/or targeted professional development, is likely to be the more powerful lever for increasing the quality of the teaching force (Goe et al. 2012)—a notion that is echoed throughout broad policy statements, but may not be supported by infrastructure or guidelines for implementation within new-generation policies (e.g. Donaldson et al. 2014). At the heart of both possible pathways is a need to identify and define what counts as effectiveness, how it can be measured (pathway one) and developed (pathway two). Therefore, the purpose of this study is to investigate how policymakers discussed and made sense of teacher effectiveness in conversations that led to the construction of state evaluation policy.

METHODOLOGICAL AND THEORETICAL PERSPECTIVE

Given that new teacher evaluation policies codify specific versions of what it means to be effective, I analyze the language of policymaking conversations in order to trace the development of such definitions in and through talk. I approach this analysis from an epistemic position described as discursive constructionism (Potter 1996; Potter and Hepburn 2008), which assumes discourse is both constructive of and constructed by the social world. I therefore assume that the meaning of teacher effectiveness is socially constructed and can be understood by examining talk-in-interaction. In order to analyze within this perspective, I used discursive psychology, an approach to discourse analysis which aims to re-specify cognitive constructs, like effectiveness in teaching, by examining talk-in-interaction. I organize my analysis around two analytic tools from existing literature related to discursive psychology: interpretative repertoires (IRs) (Wetherell 1998) and ideological dilemmas (Billig et al. 1988). Wetherell (1998) defined IRs as "a culturally familiar and habitual line of argument comprised of recognizable themes, common places and tropes...[which] comprise members' methods for making sense" (p. 400). She explained that the fragments of an IR "evoke for listeners the relevant context of argumentation-premises, claims and counter-claims." IRs are conceptually similar to the notion of "discourses" within post-structural approaches to discourse analysis (Edley 2001), in that they both describe distinctive ways of talking about objects and events in the world. The major difference is the emphasis on human agency and flexibility in the construction and use of an IR. Where the post-structuralist notion of a discourse is often monolithic in nature, and linked to an institution or discipline (e.g. the discourse of medicine, politics) under which people operate, IRs are smaller and more fragmented sets of available rhetorical resources that individuals choose to take up flexibly for different rhetorical purposes (Edley 2001). Within this study, individual speakers take up multiple, and, at times, conflicting IRs for different rhetorical purposes, sometimes within the same conversation.

The analytic category of ideological dilemmas was introduced to discourse analysis from the field of social psychology (see Billig et al. 1988), within which some researchers view everyday interactions as inherently dilemmatic in nature (Billig 1991; Billig et al. 1988). This perspective holds that ideology is not unitary, but consists of internal dilemmas that must be managed and accounted for within individual interactions. Attending to ideological dilemmas aids analysts in identifying and describing the scope and function of contrasting IRs. Competing or contrary ideologies related to a given phenomenon may have a structuring effect on constructions of effectiveness that are worked up and made relevant in talk.

As Cochran-Smith (2005) has pointed out, one of the reasons teacher effectiveness has been so difficult to define in research and policy endeavors is that so much is at stake and so much is involved. Identifying the dilemmas present in discourse allows the analyst to explore what is at stake, what interests must be balanced and how a participant or organization implicitly argues for their point of view over those of others. Like Cochran-Smith (2005), I consider how the available IRs for thinking and talking about teacher effectiveness have the potential to influence teacher education and development as part of comprehensive evaluation systems aimed at teacher quality.

Data Sources

In anticipation of a first-round R2T win, the governor of Tennessee appointed a15-member committee, the TEAC, during a special session of the state legislature in January of 2010. This TEAC held 16 meetings from May 2010 through April 2011. During this time, the committee met in person and via conference calls in order to develop and submit drafts and final recommendations to the State Board of Education. In the interim, a model plan was developed by the committee and piloted throughout the state during the 2010–2011 school year. The committee's recommendations were accepted by the State Board of Education without modification in April of 2011. The policies they outlined went into effect statewide for the 2011–2012 school year.

ANALYTIC APPROACH

I audio-recorded and transcribed every meeting of the TEAC from April 2010 through April 2011 (a total of 14 meetings, or roughly 60 hours of talk) with the permission of the committee chair with access guaranteed by the Tennessee Open Meetings Act. Transcription was completed using Transana™, a software program that synchronizes transcripts with audio files for selective and repeated listening.

After transcription, I engaged in an iterative and emergent analysis process that involved four phases of analysis. First, I conducted a transcript review within Transana in order to identify large extracts of data that were related to teacher effectiveness. This process allowed me to separate talk related to teacher effectiveness from sections of each transcript that primarily addressed other topics (e.g. presentations from test and technology vendors, document approval processes). Extracts related to teacher effectiveness were uploaded into ATLAS.TI, qualitative analysis software that was used to support the organization of analytic memos and several layers of coding. This set of extracts included anecdotes about teachers; segments of talk that used the term "effectiveness" or "quality" or "good/bad teaching/teacher"; and discussions of various measures of teaching (observation, test scores, survey, etc.). Second, identified extracts were reread multiple times while open codes and analytic memos were created in order to note patterns and create an audit trail (Anfara et al. 2002; Creswell and Miller 2000) of observations about emerging codes (see Appendix 1 for a map of iterations for coding and analysis). Third, a line-by-line analysis of coded extracts (Sacks 1992) was conducted, focused on patterns of interactions (e.g. turn-taking) that might indicate IRs and ideological dilemmas in conversation. This phase of analysis involved identifying patterns in word choice, claims, warrants and the evolution and management of conflict or difficulty in interactions between committee members and consultants. For example, a long sequence of back-and-forth interaction between two speakers and/or a long sequence of interruptions and cross talk were taken as possible indications of conversational trouble or conflict. This analysis led to the identification of two IRs related to teacher effectiveness, which outline polarized versions of effectiveness. Each includes and highlights dilemmas in the conceptualization of teacher effectiveness as either knowable or unknowable.

Fourth, I sought confirmation and disconfirmation of the patterns in constructions of teachers, effectiveness and tools for measurement from the third phase. Using examples found across the dataset, I confirmed patterns related to conceptions of teacher effectiveness and considered when and how they were presented and contested in individual interactions.

The following section includes extracts from the transcripts that are representative of patterns and themes across the dataset (see Appendix 1). They are presented in raw form, with some transcription conventions included to give a sense of timing (e.g. pauses, repetitions, false starts, overlapping speech; see Appendix 2) with the purpose of inviting readers to interpret as they read, and to add transparency to the analysis.

FINDINGS

Two patterned ways of talking about effectiveness in teaching can be traced throughout conversations of the committee: The first is the binary "call a spade a spade" IR in which teachers either are or are not effective. The second is "real situation" IR in which teachers are infinitely unique, teaching is infinitely complex and labeling one as either effective or ineffective is impossible. When taking up the "real situation" repertoire, speakers often provide a hypothetical or personal example, often in the form of an anecdote, which defies binary categorization because of particular circumstances. This IR explains the difficulties associated with teacher evaluation as the result of educational circumstances being inherently unique and complex. On the other hand, the "call a spade a spade" IR positions the difficulty of teacher evaluation as a matter of honesty about whether a teacher is "good" *or* "bad." These ways of talking about and making sense of teacher effectiveness are in conflict with one another and, when evoked in the same conversation, often framed ideological dilemmas that stymied the committee's decision-making process (Gabriel and Paulus 2014) as well as efforts to include considerations for teacher development in evaluation policies.

Call a Spade a Spade

The "call a spade a spade" IR can be identified by phrases that present an either/or relationship between possibilities for teacher effectiveness.

Phrases like "effective or not," "you are or you aren't," "can or can't teach" and the exact phrase "call a spade a spade" are used to imply the honesty of a simple yes/no set of labels or categories across conversations about teaching and learning. In the following extract, a committee member takes up the "call a spade a spade" repertoire in response to a suggestion that the labels for different levels of teaching proficiency be softened in case teacher ratings are published in newspapers. The speaker is a local entrepreneur appointed to the committee to represent a business perspective.

Extract 1[1]

> ENTREPRENEUR: Yeah I've (3.0) I never let the media (dictate) how I run my business (1.0) and (1.0) how what why not call a spade a spade? (.) I mean if they if these guys if they're teachers and they perform satisfactory and that's (.) in the paper uh it may encourage them to become to move up the ladder I mean (.) they're in the public sector they're working with public school kids and (2.0) it may make them work harder but I' m not gonna have them be I'm not gonna (.) I wouldn't I wouldn't change my evaluation wording based on the fact that it's going to be public (.) it is what it is (2.0) they either good or bad (.) I mean (.) so be it.

This extract contains examples of several features of this "call a spade a spade" IR: (1) the theme of honesty, (2) the structuring of binaries between polarized categories of teachers, (3) the call for an either/or decision about effectiveness and (4) the implication that there is no other choice. The speaker begins by positioning himself as free from the influence of the media and thus willing to be honest. The problem with calling for public recognition is that it may seem unsympathetic toward teachers. Later, he manages the dilemma of appearing to be anti-teacher by suggesting that public recognition is a good thing. It is motivation to get better, rather than humiliation. This constructs a version of effectiveness in which you are either effective or ineffective, but teachers can become effective via hard work.

Using a variety of idioms ("call a spade a spade," "it is what it is" and "either good or bad," and "so be it,") makes the binary of effective/ineffective seem familiar, casual and almost obvious (Antaki 2007; Drew and Holt 1988).

The either/or effective-or-ineffective pattern appears frequently throughout the data with a similar effect of positioning the speaker as logical and willing to be honest. One of the dilemmas at stake (Edwards and Potter 1992) when deploying the "call a spade a spade" IR is that the willingness to label someone ineffective may be perceived as anti-teacher. Extract 2 shows how one participant managed this dilemma. The extract begins with a principal's response to an earlier question about how the lowest-rating level should be defined.

Extract 2

> PRINCIPAL: . . .hopefully the Race to the Top law should be pushing us by having this um you know the value-added component to really make hard decisions and figure out who should. You know who belongs in the teaching profession and who may not. U and you know I think from what y'all have said in the past about as teachers you know if there's an ineffective teacher in your building who's not going to get better and not put the effort out there I'm sorry to say it but it's true and.
> TEACHER: but you do sometimes have a teacher=
> PRINCIPAL: =sometimes you gotta call a spade a spade. That's that's "improvement necessary" or "striving" or whatever
> CHAMBER OF COMMERCE PRESIDENT: absolutely
> PRINCIPAL: but there are some that fall into that ineffective category um
> TEACHER: I agree
> PRINCIPAL: and that's the only way to really if you get into a legal thing if you haven't used those type of words and been very very clear um you don't have a leg to stand on.

In this case, the "call a spade a spade" IR had a similar effect to the first extract by positioning the speaker as logical and willing to be honest rather than fall into the trap of excusing low achievement or unsatisfactory outcomes in order to avoid calling someone ineffective. The principal works up calling *a spade a spade* as both honest (the result of "hard decisions") and necessary for legal reasons ("if you get into a legal thing"). This works to minimize alternatives ("that's the only way to really") by suggesting any alternative would not hold up in court. At the end of her first comment, she uses a combination of a hedge and a truth claim, "sorry to say it, but it's true," as if to acknowledge that the sentiment may not be popular, but is still necessary. She also positions herself as in alignment with teachers saying, "as teachers you know if there's an ineffective teacher in your building." By aligning herself with teachers, apologizing for the comment and claiming that there is no way around it, she both reifies the binary category of ineffectiveness and mitigates the dilemma of appearing anti-teacher.

Besides appearing anti-teacher, repertoire comes with another internal dilemma: the need to be able to identify who is and is not effective. In this case, the principal makes value-added data relevant as the tool available to do this very sorting. She positions the use of value-added data as something that is "hopefully" going to occur as a result of R2T and as the way to "make really hard decisions." This acknowledges the difficulty of determining effectiveness while constructing value-added measures (VAM) as the tool to do it. This pattern of using VAM as the guarantor of objective identifications of effectiveness is in direct conflict with the other IR discussed below, and with recent evidence on confidence, stability, reliability and validity of VAMs (see Amrein-Beardsley 2012, 2014; and Baker et al. 2010 for reviews).

Real Situation

The "real situation" IR outlines a set of discursive strategies and themes that construct teachers and teaching situations as complex and unique in ways that eschew categorization. This IR represents the opposite of binary logic and thus polarizes sets of available discursive resources (Reynolds and Wetherell 2003) within conversations of the committee. Examples of the "real situation" IR often came in the form of anecdotes used to present a specific or extreme case (Pomerantz 1986) that defies generalization.

For example, in this extract, a high school math teacher is responding to a presentation delivered by representatives from Memphis City Schools who have outlined their work with the Gates Foundation's Measures of Effective Teaching (MET) project. As MET project participants, the district was collecting multiple measures of teacher effectiveness that included student and parent surveys along with value-added scores and other "lines of evidence," and will be sending them to MET project researchers to see which measures are the best predictors of student achievement. This extract is taken from a question-and-answer session following the presentation.

Extract 3

> TEACHER: ok I want to go back to something you said earlier talked about uh value-added versus some other form possibly parent student that sort of thing I had a principal interview uh several weeks ago (.) Teacher with low value added (.) Um being moved from one school to the other (1.5) for this reason and you know there's the trouble of tryin' to (.) get 'em out of the system of course they're tenured now (.) they have a great parent student following (1.0) go to all the ball games kids love em parents love em (.) but they're not performing in the classroom, and parents don't seem to care because they (.) love this person so I- how are you gonna do how are you gonna weight those if one is just as good as the other (.) you know it it just because you're popular doesn't mean you're effective.
>
> DISTRICT REPRESENTATIVE: Ah I love this question thank you...you're going to have to decide at the district level (.) you're gonna have to decide at the state level gonna have to decide this (.) as a field what we're gonna do about that (.) because (.) the way that we would weigh it out is 35,35,15,15² the love for Mr. Johnson would be great or Mrs. Johnson (.) would be great (.) value-add might tip the scales so we're seeing this as a body of evidence (.)...[my colleague] and I are just ultimate pragmatists it's like get the job done how are you going to get this out there how what does it really look like how is it going to work (.) which is one of the reasons why we're doing this pilot thing and we're bringing back results.

In this case, the "real situation" repertoire involves a firsthand account, which positions the teacher as having authentic inside information about situations that may be unavailable to others (Davies and Harré 1990). In this case, presenting a firsthand account also works to legitimize her question because she is presenting a real, rather than hypothetical, challenge to the logic of assumptions underlying the use of parent input. Within her statement above, the teacher constructs teacher effectiveness as unrelated to popularity, but suggests that one can be mistaken for the other.

On the other hand, the Memphis representative's team has decided to assume that a "great love" of teachers on the part of evaluators can be balanced or out-weighed by VAMs. His version of effectiveness, like the principal's above, relies on VAM to balance out sources of error. This positions love for a teacher—a subjective and emotional factor—as something to be balanced out, and VAMs as the way to create that balance. Here and throughout the meetings, VAMs are used as the arbiters of difficult decisions and guarantor of validity (Gabriel and Lester 2013b; Gabriel and Paulus 2014).

In addition, the dilemma surrounding the need to arrive at a rating in the face of particular complexities (a mismatch between popularity and performance) is managed by constructing VAMs as the gold standard (Gabriel and Lester 2013a, b) measure among "multiple lines of evidence." The pattern of evoking VAM as the solution to dilemmas within and between each IR is described in the following section.

Managing Conflicting Repertoires

This idea that the current state of affairs (e.g. low student achievement, wide gaps in achievement between demographic groups) can be blamed on failure to "call a spade a spade" is common both within the conversations of the committee and in the research and policy documents that informed new-generation evaluation policies. For example, the influential report, *The Widget Effect* (Weisberg et al. 2009), argued that schools have previously failed to identify effectiveness, but that evaluation systems that *do* identify who is/isn't effective will improve the teaching force—by either targeting support or dismissing poor teachers. This line of logic assumes that a rating carries an explicit meaning in terms of human capital decisions (e.g. support, promote, hire, fire). Instead, a rating may not, in itself, be transparent, reliable or meaningful enough to guide human capital decisions (Baker et al. 2013; Amrein-Beardsley and Collins 2012). Given the variety of ways to earn a low rating across multiple measures of effectiveness, it may be that some low-rated teachers should be dismissed, while others with similar ratings should be supported; or that some will be rated low under certain circumstances, but reassignment would change their ratings. This is the very point a teacher attempts to make in extract 4 in her exchange with the Memphis City School Board member wherein both IRs are deployed and create conversational difficulty marked by a series of interruptions.

Extract 4

TEACHER: . . .well let me give you a situation
SCHOOL BOARD MEMBER: =oh I II know [I'm not
TEACHER: no and I'm not] I'm talking about a real situation=

SCHOOL BOARD MEMBER: =yeah I get it=
TEACHER: =of sometimes you transfer what you have to. Right now
    we're teaching algebra two online and chemistry online=
SCHOOL BOARD MEMBER:=I get it=
TEACHER: cuz there were no teachers available=
SCHOOL BOARD MEMBER: =I get it=
TEACHER: how is how is that detrimental to the students [by having. . .
SCHOOL BOARD MEMBER: I get it and] that's why the whole state
    gotta do is eventually this is about changing all of it
CONSULTANT: right
SCHOOL BOARD MEMBER: all of that (many voices)
CONSULTANT: so if just to just clarify (.) yeah?
ENTREPRENEUR: I think (.) I don't think we can (1.0) come up with
    an evaluation process (1.0) for every little exception we can come up
    with an evaluation process that meets the majority=
CONSULTANT: =for the broad majority
ENTREPRENEUR: for the broad majority there are gonna be some
    (1.5) bad situations that we just have to deal with but we can't (.)
    we're not going to be able to deal with that in this process.
CONSULTANT: that's right that's right there will always be some sort
    of c- you know special case scenarios. Um so my recommendation is
    over the next week you are going to receive um by email a summary of
    all of the major decisions. . .

In the previous extracts, the benefit of the "real situation" IR was that it
offered the speaker the position of an insider having unique knowledge
about teaching and schools. In this extract, the school board member
neutralizes that benefit by repeating that she already "gets it" even before
(and while) the story is told. Her interruptions and the repetition of "I get
it" prevent the teacher from holding the floor to describe her "real situation." The school board member's emphasis on how the policy will change
or address "all of that," indicates that she is focused on a broader level of
decision-making, one at which individual situations are already accounted
for and do not matter.

This position is strengthened by the next two conversational turns. Each
of the next two speakers echoes the need to attend to the bigger pictures
instead of particular situations. They both use extreme case formulations to
minimize the particular ("every little exception," "some situations we just
have to deal with," "special case scenarios"). Finally, as in previous extracts,

the consultant manages the conflict by putting off any decision for informal discussions between meetings or a later meeting.

Key Implications

Findings from this study suggest that discursive resources for discussing teacher effectiveness both contain and create dilemmas that are managed in ways that affect the policymaking process as well as the contents of policies themselves. As Stokoe et al. (2012) have described, discursive psychology can be a tool for social change by illuminating social interaction minutely and focusing on how constructs are worked up, and outcomes accomplished, in talk. A major implication of this study, therefore, is awareness—both the nature and impact of polarized relationship of available resources for thinking and talking about teacher effectiveness. Awareness of this fundamental dilemma, and its impact on policy conversations, might create space for participants and/or facilitators to identify, and even resist the patterns of talk that led to the content and exclusions (i.e. mechanisms for teacher development) of Tennessee's current policy.

One important outcome of the patterned management of dilemmas related to polarized ways of talking about effectiveness was the policy's reliance on VAM. Reliance on VAM has proved to be problematic both ideologically and methodologically. Generating VAMs for every teacher every year, even in the small number of grades and subjects where this is possible, is time-consuming, expensive and difficult to accomplish in advance of the start of each school year (e.g. Sawchuk 2013). This makes it difficult to include student growth measures in decisions about placement, promotion and dismissal.

In the years since Tennessee's policy went into effect, VAM has consistently failed to be the arbiter of when administrators can "call a spade a spade." After the first year under the new teacher evaluation plan, Tennessee's Department of Education reported a "significant mismatch" between observation ratings and VAM: observations placed 76% of teachers in the top two quintiles, while VAM scored only 51% in the top two quintiles (Tennessee Department of Education 2012). They readily attributed this to human error in observation, rather than questioning the supremacy of the VA score (Goe 2013). At this point, given the very public debate about VAM in mass media outlets (Gabriel and Lester 2013a), the robust debate about VAM within academia (e.g. Amrein-Beardsley 2008; Baker et al. 2010; Briggs and Domingue 2011; McCaffery et al. 2005;

Rothstein 2012) and the failure of terminations predicated on VAM data to stand up in court (Strauss 2016; Croft and Buddin 2014), there is reason to believe that systems predicated on VAMs infallibility are vulnerable to legal and ethical attack (Amrein-Beardsley and Collins 2012; Baker et al. 2013).

Just three years after Tennessee's teacher evaluation policy went into full effect, the state legislature passed a law that prevents student growth measures from being used to revoke or non-renew a teacher's license. Other states, from California to New York, Connecticut and Massachusetts, have similarly delayed or rolled back parts of high-stakes teacher evaluation policies in the wake of delayed assessments for Common Core State Standards and changing political landscapes. The notion that simply identifying and removing "the ineffectives" (Gabriel and Lester 2013a), would improve the overall quality of the teaching force, has proven inadequate. This is not surprising in urban settings where teacher shortages and high turnover rates make it difficult to ensure a consistent, let alone effective, teaching force (Irizarry and Donaldson 2012; Jacob 2007; Rinke 2011). The problem with both available IRs is that neither includes a conception of how effectiveness might be developed—because it exists, does not exist or cannot be proven to exist. Therefore, policies themselves fail to account for mechanisms of support and development. Funding and infrastructure for linking or designing professional development in response to teacher evaluation ratings are effectively absent from otherwise comprehensive policy packages. As evaluation policies scale back over time, the future and function of professional development as a tool for reform is uncertain.

Summary

The corpus of data from these meetings suggests that no single definition of teacher effectiveness exists "pure and serene" (Rabinowitz and Travers 1953, p. 212) awaiting scientific discovery, as presumed by tools like VAM and endeavors like the MET project. Rather, there are polarized repertoires available for talking about teacher effectiveness: one in which speakers take the risk to be honest about *whether or not* a teacher is effective; and another in which any effort to measure effectiveness is futile because the possibilities of nuanced complexities are infinite.

Perhaps because neither conception of effectiveness contains a theory of action for increasing it, few policies are explicit about mechanisms for teacher development. A new evaluation system that identifies effectiveness, but does not explicitly create systems for its development, is unlikely to change teacher effectiveness or student outcomes. Likewise, a policymaking conversation in which two contrasting interpretive repertoires compete creates conflicts that must be managed by the speakers—in this case, most often by the consulting facilitators. As we have argued elsewhere (see Gabriel and Paulus 2014), this creates conditions within which unappointed paid consultants may have outsized influence on what is assumed and designed to be a democratic process.

Key Connections to Policy Research
1. Polarized interpretive repertoires caused conflicts that were mediated by (over)reliance on value-added measurement tools.
2. Limited views of effectiveness itself failed to inspire policy language that includes infrastructure or guidance for support/development activities within teacher evaluation.
3. Awareness of the patterned nature of talk in committee conversations could fuel reflections on the content and process policymaking that identify holes and biases before policies are accepted into state or federal code.

Appendix 1

Map of Iterations/Levels of Analysis (to be read from bottom-up) (Anfara et al. 2002)

Final Iteration/Level of Analysis Applied to Data Set

- IR of a "real situation"
  - Anecdotes and stories
  - Hypothetical scenarios
  - Extreme case formulations
- IR of "calling a spade a spade"
  - Teaching
  - Student achievement
  - Teacher quality
  - Positioning
  - Dilemmas

- Measurement
  - VAM—reliance
  - VAM—challenges
  - Student test scores—reliance
  - Student test scores—challenges
  - Teachers of untested subjects
  - Selection of rubrics
  - Selection of assessments

Second Iteration/Level of Analysis Applied to Data Set

- Constructions of effectiveness
  - Anecdotes and stories
  - Hypothetical scenarios
  - Extreme case formulations
  - Teaching
  - Student achievement
  - Teacher quality
- Decision-making
  - Agenda-setting
  - Purpose statements
  - Conflict/disagreement
  - Positioning
  - Hedging
  - Turn-taking
  - Consultant's role/prerogative
- Measuring effectiveness
  - Observation rubrics
  - Teachers without TVAAS
  - Problems with TVAAS
  - Reliance on TVAAS
  - Problems with test scores
  - Reliance on test scores

First Iteration/Level of Analysis Applied to Data Set

- "Other" 50% measures of teacher effectiveness
- Value-added measurement (general)
- TVAAS (specific)—Tennessee value-added assessment system

- Effectiveness
- Quality
- Conflict/disagreement
- Good/bad teaching/teacher
- Decision-making
- Ratings & levels
- Statistics & research
- Committee purpose & scope

APPENDIX 2

Transcription Symbols

...speech continues or is excerpted from a longer statement
=interruption=
(.) pause of less than one second
(#) pause of # of seconds
(...) unclear speech
[ ] overlapping speech
[researcher insertion]

NOTES

1. A key to transcription symbols appears as Appendix 2. Some periods are used to increase readability, but pauses are marked and timed in parentheses instead of laying assumed punctuation over the spoken language. Pauses, repetitions and false starts are included in these transcripts in order to provide the clearest record of talk without overly compromising readability (Ochs 1979).
2. This string of numbers in this line refers the weighting of Tennessee's teacher evaluation system: 35% student growth, 15% student achievement, 35% observation and 15% other measures.

REFERENCES

Amrein-Beardsley, A. (2008). Methodological concerns about the Education Value-Added Assessment System (EVAAS). *Educational Researcher, 37*(2), 65–75.
Amrein-Beardsley, A. (2012). Value-added measures in education: The best of the alternatives is simply not good enough. *Teachers College Record*. Retrieved from http://www.tcrecord.org/content.asp?contentid=16648

Amrein-Beardsley, A. (2014). *Rethinking value-added models in education critical perspectives on test and assessment-based accountability.* New York: Routledge.

Amrein-Beardsley, A., & Collins, C. (2012). The SAS Education Value-Added Assessment System (SAS® EVAAS®) in the Houston Independent School District (HISD): Intended and unintended consequences. *Education Policy Analysis Archives, 20*(12). Retrieved from http://epaa.asu.edu/ojs/article/view/1096

Anderson, J. (2013). Curious grade for teachers: Nearly all pass. *New York Times.* Retrieved from http://www.nytimes.com/2013/03/31/education/curious-grade-for-teachers-nearly-all-pass.html?pagewanted=all&_r=0

Anfara, V., Brown, K., & Mangione, T. (2002). Qualitative analysis on stage: Making the research process more public. *Educational Researcher, 31*(7), 28–38.

Antaki, C. (2007). Mental health practitioners' use of idiomatic expressions in summarising clients' accounts. *Journal of Pragmatics, 39,* 527–541.

Baker, E., Barton, P., Darling-Hammond, L., Haertel, E., Ladd, H., Linn, R., et al. (2010). *Problems with the use of student test scores to evaluate teachers.* Washington, DC: Economic Policy Institute.

Baker, B., Oluwole, J., Greene, P. (2013). The legal consequences of mandating high stakes decisions based on low quality information: Teacher evaluation in the race-to-the-top era. *Education Policy Analysis Archives, 21.* Retrieved from http://epaa.asu.edu/ojs/article/view/1298

Barge, J. (2012). *Overview to the 2012 TKES/LKES pilot evaluation report.* Atlanta: Georgia Department of Education.

Billig, M. (1991). *Ideology, rhetoric and opinion.* London: Sage.

Billig, M., Condor, S., Edwards, D., Gane, M., Middleton, D., & Radley, A. (1988). *Ideological dilemmas: A social psychology of everyday thinking.* London: Sage Publications.

Briggs, D., & Domingue, B. (2011). *Due diligence and the evaluation of teachers: A review of the value-added analysis underlying the effectiveness rankings of Los Angeles Unified School District teachers by the Los Angeles times.* Boulder: National Education Policy Center.

Cochran-Smith, M. (2005). The politics of teacher education and the curse of complexity. *Journal of Teacher Education, 56*(3), 181–185.

Connors, C. (2013). Commentary on two classroom observation systems: Moving toward a shared understanding of effective teaching. *School Psychology Quarterly, 28*(4), 342–346.

Creswell, J. W., & Miller, D. L. (2000). Determining validity in qualitative inquiry. *Theory Into Practice, 39,* 124–130.

Croft, M., & Buddin, R. (2014). Will courts shape value-added measurement for teacher evaluation? *ACT Working Paper Series.* Retrieved from https://forms.act.org/research/papers/pdf/WP-2014-2.pdf

Darling-Hammond, L. (1990). Teacher evaluation in transition: Emerging roles and evolving methods. In J. Millman & L. Darling-Hammond (Eds.), *The new handbook of teacher evaluation: Assessing elementary and secondary school teachers* (pp. 17–34). Newbury Park: Sage.

Darling-Hammond, L. (2013). *Getting teacher evaluation right: What really matters for effectiveness and improvement.* New York: Teachers College Press.

Davies, B., & Harré, R. (1990). Positioning: The discursive production of selves. *Journal for Theory of Social Behavior, 20*(1), 43–64.

Doherty, K., & Jacobs, S. (2013). *State of the states 2013: Connect the dots using evaluation of teacher effectiveness to inform policy.* New York: National Council on Teacher Quality.

Donaldson, M., Cobb, C., LeChasseur, K., Gabriel, R., Gonzalez, R., Woulfin, S., & Makuch, A. (2014). *An evaluation of the pilot implementation of Connecticut's system for educator evaluation and development: Final report.* Storrs: UConn Center for Education Policy Analysis.

Drew, P., & Holt, E. (1988). Complainable matters: The use of idiomatic expressions in making complaints. *Social Problems, 35*, 398–417.

Duncan, A. (2012, September 22). The Tennessee story. *Huffington Post.* Retrieved from http://www.huffingtonpost.com/arne-duncan/the-tennessee-story_b_1695467.html

Edley, N. (2001). Analysing masculinity: Interpretive repertoires, ideological dilemmas and subject positions. In M. Wetherell, S. Taylor, & S. Yates (Eds.), *Discourse as data: A guide for analysis* (pp. 189–228). London: Sage/The Open University.

Edwards, D., & Potter, J. (1992). *Discursive psychology.* London: Sage.

Firestone, W. A. (2014). Teacher evaluation policy and conflicting theories of motivation. *Educational Researcher, 43*(2), 100–107.

Gabriel, R., & Lester, J. N. (2013a). The romance quest of education reform: A discourse analysis of the LA times' reports on value-added measurement teacher effectiveness. *Teacher's College Record, 115*(12), 1–32.

Gabriel, R., & Lester, J. N. (2013b). Sentinels of trust: The discursive construction of value-added measurement in policy conversations. *Educational Policy Analysis Archives, 20*(9). Retrieved from http://epaa.asu.edu/ojs/article/view/1165

Gabriel, R., & Paulus, T. (2014). Committees and controversy: Consultants in the construction of education policy. *Educational Policy.* Retrieved from http://epx.sagepub.com/content/early/2014/08/22/0895904814531650.abstract

Garrison, J. (2014, May 20). US education secretary Arne Duncan lauds Tennessee amid reform pushback. *The Tennessean.* Retrieved from http://www.tennessean.com/story/news/education/2014/05/20/us-educationsecretary-arne-duncan-visits-nashville-today/9322449/

Goe, L. (2013, March 14). Teacher and principal evaluation webinar. *Edweek.* Retrieved from http://www.edweek.org/ew/marketplace/webinars/webinars.html

Goe, L., Biggers, K., & Croft, A. (2012). *Linking teacher evaluation to professional development: Focusing on improving teaching and learning.* Retrieved from http://files.eric.ed.gov/fulltext/ED532775.pdf

Hanushek, E. (2012). Valuing teachers: How much is a good teacher worth. *Education Next, 11*(3), 40–45.

Heitin, L. (2012). Take it from Tennessee: Lessons on teacher evaluation. *Edweek.* Retrieved from http://blogs.edweek.org/teachers/teaching_now/2012/11/take_it_from_tennessee_lessons_on_teacher_evaluation.html?intc=es

Horn, J., & Wilburn, S. (2013). *The mismeasure of education.* Cary: Information Age Publishing.

Irizarry, J. G., & Donaldson, M. L. (2012). Teach for América: The latinization of U.S. schools and the critical shortage of Latina/o teachers. *American Educational Research Journal, 49*(1), 155–194.

Jacob, B. (2007). The challenges of staffing urban schools with effective teachers. *The Future of Children, 17*(1), 129–153.

Kane, T., & Staiger, D. (2012). *Gathering feedback for teaching combining high-quality observations with student surveys and achievement gains.* Retrieved from http://k12education.gatesfoundation.org/wp-content/uploads/2016/06/MET_Gathering_Feedback_for_Teaching_Summary1.pdf

Keesler, V., & Howe, C. (2012). *Understanding educator evaluations in Michigan.* Lansing: Michigan Department of Education.

Marzano, R., Frontier, T., & Livingston, D. (2012). *Effective supervision: Supporting the art and science of great teaching.* Alexandria: ASCD.

McCaffery, D., Lockwood, J., Mariano, L., & Steodji, C. (2005). *Challenges for value-added assessment of teacher effects.* Santa Monica: RAND Corporation.

Pomerantz, A. (1986). Extreme case formulations: A way of legitimizing claims. *Human Studies, 9*(2), 219–229.

Potter, J. (1996). *Representing reality: Discourse, rhetoric, and social construction.* London: Sage.

Potter, J., & Hepburn, A. (2008). Discursive constructionism. In J. Holstein (Ed.), *Handbook of constructionist research* (pp. 275–293). New York: Guilford.

Rabinowitz, W., & Travers, R. (1953). Problems of defining and assessing teacher effectiveness. *Educational Theory, 3*(3), 212–219.

Raudenbush, S. W. (2009). The Brown legacy and the O'Connor challenge: Transforming schools in the images of children's potential. *Educational Researcher, 38*, 169–180.

Reynolds, J., & Wetherell, M. (2003). The discursive climate of singleness: The consequences for women's negotiation of a single identity. *Feminism and Psychology, 13*, 489–510.

Rinke, C. R. (2011). Career trajectories of urban teachers: A continuum of perspectives, participation, and plans shaping retention in the educational system. *Urban Education, 46*(4), 639–662.

Rothstein, J. (2012). *Review of learning about teaching.* Denver: National Education Policy Center.

Sacks, H. (1992). *Lectures on conversation.* Oxford: Blackwell.

Sawchuk, S. (2013). What will new evaluation systems cost? *EdWeek.* Retrieved from   http://blogs.edweek.org/edweek/teacherbeat/2013/04/What_will_new_evaluation.html

Stokoe, E., Hepburn, A., & Antaki, C. (2012). Beware the 'Loughborough School' of social psychology? Interaction and the politics of intervention. *Journal of Social Psychology, 51*(3), 41–96.

Strauss, V. (2016). Retrieved from https://www.washingtonpost.com/news/answer-sheet/wp/2016/05/10/judge-calls-evaluation-of-n-y-teacher-arbitrary-and-capricious-in-case-against-new-u-s-secretary-of-education/

Tennessee Department of Education. (2012). *Teacher evaluation in Tennessee: A report on year 1 implementation.* Retrieved from http://www.tn.gov/education/doc/yr_1_tchr_eval_rpt.pdf

Weisberg, D., Sexton, S., Mulhern, J., & Keeling, D. (2009). *The widget effect.* New York: The New Teacher Project.

Wetherell, M. (1998). Positioning and interpretative repertoires: Conversation analysis and post-structuralism in dialogue. *Discourse and Society, 9*(3), 387–412.

Rachael E. Gabriel is Assistant Professor of Literacy Education at the University of Connecticut. She is an associate of the Center for Education Policy Analysis and the Center on Post-Secondary Education and Disability at the University of Connecticut. Her research interests include teacher preparation, development and evaluation, as well as literacy instruction, interventions, and related policies. She is the author of *Reading's Non-Negotiables: Elements of Effective Reading Instruction* (2013) and co-editor of *Evaluating Literacy Instruction: Principles and Promising Practices* (2015) and *Performances of Research: Critical Issues in K-12 Education* (2013). In addition to serving as an associate editor of *Educational Administration Quarterly,* Gabriel is also on the editorial boards of the *American Educational Research Journal, Educational Policy Analysis Archives, Journal of Literacy Research,* and *Reading & Writing Quarterly.*

CHAPTER 12

Future Directions for Education Policy Research and Language-Based Methods

Chad R. Lochmiller and Jessica Nina Lester

Introduction

This chapter brings together the key contributions that this volume's authors make at both a methodological and substantive level. Specifically, we use this chapter to offer our interpretation of the key points or primary considerations from each chapter in this volume. Then, we identify the key methodological contributions that readers might derive when engaging with this volume. Notably, we highlight the possibilities that exist at the intersection of education policy and discourse analysis. Thus, we also proffer several key contributions that we believe this volume makes to education policy conversations. To conclude, we offer considerations for next steps, noting possibilities for future directions for education policy scholars interested in taking up language-based methods writ large.

C.R. Lochmiller (✉) • J.N. Lester
Indiana University, Bloomington, IN, USA

© The Author(s) 2017   241
J.N. Lester et al. (eds.), *Discursive Perspectives on Education Policy and Implementation*, DOI 10.1007/978-3-319-58984-8_12

REVISITING THE VOLUME'S GOALS

When we began developing this volume, our primary goal was to create a resource for scholars to explore the utility of language-based methods as related to education policy research. In particular, we sought to highlight how the study of education policy, particularly policy implementation, could be studied using a variety of language-based methods. We saw the use of these methods as valuable for the study of policy within federal, state, local, and organizational contexts. Moreover, we believed that such methods opened the possibility of using new and novel data sources and potentially posing substantive questions not yet explored within the broader policy literature. Thanks to the contributions of the chapter authors, we believe we have created a resource for scholars—both novice and experienced—to examine the potential applications of language-based methods to education policy, particularly discourse analytic perspectives and conversation analysis. Indeed, across the chapters, the authors have highlighted how language-based methods could be used to study policy, which serve various audiences and may be focused on different educational goals. Further, one of our primary hopes was to showcase how vastly different policy issues could be studied using a relatively coherent suite of methods—all of which focus on the study of language at varying levels.

Before discussing specific methodological and substantive contributions that we believe this volume offers, we think it is important to highlight the primary purpose of each of the chapters as related to the overarching goals of this volume. In Chap. 2, Lochmiller and Hedges provide helpful insights for education policy scholars who may be unfamiliar with both the origins of policy implementation research, as well as its dominant methodological reliance on the qualitative case study. In doing so, they ground their call for the potential utility of using language-based methods to study policy in the literature base. In Chap. 3, Lester, White, and Lochmiller provide the technical and methodological core for the volume. Their chapter highlights theoretical and methodological issues related to the use of language-based methods, while connecting methodological possibilities of using critical discourse analysis, discursive psychology, and conversation analysis, in particular, to the study of policy. In varying ways, Chaps. 4, 5, 6, 7, 8, 9, 10, and 11 provide empirical examples for the reader to review how language-based methods may be used. In Chap. 4, Burman offers a rich perspective on the uses of a Foucauldian discursive approach (Foucault 1980), connecting it specifically to a UK-based study of the educational impacts of welfare reform. Offering a more micro-oriented approach to the study of language, in Chap. 5, Paulsen provides an overview to Membership Categorization Analysis (Sacks 1992; Stokoe 2012), illustrating his discussion of Membership Categorization Analysis with a close analysis of how varying organizations in Bangladesh construct the category of teacher. Gildersleeve and Kleinhesselink, in Chap. 6, position policy discourse analysis as a method for critical policy analysis, while calling upon a post-humanist and materialist orientation (Deleuze 2004) to the work. In Chap. 7, Willinski foregrounds Bakhtin's (1981) writing around dialogism as she illustrates how a local pre-Kindergarten partnership deviated from a state-level vision of partnership. In Chap. 8, Lustick draws upon CDA, Fairclough's (1992) writing in particular, to analyze a governmental initiative aimed at addressing suspension rates and disciplinary practices that impact students of color far more than their white counterparts. Her analyses points to underlying ideologies that construct "mis-behavior" as bound within notions of school climate. Also drawing upon CDA, Ulmer and Lenhoff examine discourses of education reform particularly related to twenty-first-century policies that claim to produce more productive citizens in Chap. 9. Indeed, both Lustick's and Ulmer and Lenhoff's chapters unearth taken-for-granted knowledge and practices, and point to the discourses that shape policy initiatives and practices. In Chap. 10, Gabriel and Woulfin draw upon framing theory (Goffman 1974) to conduct a discourse analysis of education policy problems as constructed in written testimony, particularly as related to reading achievement. And, finally, in Chap. 11, Gabriel draws upon discursive psychology, specifically the notion of interpretative repertoires (Wetherell 1998) and ideological dilemmas (Billig et al. 1988)—analytic constructs most often drawn upon when engaging in critical discursive psychology. In this chapter, Gabriel analyzes transcripts from Tennessee's Teacher Evaluation Advisory Committee meetings in which teacher evaluation policies were being generated.

When viewed in its entirety, we believe that the volume's focus on the applicability of language-based methods is compelling and serves to foreground the possibilities for building what we have loosely referred to as third-generation policy research (see Chap. 1 in this volume for further discussion). While selective and partial, the authors within this volume contribute to scholarly conversations positioned at the intersection of education policy and discourse analysis. In this concluding chapter, we thus highlight some of these key contributions as a means of weaving the seemingly disparate arguments together. We conclude this chapter by offering future directions that education policy scholars might pursue when using language-based methods.

CONTRIBUTIONS TO METHODOLOGY

When considering the methodological contributions this volume makes, we believe it is important to foreground our own view of theory and methodology. We orient to the very notion of theory, as well as methodology, as constructions. As Noblit (1999) noted, "theory. . .is historicism. Theory is not truth" (p. 11). Further, in our own empirical work, we assume that theoretical and methodological understandings will be challenged and even altered as we engage with data, theory, and the research process more generally (Lather 1986). In other words, we position methodological and theoretical perspectives as situated, historically and culturally specific, and in need of ongoing critique. As such, we seek to unearth ways in which methodology and theory might be reframed and crafted in creative and useful ways. Thus, when considering the chapters in this volume, we were particularly struck by the methodological possibilities unearthed by the authors.

Specifically, we suggest that the most significant methodological contribution this volume makes is highlighting methodological approaches that have been less commonly used within education policy research. Notably, CDA is perhaps the most commonly used discourse analytic perspective used within policy research (see Chap. 3 of this volume for further discussion of this). Yet, we recognize that CDA does not represent a single methodology but rather a diverse set of approaches. Nonetheless, beyond CDA, other language-based methods have been less commonly employed. This volume's contributors, therefore, provide examples of new methodological possibilities for education policy research. In Chap. 4, Burman illuminates the potential for aligning closely with the work of Foucault and engaging in a Foucauldian-informed discourse analysis. In Chap. 5, Paulsen positions Membership Categorization Analysis as a meaningful methodological and analytical approach for studying categories of interest to policy researchers—particularly categories made explicit in text and talk. In Chap. 6, Gildersleeve and Kleinhesselink offer an addendum to policy discourse analysis, arguing for a post-humanist and materialist informed approach. In many ways, this argument works at the "edges" of methodological possibilities. In Chap. 7, Willinski centers Bakhtin's notion of dialogism and offers an example of how such an idea might be drawn upon when studying language. In both Chaps. 8 and 9, CDA is drawn upon in ways that illustrate its continual potential for making sense of policy issues. In Chap. 10, Gabriel and Woulfin produce a synthetic approach to discourse analysis, offering a useful example of how multiple theories and methodological positions might coalesce to produce a nuanced and layered understanding of the policymaking process. Finally, in Chap. 11, Gabriel draws upon discursive psychology to study policymaking conversations. To summarize, then, contributing authors bring to the fore several methodological perspectives that have been less commonly used within policy research, including Foucauldian-informed discourse analysis, Membership Categorization Analysis, post-qualitative perspectives on discourse analysis, a Bakhtinian informed approach, and discursive psychology. Further, in Chap. 3, Lester, White, and Lochmiller pointed to additional possibilities when noting that conversation analysis has rarely been drawn upon in education policy research (see Bonacina-Pugh 2012, for an exception).

The authors in this volume also provide diverse examples of varying data sources that might be used by policy scholars when working at the intersection of education policy and discourse analysis. Specifically, the authors drew upon data sources ranging from written testimony to policy documents to policymaking conversations to more traditional forms of qualitative data, such as interviews, among other sources. Beyond these data sources, there is ample opportunity for future language-based policy research to draw upon an even wider range of data sources. For instance, in a recent special issue in *Education Analysis Policy Archives* (Lester et al. 2017), Supovitz and Reinkordt (2017) collected tweets related to the Common Core State Standards (CCSS) and analyzed how the language used served to frame CCSS as a policy issue in which broad opposition exists. Similarly, Hurst (2017) collected a corpus of tweets and drew upon discursive psychology to examine how superintendents represent their engagement with the public. Indeed, there are new and emergent forms of data that might be drawn upon to explore policy issues in varied and even innovative ways. We suggest that this volume serves as a useful starting point, with variable examples, and yet also points to ways in which even more expansive conceptions of data relevant to policy scholars interested in language use are needed.

Contributions to Education Policy Conversations

Substantively, the chapters in this volume present new ways of thinking about a variety of contemporary policy issues in both the US and international contexts. Within the US context, the authors attend to issues related to early childhood education, school discipline, twenty-first-century education reform, reading and dyslexia, and teacher effectiveness. Each of these policies has received considerable attention from policymakers, particularly as the US public education system has increasingly focused on student achievement outcomes and elevated the importance of educational practice as the primary determinant of these outcomes. Collectively, these discussions illuminate various competing agendas and interests within the US policy system, as well as in various policy debates. Further, these chapters highlight how scholars can use language-based methods to unpack differences in meaning ascribed to various policy choices. Internationally, some of the authors consider issues related to the categorization of teachers within Bangladesh, as well as the impact of welfare reform on families in the UK. These studies operationalize applications of language-based approaches within international contexts and thereby demonstrate how understanding(s) of policy vary outside US contexts. Indeed, we think the international contributions to this volume are instructive in informing how language-based methods might be used within and across international education policy contexts.

What is striking about each of the chapters within the volume is the extent to which the policy issues are enmeshed within particular social and political contexts. Indeed, as Stephen Ball (2006) has noted, "Research is thoroughly enmeshed 'in' the social and 'in' the political and developments and innovations within the human sciences, like education, are intimately imbricated in the practical management of social and political problems" (p. 15). Policy issues are thus intertwined with the cultures, politics, and identities that exist within social and political circumstances. We argue that the language-based methods highlighted in this volume provide a more nuanced tool for education policy scholars to determine how this "intertwining" influences both the meanings conveyed by the policy, as well as the ways in which actors who participated in the policy's development shape this meaning throughout the policymaking process. For instance, Burman's discussion in Chap. 4 of the educational impacts of welfare reforms on poor families within the UK illustrates both the overarching government narrative of the time and the localized impressions of policy as it relates to those who are most directly impacted. Likewise, were it not for the massive federal investment in educator evaluation within the US spurred by Race to the Top, issues of teacher effectiveness might be viewed as mundane state policy debates. Yet, as Gabriel highlights in her analyses in Chap. 11, these debates and the forums within which they are occurring serve as important opportunities to unpack and more deeply understand how education policymakers ascribed particular meaning to concepts related to teacher effectiveness. Indeed, both cases remind us that education policy research "displays a variety of stances, styles and preoccupations" (Ball 2006, p. 15). We suggest that language-based methods help us unpack and examine these stances, styles, and preoccupations in a more incisive fashion.

What is more, the approaches taken up by each of the authors contribute to our collective understanding of how particular policy actors contribute to the implementation of policy at the school, district, state, and federal level. Indeed, the chapters within this volume highlight how actors across multiple policy arenas use discourse broadly construed to influence how policy is designed, as well as how policy comes to be understood by actors at different levels of the policy system. Political scientists have long investigated the role of policy actors in the policymaking process. For instance, Mazzoni (1991) conceived of policy actors entering and leaving policy arenas as particular issues arise. The analyses presented within this volume suggest that even as actors leave the policy arena, their understanding(s) of policy issues, the images they have constructed about particular policies through their discourse, and the agendas which they have set in place continue to influence the policy process. Willinski's description of pre-Kindergarten partnerships, for example, offers some instructive insights in this regard. Drawing upon Bakhtin's (1981) notion of dialogism, she demonstrates how a local pre-Kindergarten partnership deviated from the vision animated by state policy discourses in Lakeville, Wisconsin. Her analysis reveals that even when a policy prescription (i.e., partnerships) is considered a positive practice, the ways in which actors in different policy arenas take up these policy ideas and imbed them within their own practice can vary greatly. Such is the case in many of the chapters presented in this volume.

Although not specified in this way, many of the chapters in the volume also attend to problem-framing as a central policy concern. Gabriel and Woulfin, for example, illustrate how reading is effectively problematized within the context of policymaking. Their analysis presents insights into the ways in which discourse analysis can be used to examine how actors formulate policy problems that can be addressed through formalized policy action. While reading is certainly a dominant issue, we think other issues may well be ripe for examination. For instance, recent debates (re)framing the Common Core, deliberations concerning the equity of school funding levels, and localized discussions concerning the need for school closure or consolidation all would provide important insights into how policy actors problematize the issues which they hope policy will ultimately address. Some of these topics have been addressed in special issues featured in *Educational Policy Analysis Archives,* as well (Lester et al. 2016, 2017).

One aspect of problem-framing that may be especially worthy of study using language-based methods relates to the ways in which political agendas influence policy. While political scientists have formulated these using a variety of macro-level constructs, such as advocacy coalitions (Sabatier 1988), language-based methods provide an opportunity to study the formulation of political agendas at the level of text and talk. This opens up new and potentially useful ways of exploring how actors disclose their interests, position their interests relative to policy issues, and create opportunities to advance policy-based goals. Such an approach could be especially useful in exploring how, for instance, for-profit charter school operators have framed the debate about charter schools and created an opening for them to provide services once offered exclusively by nonprofit educational entities. Likewise, these approaches might be useful in exploring how teachers' unions manifest influence over issues related to teacher evaluation, compensation, and, more globally, school funding. In both cases, an education policy scholar might turn to public testimony offered during legislative hearings, press releases, or policy reports to determine how the policy issue was framed, agendas were articulated, and resistance (or support) was presented.

ESTABLISHING FUTURE DIRECTIONS

We think it appropriate to conclude this chapter and the volume by setting out some of the future directions for the use of language-based methodologies in the study of education policy. First and perhaps foremost, we see the use of language-based methods as offering education policy scholars new ways to hold policymakers accountable. Given the hyper-partisan, anti-factual policy environment emerging in the USA, the use of language-based methods provides an important avenue for education policy scholars to disassociate unproductive, disingenuous rhetoric from key policy issues in schools. Indeed, as Sirotnik (2004) noted, "just as educators need to be held accountable, so do policy makers and the public as a whole for the validity of the educational accountability systems they establish" (p. 155). While language-based methods are not exclusively critical in their orientation, we think their capacity to adopt a critical lens and make visible issues of power, privilege, and (in)justice within the discourses found in these accountability systems is essential. Indeed, one future direction might well be to consider how discourses within the context of accountability systems position public schools as failures and thus fuel the anti-public school policy prescriptions which the hyper-partisan, anti-factual policy environment seems to demand.

Second, as part of an attempt to hold policymakers accountable, we see the opportunity to examine various discourses for notable "silences" as key to identifying whom the policy system neglects. Silence has long been studied (Jefferson 1989; Lester 2012; Mushin and Gardner 2009), yet few have specifically considered its role in the policymaking process. Working from the assumption that language is always doing something (Jørgensen and Phillips 2002), it becomes apparent that silence may well convey more than disapproval. Indeed, if education reform discourses do not focus substantially on the educational needs of students with disabilities, English language learners, or students living in poverty, then it raises the question about whose interests the policy and/or the policymakers actually serve. Further, when key constituencies who work closely with these students are not participants in the education discourse, it raises questions about the extent to which the policy process hears and responds to their needs. Indeed, Oakes et al. (2004) asserted that "the uneven distribution of basic educational tools places the burden of the system's deficiencies squarely on the backs of low-income students and students of color" (p. 88). Yet, this distribution reflects power arrangements and policymaking activities that exist far from the classroom. Without appropriate and meaningful avenues within the policymaking for individuals who work with these students to share their views, it becomes difficult to see how this distribution can be changed. Silence may well convey a systematic discrimination toward the interests of all but the most elite constituencies. Language-based methods, we argue, might provide an avenue for education policy scholars to examine whether and how this may be the case.

SUMMARY

In this chapter, we summarized the key contributions of this volume. To do so, we first revisited the aims of the volume, offering a brief summary of each of the included chapters. Then, we discussed what we view as some of the primary methodological contributions that the contributing authors make, specifically contributions at the intersection of education policy and discourse analysis. Following this, we provided a synthesized discussion of some of the key policy contributions this volume offers, which served as a foundation for considering future research directions for education policy researchers.

Key Connections to Policy Research
1. Language-based methods enable policy scholars to understand more deeply how policy issues emerge, how they are presented within the context of discourse, and, ultimately, how actors within the policy process position themselves in order to achieve their individual and collective agendas.
2. The chapters within this volume collectively demonstrate the potential intersection(s) of education policy research and language-based methods. Specifically, the volume highlights the utility of language-based methods in unpacking the intersection (s) between policy research and language as the primary medium for advocacy and influence.

REFERENCES

Bakhtin, M. M. (1981). Discourse in the novel. In M. Holquist (Ed.), *The dialogic imagination: Four essays by M. M. Bakhtin* (pp. 259–422). Austin: University of Texas Press.

Ball, S. J. (2006). *Education policy and social class: The selected works of Stephen J. Ball*. Abingdon: Routledge.

Billig, M., Condor, S., Edwards, D., Gane, M., Middleton, D., & Radley, A. (1988). *Ideological dilemmas: A social psychology of everyday thinking*. London: Sage.

Bonacina-Pugh, F. (2012). Researching 'practiced language policies': Insights from conversation analysis. *Language Policy, 11*(3), 213–234.

Deleuze, G. (2004). In C. Boundas (Ed.), *The logic of sense* (trans: Lester, M.). London: Continuum.

Fairclough, N. (1992). *Discourse and social change*. Cambridge: Polity Press.

Foucault, M. (1980). Prison talk. In C. Gordon (Ed.), *Power/knowledge: Selected interviews and other writings,1972–1977* (pp. 37–54). Brighton: Harvester.

Goffman, I. (1974). *Frame analysis: An essay on the organization of experience*. Boston: Northwestern University Press.

Hurst, T. (2017). The discursive construction of superintendent statesmanship on Twitter. *Education Policy Analysis Archives, 25*, 29.

Jefferson, G. (1989). Preliminary notes on a possible metric which provides for a 'standard maximum' silence of approximately one second in conversation. In P. Bull & R. Derek (Eds.), *Conversation: An interdisciplinary approach* (pp. 166–196). Clevedon: Multilingual Matters.

Jørgensen, M. W., & Phillips, L. J. (2002). *Discourse analysis as theory and method*. London: Sage.

Lather, P. (1986). Issues of validity in openly ideological research: Between a rock and a soft place. *Interchange, 17*(4), 63–84.

Lester, J. N. (2012). Researching the discursive function of silence: A reconsideration of the normative communication patterns in the talk of children with autism labels. In G. S. Cannella & S. R. Steinberg (Eds.), *Critical qualitative research reader* (pp. 329–340). New York: Peter Lang.

Lester, J. N., Lochmiller, C. R., & Gabriel, R. (2016). Locating and applying critical discourse analysis within education policy: An introduction. *Education Policy Analysis Archives, 24*(102). doi:10.14507/epaa.24.2768

Lester, J. N., Lochmiller, C. R., & Gabriel, R. (2017). Exploring the intersection of education policy and discourse analysis: An introduction. *Education Policy Analysis Archives, 25*, 25.

Mazzoni, T. L. (1991). Analyzing state school policymaking: An arena model. *Educational Evaluation and Policy Analysis, 13*(2), 115–138.

Mushin, I., & Gardner, R. (2009). Silence is talk: Conversational silence in Australian Aboriginal talk-in-interaction. *Journal of Pragmatics, 41*, 2033–2052.

Noblit, G. W. (1999). *Particularities: Collected essays on ethnography and education*. New York: Peter Lang Publishing.

Oakes, J., Blasi, G., & Rogers, J. (2004). Accountability for adequate and equitable opportunities to learn. In *Holding accountability accountable: What ought to matter in public education* (pp. 82–99). New York: Teachers College Press.

Sabatier, P. A. (1988). An advocacy coalition framework of policy change and the role of policy-oriented learning therein. *Policy Sciences, 21*(2), 129–168.

Sacks, H. (1992). *Lectures on conversation*. Oxford: Blackwell.

Sirotnik, K. A. (Ed.). (2004). *Holding accountability accountable: What ought to matter in public education*. New York: Teachers College Press.

Stokoe, E. (2012). Moving forward with membership categorization analysis: Methods for systematic analysis. *Discourse Studies, 14*(3), 277–303.

Supovitz, J., & Reinkordt, E. (2017). Keep your eye on the metaphor – The framing of the Common Core on Twitter. *Education Policy Analysis Archives, 25,* 30.

Wetherell, M. (1998). Positioning and interpretative repertoires: Conversation analysis and post-structuralism in dialogue. *Discourse & Society, 9*(3), 387–412.

Chad R. Lochmiller is Assistant Professor of Educational Leadership in the Department of Educational Leadership & Policy Studies in the School of Education at Indiana University. His current research focuses on education policy issues, particularly those related to school finance, human resource management, and leadership development. Lochmiller's research has been published in *Educational Administration Quarterly, Journal of Educational Administration, Journal of School Leadership, Education Policy Analysis Archives, Leadership and Policy in Schools,* and edited volumes.

Jessica Nina Lester is Assistant Professor of Inquiry Methodology in the Department of Counseling & Educational Psychology in the School of Education at Indiana University. Much of her research is positioned at the intersection of discourse studies and disability studies. Lester recently co-edited a book focused on performance ethnographies and co-authored a book focused on the use of digital tools across the qualitative research process. She also co-authored a research methods textbook and is the co-editor of *The Palgrave Handbook of Child Mental Health: Discourse and Conversation Studies* and *The Palgrave Handbook of Adult Mental Health: Discourse and Conversation Studies.* Her most recent article has appeared in journals such as *Qualitative Inquiry, Qualitative Research,* and *Discourse Studies.*

INDEX

Note: Page numbers followed by 'n' denote end notes.

© The Author(s) 2017   253
J.N. Lester et al. (eds.), *Discursive Perspectives on Education Policy and Implementation*, DOI 10.1007/978-3-319-58984-8